What Men Say
What Women Hear

Dr Linda Papadopoulos is widely published in both the academic and popular arena. She has published over 40 research articles and co-authored five academic books. Her expert advise is much sought after and she provides commentary for national newspapers and news channels. She is a contributing editor for Cosmopolitan magazine and appears regularly on TV and radio both in the UK and in America. She has a private practice in London where she lives with her daughter and husband.

What Men Say
What Women Hear

Dr Linda Papadopoulos

Dún Droma
Dundrum Library
Tel: 2985000

arrow books

Published in the United Kingdom by Arrow Books in 2009

1 3 5 7 9 10 8 6 4 2

Copyright © Dr Linda Papadopoulos, 2008

Dr Linda Papadopoulos has asserted her right under the Copyright, Designs and
Patents Act, 1988 to be identified as the author of this work.

This book is sold subject to the condition that it shall not,
by way of trade or otherwise, be lent, resold, hired out,
or otherwise circulated without the publisher's prior
consent in any form of binding or cover other than that
in which it is published and without a similar condition,
including this condition, being imposed on the
subsequent purchaser

First published in Great Britain in 2008 by
Century

Arrow Books
Random House, 20 Vauxhall Bridge Road,
London SW1V 2SA

www.rbooks.co.uk

Addresses for companies within The Random House Group Limited can be found at:
www.randomhouse.co.uk/offices.htm

The Random House Group Limited Reg. No. 954009

A CIP catalogue record for this book
is available from the British Library

ISBN 9780099478690

The Random House Group Limited supports The Forest Stewardship Council
(FSC), the leading international forest certification organisation. All our titles
that are printed on Greenpeace approved FSC certified paper carry the
FSC logo. Our paper procurement policy can be found at:
www.rbooks.co.uk/environment

Typeset by SX Composing DTP, Rayleigh, Essex

Printed and bound in Great Britain by
CPI Cox & Wyman, Reading , RG1 8EX

To my wonderful family.

To my parents for making me feel safe, secure and loved enough to face any challenge or go after any dream.

To my husband for making me laugh when I need it, letting me cry when I need it and for making sure that I always feel there is someone looking out for me.

To my amazing little daughter, Jessica, for helping me to see the world more beautifully and more clearly through her eyes.

Acknowledgements

It has taken a lot of input from a lot of great people to bring this book to fruition. Alexandra Mizara, Amy Lawson, Jaine Brent, Mark Booth, Charlotte Haycock, Rina Gill, Rebecca Morrison, Richard Ogle — I feel a great deal of gratitude to you all, thank you for believing in me and in this project. Thank you also to all those who read my books and take the time to share their thoughts and experiences with me, to those that believe in relationships and hope and love. This book would not have been possible without you, nor would it have been worth writing.

Contents

Introduction:
What Men Say, What Women Hear

I t should be so easy. Evolution should have prepared us for this after years and years of development and progression, centuries of socialisation and civilisation. We've sent men into space, women to the voting booths and cloned a pretty impressive little sheep. So when it comes to communication between the sexes, why does it feel like we're still at the 'Me Tarzan, you Jane' stage?

How does 'You look great!' become 'I feel sorry for you, you fat moose' in a matter of seconds? Why does 'I'll do the washing-up after the football' seamlessly transform into 'I don't even love you enough to respect our kitchen.' And why do we ever ask the question 'Does my bum look big in this?' when no answer on the face of the planet (this one, or Mars) is ever correct?

The fact is that men and women speak different languages. We live in a society that values men and women very differently, and this plays a major part in how we communicate. Of course this can work very effectively as any woman who's ever flirted with a traffic warden can testify. On a daily basis we negotiate the hurdles and pitfalls of cross-gender com-munication, professionally and personally.

However, every now and then the system breaks down. Every now and then we listen in our own gender-specific tongues. So, we don't hear 'You look great', because by the time the compliment has passed through our portable translation guide and endured a mauling by a set of deep-rooted insecurities and an attack from years of personal experience, it becomes something rather different. Rather than accepting the compliment in the context in which it was meant, by interpreting it in 'man language', we decipher it into 'woman language' and it all gets a little messy . . .

Cognitive Behaviour Therapy (CBT)

This book will help you understand these messy transactions and guide you through the minefield of romantic relationships using Cognitive Behaviour Therapy. Put simply, CBT examines the link between our cognitions and our behaviour. So, how does what we think affect what we do? How do the processes in our mind influence the action we take and the choices we make?

CBT is generally regarded as one of the most effective and useful psychological therapies available today. From anxiety disorders and depression, to relationship and interpersonal problems, CBT is seen as the treatment of choice by the majority of clinicians in the UK and America. Its popularity lies in its straight-forward, hands-on approach, involving the patient directly rather than in the distant, removed way for which many other therapies are criticised.

So, the premise of CBT is relatively simple: it basically states that first we think and then we have an emotional reaction to something. Here are a few examples of common thinking errors when it comes to relationships:

All or nothing thinking: this is when a person thinks in complete extremes. So, for example, 'Either he tells me he loves me or our relationship is doomed' or 'If he hasn't asked me on a second date by Tuesday, I'm never answering his calls again.'

Maximising the negatives: attending only to the negative aspects of a situation. So what if he's the love of your life and he's reliable, handsome and kind? You just can't shake the memories of that disagreement he had with your uncle at a family party last week, so he'll probably hate everyone in your life, and eventually he'll start to hate you too. Right?

Making everything about you: feeling responsible for things that have nothing to do with you. 'He's in a foul mood, it must be my fault. Clearly he's gone off me, and he's trying to push me away so I'll back off and eventually finish it.'

Jumping to conclusions: reaching inaccurate conclusions based on insufficient or inadequate evidence: 'I can't believe he asked how old my sister is! Blatantly he's fantasising about how young and nubile she is. He must fancy her more than me!'

Seeing everything as a catastrophe: focusing on the worst-case scenario and exaggerating the possible consequences: 'I've gone up a dress size since I saw John last time, I bet I'll be too big for the seat at the cinema and everyone will point and stare at my huge backside. That's it, I'm not going!'

Generalising the negatives: exaggerating the memory of an unpleasant experience causing It to affect other parts of your life, even if they are entirely unrelated. So, that throwaway comment from your ex-boyfriend about how he's not really into blondes, turns into: blonde hair looks rubbish, and 'If he thinks so, so will every other guy, and I'll die a lonely old woman who never found love.'

And in turn, these thinking errors affect the way we behave. One woman might sleep with every man who takes her out for a drink, because she's established a false belief that sex is the way to make men fall in love with her. Another might starve herself for a week before every date, because someone told her she had 'womanly curves'. And, in an extreme example, a person may completely avoid dating altogether, and close off the option of meeting anyone, because they don't believe they deserve to find love.

CBT in Action

Having established this inextricable link between our thoughts and our behaviour, how does CBT work to address these problems? Well, the key is perspective. Getting a grip on all those nonsensical, yet strangely powerful thoughts is all down to establishing how realistic your fears are, and replacing them with a set of more reasonable expectations. *What Men Say, What Women Hear* will examine specific communication problems between men and women, placing some psychological context behind what is happening, and then suggesting a more realistic way to approach the problem. Often, the trick is as simple as accepting that 'I'm a bit busy tonight' doesn't mean 'I'm too busy to have you in my life', or that 'I love the blue dress on you' doesn't mean 'I hate the red dress'. Sometimes, it's a bit more complex and involves replacing deep-rooted thoughts and insecurities with a set of more sensible expectations. The answer is always perspective, perspective, perspective. Once we take a step back from the problem and learn to view it with impartiality and objectivity, we're one step closer to finding the holy grail of relationships . . . a common dialogue.

This book addresses problems that can occur at vital stages of your relationship, from that initial longing gaze across the crowded city bar, to that scary first family gathering, to parenting, or separation. Initially, we will present a framework of psychological research, regarding the problem, then we will go on to translate these studies into real-life scenarios, establish what it means for your relationship and how you can address and work through it with your partner. We will examine issues that arise as crucial elements of any relationship, and the following chapters will act as a guidebook for anyone who has ever second-guessed exactly what a man means, misinterpreted a man's inner thoughts and feelings or hurled a phone across the room and screamed in fury, 'Well, why didn't he just *say* that!'

In Chapter 1 the focus is on the anxieties of asking someone out on a date, and how our own insecurities and past experiences factor into this process. The chapter begins with some research into the different ways men and women interpret non-verbal communication to help establish why you might just be moving your hair out of your eyes, but to him you're effectively saying, 'Come get it, tiger!' It deals with those awkward water-cooler moments where you flirt, fluster and faff, desperately trying to suss out if you're actually into each other. Just as we misinterpret male communication, they are as likely to misinterpret the things we say and do – and before you have established exactly how you feel about one another, this can add up to a mish mash of misunderstandings. As a woman you have to address the challenge of managing your own communication as much as you have to work on reading his. And even once you've established that there is some kind of mutual interest, there are still complicated issues such as where you go, what you do and who pays when it comes to that crucial first date. Different societal expectations between men and women, and how these influence the way we interact with each other will also be addressed.

So, you've negotiated that tricky first date. You've established you're pretty compatible on a dinner, drinks and walks in the park basis but you both know the next big hurdle will soon be looming its grubby little head. Because, after discovering that you like each other in a clothes-on environ-ment, the next step is negotiating the clothes-off side of things. So, in Chapter 2, our focus will move onto what sex means to men, what it means to women and why the two are so different, beginning with research that throws up some interesting revelations on the 'men think about sex every six seconds' cliché. Why do women turn 'I'll call you next week' into 'Next week?! Next week?! Why not tomorrow? He's obviously not bothered about me now he's had his wicked way!'? When is sex 'just sex'? When is it something more? And what is the psychological context behind each scenario? We'll examine both the verbal and non-verbal language we use in the bedroom and provide a glossary for the most crucial sexual communication errors.

Now this is when it starts getting serious. You know you like this fantastic guy, but will your Great-Aunt Mildred? Will he take one look at those circa 1970 baby photos and run a mile? Introducing your partner to your friends and family is always a potential minefield. This is often due to the fact that the person you are when you are with your best mate, your mum, or your Uncle Gerald is very different to the person you are when you're with the potential love of your life. In Chapter 3 we'll address this discrepancy and provide guidance in sailing through these important first meetings. The psychological framework is provided by a study that suggests it's not your mother-in-law who's the problem – contrary to all those rubbish male-orientated mother-in-law jokes – it's actually likely to be your relationship with his mother that throws a spanner in the works.

Relationships are pretty worthless if they don't further our knowledge about ourselves and the world we live in. Once you've endured a few crucial beginning stages, this is the time when you really get to the crux of your relationship, and your identity as a couple. The next chapter, Chapter 4, examines how emotional intelligence develops and also looks at factors that have the potential to stunt our emotional growth. Emotional unavailability and its symptoms will be studied on both sides of a romantic relationship, and suggestions that will keep a relationship progressing from emotional strength to strength will be discussed. It kicks off with some interesting research that looks at why big boys don't cry, what happens when they do and how you and your partner can embrace and encourage your emotional differences.

One of the hardest things that a relationship will have to contend with is infidelity, which is responsible for over 50 per cent of relationship break-ups. And unsurprisingly, the way we respond to infidelity varies greatly according to gender. So in Chapter 5 we'll look at why it happens, how we try and justify it, and how the only way to move forward is for everyone involved to take responsibility. The language we use to define the experience will be analysed, and used to reflect the importance of the infidelity in relation to beliefs about the relationship.

And of course sometimes two individuals will decide they aren't quite the perfect fit and they're both better off going their own separate ways. Maybe because they've been faced with a big horrible issue like one partner's infidelity, perhaps because they've run out of conversation and the silences are far from comfortable – or maybe because, despite perseverance, they just couldn't find a common language to combat the 'he says, she says' barrier. We look at when it is the right time to work through problems, when it is the right time to say goodbye, and how developing positive and moderate language can make the whole process a lot less painful for everyone involved. Oh, and we examine some evidence that might go some way to explain why all the best break-up love songs are written by men!

You really don't know somebody until you live with them. Sure, we all have cohabitation images of cosy Sunday lie-ins and blissful winter nights in front of the fire, but sometimes, just sometimes, the reality is a little different. Moving in together is a huge step in any relationship, and we start Chapter 6 by looking at the British Household Panel Survey of over 5,000 UK households for some statistics on moving in and mental health. It seems it isn't all Habitat and beautiful paint swatches. Here, we go through exercises that will allow you to examine both parties' motivations for moving in together, and ensure the process runs as smoothly as possible. If you can't agree on home furnishings, at least you'll be able to agree on why you want to wake up every morning next to each other. Once again an analysis of the way we approach and speak about moving in together will be outlined.

So . . . are you waiting with bated breath (and a clutch of bridal magazines) for him to get down on that knee? Do you come out in a cold sweat every time he goes to tie his shoelace? In Chapter 7 we will take a social psychological view of how and why men and women approach marriage differently, and look at what the language we use to talk about marriage says about us and our relationships. While you're single or struggling to coax a relationship up the aisle, getting that ring on your finger can feel like the final frontier, the icing on the cake, the answer to all your problems. If only. In many ways, it's only the beginning. Marriage, wonderful as it is, brings its own set of challenges. In the remaining chapters, we take a look at some of these challenges, place them in psychological context and guide you through methods of confronting them. For example, the next stop for many of us, after we've tied the knot, is baby central (see Chapter 8). And the tiny pitter patter of Gucci booties can raise a whole load of questions you never thought you'd be asking. Who has to stop being a baby once the little one arrives? How do you share breasts between a screaming brat and a newborn baby? How do you develop a language that takes you from the boardroom to the nursery? And how on earth do you deal with that awful time-warp moment when you realise you've turned into your parents?

And even once there's a ring on your finger, there's no guarantee that you and your partner will live happily ever after. When you've had the 175th argument about the same issue, or when you realise you've ceased being lovers and are actually just best friends, or when the marriage has become a burden rather than an added bonus to your life, sometimes the only solution is to say goodbye. Focusing specifically on divorce, in Chapter 10 we'll look closely at how you can contemplate life without each other and divide your lives in an amicable way that will ensure minimum pain for everyone involved. The statistics don't lie: a sizeable proportion of marriages end in divorce. So we examine the psychology behind this life upheaval, how you can use language to reach a neutral, non-confrontational conclusion and amicable ways of resolving property and childcare issues.

All relationships (or at least relationship self-help books) should finish with a happy ending. In the final chapter, Living Happily Ever After, there are some tips to ensure your relationship works for you and your partner and that you grow old together happily, simply by learning to speak the same language.

People try to address relationship problems in a million different ways. We make unreasonable demands, we come up with unrealistic promises, we buy big gift-wrapped boxes of chocolates. And largely, these strategies are useless. Even the chocolates – they're yummy, but useless. This is because the underlying problem remains. It's impossible to tell somebody what they want to hear when you can't understand what they're saying in the first place. It's impossible to read what is going on in a relationship when we're only referring to one translation guide – our own, slightly gender-skewed version. Men and women will always find it hard to understand each other, unless we start speaking the same language. This doesn't mean evening classes. It means we need to understand that every day of our lives we are socialised – meaning that we learn from and adopt the common beliefs of the society in which we live – to speak and listen as a man or a woman, and there isn't a whole load of common ground. Understanding this is the first step.

This book explains and examines this first step, looking at psychological research and individual case studies. We also look at how you and your partner can develop a universal language. That doesn't mean he's suddenly going to chirp, 'Of course darling, I'm right on it!' as soon as you ask him to get his filthy laundry out of your pristine bedroom. It just means that perhaps you learn to interpret his distracted grunt as just that, rather than an intentional insult to your whole relationship. Likewise, it might also mean that he learns that your asking him is not an attempt to run his life or cage him into a boring domesticated relationship, just a plea to prevent a visit from the health authority. And maybe he will learn that a quick, 'No worries, I'll do it now' is far easier in the long run. Well, stranger things have happened . . .

It sounds obvious but if we learn to understand and speak to each other in a generic dialect, the battle's almost won. *What Men Say, What Women Hear* is like your portable translation guide to the various 'he says, she says' relationship minefields. You can't change the fact that you feel things differently because you are male or female, but you can establish a common language that allows you to identify, address and work through these differences to achieve your very own happy ever after.

Chapter 1

Dating

In 1988, Shotland and Craig set out to establish the differences in the way males and females evaluated the sexual connotations behind a potential partner's behaviour. A mixed group of actors was divided into five role-play pairs. Each pair was asked to enact four role plays; these covered a scenario where both partners were acting in a friendly way, one where both were acting as though they were 'interested' and two that looked at a situation where each sex was in turn 'interested' while their partner's behaviour was just friendly.

In each case the pairs were asked to act out a scene where two people had just met adopting the relevant behaviour. The role plays were filmed and later shown to eighty students who were asked to analyse and rate the intentions of each 'character' using a five-point likert scale and a specially developed 'Sexual Interest Scale'. (A likert scale is a numerical scale, usually from 1 to 4, where people rate how they feel about a particular issue.)

This sounds pretty simple, doesn't it? Even without hearing the actors' original instructions, we should all be able to pinpoint behaviour that implies romantic interest. At the very least we should be able to glean from the interaction between two characters who is going for 'just friends' and who is gunning for a little something more.

But here is what Shotland and Craig found: men always perceived *the actors, male or female, to be more interested in their role-playing partner than the women did. Men perceived situations to be more sexually orientated than women. Although both genders were credited with being able to spot the difference between interested and friendly behaviour, men have a far lower threshold for what constitutes 'interested' behaviour. In other words, men are far quicker to jump to the conclusion that something is ... um ... far more promising, shall we say, than it actually is. So what do these key differences actually mean for male–female communication in the potential minefield that is modern dating?*

It isn't just these charged, potentially romantic scenarios that can highlight the differences between men and women. From car navigation, to fashion, to how many days you can leave a takeaway container before it becomes a health risk, there's likely to be little or no consensus between your average male and female. The weird and wonderful world of dating just provides us with opportunities for a whole new level of misunderstanding. Dating has become the primary form of premarital involvement in our contemporary world. In fact, it has become a crucial hurdle almost every relationship must negotiate in the transition from platonic to romantic. In particular, the famous 'first date' is recognised as a hugely important event in a relationship's evolution (Morr and Mongeau, 2004).

New romantic relationships are remarkably fragile. Like any relationship they take time to solidify, and become dependable. In order to survive, they must recognise the expectations of each party, and endure possible violations of these expectations. Research suggests that what we come to expect from our relationships is the result of a range of variables: sexual stereotypes, personalities, beliefs, past relationships and previous experiences. The study above shows us that even before embarking on that crucial first date, establishing exactly what each other's expectations are is important. For example, it's usually helpful to find out if the man is even interested in dating in the first place. No point wasting all that eyelash-batting and rear-wiggling if he's been married for ten years. Or gay. Or your best friend's new boyfriend. Yes, right from the beginning, you can count on some awkward conversations, a sackload of uncertainty and your fair share of embarrassment, experienced in equal amounts by everyone involved. All this before you've even picked a restaurant.

The confusing complexities of dating, the panic it often evokes, and the results it produces (ranging from massive success to complete mess) make it a prime area of theoretical study. Shotland and Craig's role play and observation study is one of millions searching for the hows and whys behind cross-gender interaction. For years, research has been done into the reasons why people date, who they choose to date, how all of this is affected by peer pressure and the gender roles society expects us to adopt. Certainly, it is agreed that dating is a practice that is highly filtered by gender differences. A man's experience of a dating scenario will be viewed entirely differently by a woman. The first date will be experienced differently. The pace of the initial stages will be viewed differently, and ultimately, the reality of being part of a couple will be felt differently. This chapter will identify and explain some of these differences and examine the influence our past experiences and personal insecurities have on dating. We will also cover the different societal expectations between men and women and how these will inevitably affect the way they interact. Somewhere along the way, we will establish why 'Would you like to grab a coffee?' means 'Would you like to grab a coffee?' to a woman and something entirely different to your average man . . .

Lost in Translation – How and Why we Speak Different Languages

The beginning is a very good place to start. Let's go back to the basics of being a human being, looking at the two fundamental strands that make us who we are: the way we are conditioned psychologically and the way we are conditioned by the world around us via the heavy weight of societal expectation. Before we look at men and women as dating participants, it's helpful to look at men and women as, well, men and women.

Psychological Factors

Schemas

CBT works on the premise that our behaviour is strongly linked to our cognitions. The actions we choose to take are largely down to our thoughts, feelings and emotions. According to cognitive-behavioural literature, when evaluating a situation we must look primarily at the underlying beliefs we hold. These beliefs are embedded within a relatively stable structure, known as a schema, which operates subconsciously, outside awareness (Beck, 1964, 1967; Beck et al.,1979). Schemas form a person's picture of themselves and they are regarded to be fundamental units of personality. They select and synthesise incoming data and can be classified into a variety of useful categories such as personal familial, cultural, religious, gender or occupational. They develop initially in childhood, beginning with experiences that relate to our families, our primary care givers or our early schooldays. Eventually, schemas become part of us and long after these early experiences we continue to find ourselves in situations that evoke them.

These schemas influence the choices we make on a day-to-day basis. They affect the way we react to various stimuli and they colour our interaction with others. Every minute we make interpretations, judgements, assumptions about the feelings and motivations of others, predict outcomes and try to figure out what things mean (McKay and Fanning, 1991). This inner monologue is adaptive and frequently reflects our schemas. If we hold negative beliefs about ourselves, this can cause us to interpret others in a particularly negative way. For example, if you are somebody who displays negative schemas concerning your self-worth and you hear, 'I would really like to spend more time with you and get to know you better,' this may actually trigger a nervous, anxious response. Your deeply ingrained beliefs will convince you that, if this new person gets any closer, you will discover the unattractive traits you believe exist. Consequently, such a statement is filtered through your basic beliefs about yourself, which are generally negative; therefore you interpretation of the statement is also negative or biased. Our negative schemas can have the same effect as a hall of mirrors in the circus. A stimulus is fed to the schema, or mirror, and an image is fed back to us which, although incorrect, appears totally authentic. Researchers have suggested that these negative, or maladaptive schemas can be grouped into broader 'schema domains'. These are outlined below.

DOMAIN	SCHEMAS
Disconnection and rejection	• Abandonment/instability • Mistrust/abuse • Emotional deprivation • Defectiveness /shame • Social isolation/alienation
Impaired autonomy	• Dependence/incompetence • Vulnerability to harm or illness • Failure
Impaired limits	• Entitlement/grandiosity • Insufficient self-control/ self-discipline
Other directedness	• Subjugation • Self-sacrifice
Over vigilance	• Emotional inhibition • Unrelenting standards

Classification of schemas and their corresponding domains

This research has gone on to conclude that we can also predict the origins of these schemas, and how they affect behaviour according to their domains. For example, people whose underlying schemas fit into the 'other directedness' domain often display an excessive emphasis on meeting the needs of others. This can originate from a family background that places conditional value on acceptance and approval. So, a child who is only shown affection when they perform well in school exams might find themselves ignoring their own needs and desires in an adult romantic relationship, in order to please their partner. Consequently, schemas factor into the dating process not only as an important part of our expectations about others and relationships, but also as an influence on how we conduct ourselves.

Let's take Margaret as an example. Since childhood, she has viewed herself as flawed and unworthy. Her parents were highly critical, and she never felt good enough to please them. To compensate, she has worked hard to construct a facade that will be acceptable to others: an attractive appearance, a successful career and a warm personality. However, she still believes that anyone who gets to know her intimately will see through her immaculate exterior to the unworthy, empty person beneath. Her schema is: 'I am not good enough.' Therefore she cannot risk getting too close to somebody, or letting them see her on an intimate basis.

Consider Mike, who sees himself as incompetent. His schema is: 'Nothing I ever do really works.' In the past he has been deeply hurt in his relationships which has reinforced even further his sense of being unable to make the right decision. He simply drifts along, allowing events to happen, scared of making his own independent choices or taking the risks he needs to in order to lead the life he desires.

And now let's look at these two case studies in a dating scenario. When Margaret is on a date, she will filter any new information through her inbuilt schema of inadequacy. So if her date tells her 'I had a fantastic time tonight', instead of accepting and enjoying the compliment, Margaret will interpret it as, 'He's only being nice because he doesn't know me. Or he's probably just trying to sleep with me. What a pig.' Meanwhile, Mike, after months of deliberation, finally summons the courage to ask the object of his affection out to dinner. She agrees and all goes well, until she mentions that next time they should see a film, and Mike interprets this as, 'She probably hated the restaurant I chose tonight, so now she's trying to be polite and avoid such a disastrous evening on our next date.' So maybe Mike stutters, stammers and stumbles his way through a dejected goodbye speech before ushering his date out of the car before she even has a chance to hang around with glazed eyes doing the whole first-date 'Will we? Won't we?' kiss-thing.

These two examples illustrate how schemas can be activated, and when activated how they bias information processing. By the time the message is translated by Margaret or Mike, their schemas have far more influence than the original meaning. In fact, the original meaning is lost, so powerful are the established schemas. Both of their schemas are manifested by assigning a consistent meaning whenever a particular event occurs with their date. Both moulded information about their dates' behaviour to fit their schemas. Their schemas influence their perception and they supersede other more reasonable beliefs that might have been more appropriate on each occasion. The possibility that their polite, charming date might actually be telling the truth is immediately eliminated. Their inner dialogue is self-defeating and it immobilises them. Consequently, a common behavioural response for both Margaret and Mike is avoidance. So, restricted by their negative schemas, they may just simply refuse to talk about their thoughts, or ruminate alone on what is bothering them. And eventually, they may well find themselves avoiding dating altogether.

Past Experiences in Prior Relationships

Although cognitive-behaviour theory emphasises patterns and themes occurring in the here and now, past experiences of relationships shape our broader behavioural, cognitive and affective (emotional) responses too, so they can be equally important. The way we conduct ourselves within relationships and what we expect from them is inextricably linked to the relationships we have encountered in the past. Our relationship history casts a long and often formidable shadow over our future relationship success. We're not just talking about romantic interactions here. The bonds we build with family, friends and peers can also have an impact, even on elements as seemingly unrelated as sexual behaviour and intimacy. So, when an individual is flirting, or proposing a date, or out for dinner with a potential partner, every conversation, or action or event, is filtered through the net constructed by our past relationships.

Attachment theory (Bowlby, 1988) represents a theoretical framework that focuses on the strong, innate, emotional bonds between children and their primary care givers. According to this theory, children develop 'internal working models' (or in cognitive terms, schemas) concerning the degree of dependability and security that they come to expect in their relationships with care givers. Attachment theory asserts that the schemas developed by these early bonds will extend into our adult romantic relationships. More specifically, It describes how individuals develop behaviour tendencies in order to fulfil their intimacy and care-taking needs. So, for example, an individual with a secure model of attachment is likely to be more comfortable expressing thoughts and emotions and communicating needs and desires to a partner (Kobak, Ruckdeschel and Hazan, 1994). Conversely, the opposite is true for an individual with insecure attachment schemas, who are more likely to communicate their requirements in an unclear indirect manner. This can even extend to a point where the individual actually denies the existence of their own needs, alienating themselves as a romantic partner and as a person. So, for example, a man who has always shared an open trusting relationship with his parents and close family may feel comfortable expressing needs such as, 'I feel closer to you when we spend more time together, I hate it when we don't make time for each other. Can we spend at least two nights a week together?' On the other hand, if his girlfriend has experience of not having her needs met by those who she wants to trust, her expression of her needs may not be quite so clear. Suddenly 'I appreciate your feelings, but I need you to understand how busy I am with work, and how I also value my relationships with other people in my life – they also require time and maintenance' becomes 'Stop suffocating me you stalker! Right, I'm going out. I'll call you next year.'

As we can see, the attachment theory extends beyond the nursery, and produces the same conclusions about our romantic affiliations as adults. These bonds play an equally important role in shaping an individual's expectations of relationships, as they create opportunities to challenge pre-existing views (Furman and Flanagan, 1997). If the individual's later experiences of romantic relationships differ from their established relationship history, then their views and beliefs can be changed. In contrast, if we embark on a new relationship and experience similar treatment or feelings to those we have experienced in past relationships our beliefs and expectations are further reinforced and elaborated. For example, if Jane leaves an abusive relationship believing she is worthless and unattractive, her next relationship will have a massive impact on these feelings. If she embarks on another destructive relationship, it is likely it will only serve as further evidence of the negative schemas Jane has developed. Conversely, if Jane begins to date a man who tells her she is beautiful, intelligent and kind, she now has the ammunition she needs to begin to shoot down some of her negative beliefs. Schemas are deeply ingrained but the benefit of experience, or a conscientious effort to hold them up to scrutiny and consider other explanations can be very powerful.

We can look at this in a different way. Mary is a happy, confident woman. She grew up in a secure, loving family where she felt safe, cared for and believed in. She has been in two serious romantic relationships and is now back in the dating game.

Then we have Lisa. Lisa's father left the family home when she was three, as a result she spent much of her early life being taxied from relative to family friend, to the local crèche. She had sporadic contact with her father and his new family. Lisa has recently come out of a six-year relationship with a bullying, aggressive man who, for much of the time, she was just too scared to leave. Consequently, she has managed to develop some pretty robust schemas that scream, 'I am unlovable! I am worthless! I don't deserve to be happy.'

Now imagine Mary and Lisa go on the same date – same restaurant, same food, same flowers, same man. Let's call him Pete. If Pete picks up Mary and compliments her on her pretty earrings, she will probably hear, 'I want to make you feel good, and I'm particularly drawn to your jewellery, it looks fantastic!' Mary is comfortable receiving compliments and will respond accordingly. However, when Lisa hears, 'I like your earrings', her inner schemas will maul the compliment until it eventually becomes something like, 'Oh God, that dress is disgusting, maybe I can distract myself from its hideousness by concentrating on her mildly interesting earrings.' Lisa's inner feelings of insecurity and lack of confidence in her own attractiveness mean the compliment falls on deaf ears. Or rather, the compliment dive bombs and lands like the proverbial lead balloon.

Let's move the scenario on, the dreaded doorstep moment has arrived. That moment where you are forced to choose between a sweet goodnight kiss, a 'coffee', a promise to call and definitely meet up soon, and walking out of each other's lives never to be seen again. Maybe Pete volunteers the first suggestion: 'I had a great night, can I call you in the week to arrange another drink some time?' Mary will hear exactly that, maybe offer a compliment in return and coolly arrange to meet up again (then close the door, wait for the sound of Pete's car leaving, and call every single girlfriend to extol the joys of her wonderful date!).

Conversely, Lisa's previous relationship experiences might tell her that Pete is only asking to be polite. Years of feeling 'in the way' and slightly unwanted have taught her to feel that spending time with her is an inconvenience. So, she's more likely to knock Pete back, by saying something like, 'Erm . . . well, I'm really busy next week, so don't worry, I guess I'll just see you when I see you.'

And thus, we see how past relationship experiences can cast a long shadow over our future endeavours. These examples also illustrate how what men actually say can be interpreted so vastly differently, depending on our own issues and insecurities.

It is fair to say that attachment theory shows our past experiences play a part in our future encounters. Cliché's like 'once bitten, twice shy' are often trotted out when describing relationship behaviour, but they ring very true. The fact is, it's impossible to approach each new romantic opportunity like a blank canvas, untainted by the woes and wonders of our last relationship. We do carry the memories from past encounters with us and, negative or positive, they are likely to colour our behaviour and our expectations when we begin to date again.

Social Factors

If all this wasn't complicated enough, there are yet more factors that can shape the plot of our love-life dramas because what you hear when the object of your affections asks you out, pays you a compliment, or indeed, breaks up with you, is not only dependent on your individual history and emotional make up, but also on a whole load of external factors. Dating behaviour is closely tied to social variables as well as the individual psychological variables we have already looked at. It is well known that men and women are somewhat different in personality and it seems important to understand how sex differences arise and how they influence our interactions with the opposite sex.

Traditionally, sex differences have been explained by referring to the process of socialisation. Men and women develop different attitudes because they are treated differently by society. Fact. We develop by modelling cultural norms of gender-appropriate behaviour. Children learn what behaviours go with being a boy or a girl by learning the sex roles appropriate for their gender. Basically, we learn how to fit in with our gender roles by observing those around us, and this starts to manifest itself even before we are handed that first doll or train set. Stereotyping on the basis of gender begins even before birth. Parents attribute different sexes to their unborn babies on the basis of their prenatal behavioural characteristics – i.e. an active, kicking foetus is presumed to be a boy (Unger, 1979).

By age three or four children can assign occupations, toys and activities to stereotypic gender (Bee, 1999). Kids of this age are very, very clear about what constitutes a 'boy's toy' or a 'girl's toy'. It's impossible to argue that we don't box our children into gender-specific behaviour once you've witnessed three-year-old Molly gleefully unwrap a baby doll and a miniature kitchen complete with pots and pans, or four-year-old Johnny tear round the garden in his new army fatigues, with his brand-new football. Whether it occurs as blatantly as this or on more subtle levels, parents reinforce stereotypical activities and reward behaviours appropriate for women and men. So boys are encouraged to engage in rough and tumble play, are bought toy guns and discouraged from expressing or exhibiting their feelings (big boys don't cry), whereas girls are bought dolls and encouraged to be modest and demure (Workman and Reader, 2004).

These early socialisation experiences lead to acquisition of gender schemas. Whether we are socialised into being a boy or girl affects the way we think. It encourages the development of gender-specific schemas, far beyond whether we find it acceptable to leave the toilet seat up (every time!) or whether we think owning seventeen handbags in the same colour is perfectly normal. We learn to recognise gender differences and conform to existing gender-role stereotypes, defining what is 'feminine' and 'masculine' and how one ought to behave as they interact with others. These behavioural stereotypes become second nature to us. Women are supposed to inhibit aggressive and sexual urges (even when it comes to the Selfridges sale), be passive, nurturing, attractive and maintain poised and friendly postures. Conversely, males should be sexually aggressive, independent and suppressor of strong emotions (Workman and Reader, 2004). These differences are maintained by social constructions; the sociocultural environment influences the psychology of men and women.

Social learning theory is the framework that emphasises the role of learning and of the environment in shaping our behaviour and accounts for the gender-role development is social learning theory. According to this theory, people and their environments have a reciprocal effect on each other: we influence the society we live in and that society influences us. The acquisition and maintenance of behaviour are not passive processes, we don't just soak up information from our ever-changing society without feeding back into it. Individuals are actively involved in appraising their environments. By observing others, an individual can learn appropriate actions for particular situations. From these observations, we develop schemas. In this context, the schemas serve to determine the following:

- Which environmental influences are attended to: the things we pick up, the stimuli we notice, will be determined by our schemas. For example, if you caught your last boyfriend cheating on you when you found a sexy text on his phone, you are going to be much more aware and suspicious of your partner's habit of deleting texts after he has read them – whereas another woman in that situation may not even notice this habit.

- How these influences are perceived: the way we interpret these stimuli will also be steered by schemas. So, for example, your new date forgets to text you on your birthday – this might be a huge issue to some people and completely acceptable to others.
- Whether they will be remembered: you know how some people seem able to put things behind them and move on while others bear grudges and let the bad times fester with them for ever? The impact an influence has on us will be intrinsically tied to our schemas. Your boyfriend may have quickly forgotten that row you had over him being late to that party, while you remember it for months.
- How they affect future behaviour: it doesn't take a genius to know that we learn from the past. Our schemas will affect how we interpret and respond to situations, and they also affect how the whole experience will alter our behaviour in the future.
- In generating motivation to initiate and sustain behaviour: in general, schemas will have a lasting, ongoing effect on how we behave. So, the experience of him getting a text message late at night, coupled with him being protective over his phone, combined with him not kissing you goodbye one morning will filter through your own personal schemas, and eventually this could add up to a longer-lasting effect on your behaviour – you might feel more suspicious in general, you might check his messages etc., etc.

Assimilation of self-concept to the gender schema
- We learn the contents of society's gender schema and which attributes are linked to our own sex and, thus, to ourselves.
- We learn the deeper lesson that the dimensions are differentially applicable to each sex.
- We learn to evaluate adequacy as a person according to our gender schema.

One important domain in which these differences between genders have been demonstrated is the degree to which women and men see themselves as separate to or connected with others (Pervin and John,

2001). As mentioned earlier, men are more likely to have 'independent' or 'autonomous' schemas, while women are more likely to have 'collectivist' and 'connected' schemas. This could explain why women go to the ladies in pairs . . . on a more useful note, it could also explain how, in the initial stages, women often seem more eager to embrace a serious commitment than men.

Gender Roles, Norms and Dating

So this stereotyping socialisation process can give us some handy clues to deciphering the separate way different genders might approach relationships. And often, studying this process helps us to establish what different genders might seek from their relationships. It also goes some way to explaining the results of Shotland and Craig's observation exercise. Maybe men and women extrapolate different things from the same scenario because every bit of their make up has taught them to.

We can begin to draw some fairly firm predictions from this evidence. For one, women tend to be more anxious to get emotionally attached more quickly. All it takes for many women is one date and they're already trying to work out what pet names will suit their obvious husband-to-be, and what colour her bridal posy should be so that it's an *exact* match with his eyes. Women like the idea of settling down and exclusivity and commitment. Men like variety; they're far more into the idea of dating lots of women. To a woman, a drink at the pub might mean another step closer to that jewellery shop, to him it might be just that – a drink at the pub. In an attempt to delineate differences in male and female dating behaviour, let's look at some areas where this disparity between men and women is particularly noticeable.

Emotions

In general, women talk about intimate issues such as feelings and insecurities. In contrast, men look for similar interests in their relationships, place more emphasis on the undertaking of joint activities and avoid discussing feelings (Buunk, 2001). So if you introduce two women, it's likely that within the first hour (if not sooner) they will have moved onto 'relationship talk', swapping experiences or comparing their personal lives. Two men, however, are far more likely to identify immediately what football teams they support or what gym they attend, so they can stick to the safe neutral ground of common interest, without straying near any messy, yucky emotional rubbish.

It is apparent that men apply different criteria for intimacy and they simply show a preference for avoiding intimate interactions on many occasions. Whereas a group of women can dissect and analyse a world-threatening problem such as, 'Does my boss hate me?', 'Can I wear this dress with those shoes?' or 'Will I ever find the one?' for hours on end, men simply prefer, the majority of the time, not to talk about it. It's a fact of life. If your idea of a great first date is a show-and-tell session where you proudly exhibit your former relationships and detail exactly how they went wrong, and the effect that had on your poor crippled heart, don't expect him to reciprocate. Caldwell and Peplau (1982) asked ninety-eight under-graduates if they would rather do an activity or have a conversation with friends. Twice as many men to women preferred to get on with an activity, and three times as many women to men preferred the idea of a good old chat. The fact is, a man would rather get on with it than sit around and talk about it, whatever 'it' may be.

Physical Attractiveness

Differences also exist in the degree that physical attractiveness affects romantic attraction. Over the past years, research has shown that physical attractiveness carries positive connotations – as if we didn't know that already. Physically attractive people are perceived as having far more socially desirable qualities; they are also seen as being professionally successful, content in their personal relationships and just more happy in general. You can see why – try and think of five things that Cindy, Kate and Naomi have the need to moan about. OK, try and think of two.

However, physical attractiveness has different implications for men and women. Research has found that the physical attractiveness of a woman has far more bearing on the impact of a man's behaviour than in the reverse scenario. Large-scale studies of dating reveal that the good looks of a date are more important to men than to women (Unger, 1979). In other words, men are more likely to select a date on the basis of looks and will react more favourably towards an attractive woman.

Status

Despite the male focus on physical attractiveness, women actually have higher overall requirements for their dating partners. Women are far more interested in the security a mate can provide, so factors such as career, finances and social status are considered very important. Women seem to be more immune to 'superficial' characteristics and more concerned with a man's ability to provide. Feminine beauty is such a valuable commodity, it is assumed that to earn the right to be with an attractive female, a man must provide other socially valued material rewards.

The importance of physical attractiveness to men, and the tendency of women to value financial success and social status can be attributed to the evolutionary theory. Apparently, men subconsciously seek out mates who are likely to produce healthy babies, and are likely to raise babies successfully. This fertility and childrearing competence is represented through physical attributes – i.e. a young, nubile, attractive woman will be seen as a desirable mate. This theory argues that men have become particularly sensitive to signs of youth, health and reproductive value.

Women subconsciously seek a mate who will provide for the family while she is raising it. Thousands of years ago, the cavemen topping the Most Eligible Bachelor lists weren't the ones with the prettiest blue eyes, or sharpest six packs. Oh no. All the girls wanted the guy who could bring home the biggest mammoth for dinner. Evolutionary theorists claim that years on, these social trends continue and, unknowingly, we still want the same things from our partners.

Sexuality

Sexual attraction is also important in the choice of romantic partners in fact, it often becomes a central aspect of dating. Men are more inclined to engage in sexual behaviour and are less discriminating with regard to quality and quantity of sexual partners (Baumeister, Catanese and Vohs,

2001). And, as we've seen, men are far quicker to interpret a situation, or a woman's behaviour as sexually motivated. The 'notches on the bedpost' mentality is thought to be a particularly male way of viewing sexual conquests. They are more approving of casual sex and desire higher levels of sexual activity in their first dates than women. In other words, your average man is definitely going for quantity over quality. Conversely, women report more sexual caution and are expected to be less sexually permissive. Most women are expected to be strong subscribers to the 'nice girls don't' school of thought, disapproving of and avoiding sexual behaviour on first dates (Rose and Frieze, 1993). Again, evolutionary psychologists put this down to the fact that ancient man was primarily concerned with two main objectives: hunting and breeding. Hence, when you fast forward a few thousand years, you can see why men still hunt in packs, although now the territory is likely to be a swanky city bar, and the 'prey' are any females who happen to stray into view. The innate need to continue the species meant that multiple partners, and plenty of behind-cave-door action was the order of the day. And although mass production may well be the last thing the modern male strives for, evolutionary theorists argue that this inbuilt historical urge still affects male sexual behaviour.

Implications for First Dates

If these variables hold true, there is good reason to concur with Shotland and Craig's results and predict that males and females will approach dating differently, although anybody who's ever been on a date will tell you this anyway. People put themselves through the weird and wonderful world of social dating for a variety of reasons, and these reasons are likely to differ between men and women. In one study, respondents cited goals such as sexual activity, recreation, socialisation, mate selection/courtship, companionship, emotional intimacy and status grading as possible motivations for dating (Roscoe et al., 1987). Gender-linked differences emerged for two of these items: women more frequently mentioned emotional intimacy, whereas men more frequently cited sexual activity as a motivation for dating. In another study that focused specifically on sexuality, college dating couples were asked to rate the importance of 'desire for sexual activity' as a dating goal (Peplau et al., 1977). Male respondents rated this goal as significantly more important than females. Thus it seems reasonable to predict that women's dating goals are objectives such as emotional intimacy and a sense of security, whereas men are far more focused on moving things towards the bedroom.

Gender differences in dating goals will undoubtedly produce different expectations of normal partner behaviour for different types of dates. Gender roles are believed to be more important earlier in relationships, as individuals tend to rely on socially defined roles to guide their behaviour. So, before you feel comfortable enough to show your new love interest your repertoire of party tricks, including burping the alphabet and downing a pint in five seconds, you might feel it's safer to stick to playing the demure, sweet female that society has defined as 'ladylike'.

First dates particularly represent highly scripted situations. One can readily generate male and female scripts for a hypothetical 'first date' (Rose and Frieze, 1989). The man's role encompasses initiating the process, such as asking for a date and planning it; controlling the public domain, such as driving and opening doors; and starting sexual interaction, such as initiating physical contact, making out and kissing goodnight.

So, if he's taking care of all of that, what is the woman supposed to be doing? Well, apparently, the woman's role focuses on the private domain, showing concern about her appearance and enjoying the date, responding to the man's initiative – agreeing to be picked up and having doors opened, as well as responding to his sexual overtures (Morr and Mongeau, 2004). A degree of male dominance and control is expected on the first date, and this inevitably gives men more power in the initial stage of a relationship. Consequently, women appear to view their first dates as highly dependent on their male partner.

Having said this, there have been big shifts in society's expectations of typical male and female roles, particularly since the 1960s. These cultural shifts have affected the workplace, the home and the political landscape, so it would be fair to assume they will have touched on dating too. Dating appears to be a much less formal ritualised process these days, and is as likely to involve getting together for a drink after work, or in a group, as the practised ritual where the man shows up on the front doorstep with flowers and a dinner reservation.

Along with changes in the formality of dating, there are a few changes in roles. The expanding role of women in our society comes into the equation. With equality has come a whole heap of confusion about what role men and women should take in a relationship. For example, questions have arisen, such as: should men expect to pay on a date, or will this offend his companion? One of the biggest areas of confusion that stems from defining gender roles is the issue of who asks whom on a date. Traditionally, men were the ones who were expected to pop the question. However, with the expanded roles and accomplishments of women, this role also appears to have shifted. Women are often encouraged to be more proactive in seeking a relationship and asking men out. Cue thousands of sighs of relief from the world's male population . . .

Still, research indicates that traditional gender roles continue to define courtship today (Rose and Frieze, 1993). Women continue to want men to make the first move. Some aspects are surprisingly unchanging. Despite the 'go get him' girl-power messages churned out by the mass media, it appears we're all still waiting to be asked out. Studies during the mid- to late-1990s showed repeatedly that if a woman asked a man out, she was likely to be seen as a 'non-serious dater' and more sexually active or permissive than a woman who was asked out by a man. In other words, once women begin to adopt certain 'male' dating traits, such as pro-actively initiating a date, they are also assumed to have adopted other traditionally male objectives – i.e. non-committal sex. A majority of men in one study also reported they had higher expectations for sex on a date when a woman asked them out than vice versa. Though, interestingly, men who were asked out on a date by a woman ended up having sex less frequently than did those who asked a woman out.

Where do we Go from Here?

So it seems that while men and women all want meaningful relationships, they are both waiting for the other gender to make the first move. Shifts in society's expectations mean that men are unsure whether to make the first move, at the same time as women are desperately trying to conform to an outdated societal structure that suggests they should be sitting at home with the hair straighteners ready just in case the phone rings. It's confusing stuff.

It's important to realise that people are still looking for the same qualities in a mate that they've always been looking for: a sense of humour, a kind nature, in short an ability to meet or complement each other's emotional and physical needs. The problem isn't that men and women are seeking vastly different things. The problem is that they are seeking them for different reasons, and often their 'seeking' methods are very different. So while men and women are both, ultimately, looking for somebody to ride off into the sunset with and have beautiful kids, or someone to read the papers with on Sunday morning, or someone to accompany them in their Friday night takeaway ritual, they are looking for these things for different reasons. A typical male might think he wants these things so he can have regular sex and carry on the family name. A woman might think she needs these things for financial and emotional security. But, at the end of the day, we're all chasing the same carrot. It's recognising these key needs that is important, because then we stop ourselves wasting time trying to meet needs that don't actually exist. If we are truly committed to valuing the opposite sex, we must firstly understand and appreciate our partner's differences and secondly commit ourselves to meeting his or her unique needs. To get this point, we need to learn how to communicate these needs. Many clinicians look to communication training as the first step in improving a couple's general functioning. By assisting couples to communicate they can improve the individuals' understanding of one another.

How CBT can Help

CBT has traditionally focused on the impact of specific thoughts and beliefs on our emotional and behavioural reactions. So if we perceive an event negatively, we feel more negatively or more pessimistic about that event. We may become defensive, guarded and difficult to open up. However, if we are able to think more rationally or more positively about a particular event then, consequently, we feel more positive about it. We may be more open and less defensive when expressing what we want. What one needs to do in order to produce changes in negative or pessimistic thinking is to identify those thoughts and dispute them. However, the problem is that these thoughts are so deeply ingrained we don't even know they're there. Such thoughts pop into our stream of consciousness automatically and affect the way we hear, analyse and break down information. Of course, this in turn affects the way we communicate.

By learning to employ CBT techniques we can improve our method of communicating with the other gender and learn to speak the same language. Consider the following case: Mat is a twenty-eight-year-old man who experienced problems in socialising with women, particularly when he was interested in them romantically. Mat assumes, therefore, that women will never be interested in him. So, he approaches a date thinking: 'I am boring', 'She will have a lousy time', 'She won't want to go out again', 'There is no point going out after all'. According to CBT, Mat's plan of action should be a critical examination of his thoughts and a search for any genuine indications that any of these negative summaries are accurate. By realistically examining his thoughts, Mat will be able to see he did not have sufficient information to make these negative assumptions. He could switch his thoughts into "I am an interesting and attentive guy', and 'She will have a great time'. So if he adopted a less pessimistic and more balanced outlook, it would make a big difference both to his mood and to his behaviour. He would not feel so anxious about going on a date and be able to date freely.

OK, so you're thinking this all sounds a bit too straightforward. How could somebody with such a damning self-assessment simply convert his thoughts into positive predictions? Of course, it is possible that his subsequent experiences on his date could confirm his old views. Yes, new schemas are likely to be transitory. In order for enduring changes to occur, Mat needs to keep working on strengthening his alternative, balanced views and try adopting a more permanent optimistic outlook. He needs to examine his beliefs constantly and adopt alternative views if these are dysfunctional.

We can use CBT to challenge our negative schemas explicitly, to enhance rational thinking and to increase optimistic thought. A variety of cognitive-behavioural techniques can be used to modify behaviours that are maintained by negative, destructive schemas. This process as a whole can help both sexes recognise that their anticipation of the outcome of a date may be unduly negative; it can therefore increase the ability to appreciate the positive aspects of interaction and perhaps, most importantly, to feel comfortable with dating.

A standard CBT technique will be:	
Identify –	What thoughts pop into my mind? What am I saying to myself?
Dispute –	Is there an alternative way of seeing things? Is there any bias in what I am saying to myself?
Modify –	How can I change my automatic thought into a more balanced one?
Replace –	Swap your initial thought with a more balanced thought.

Conclusion

So, let's regress for a moment. At the beginning of the chapter we examined a study suggesting that when it comes to male–female interaction, although both sexes are sensitive to the differences between friendliness and flirtation, their interpretation of the two types of communication are very different. Now it's clear why. As human beings there is a gulf in meaning between what we say and what is heard by whomever we are talking to. That is true of any conversation and, as discussed, that's down to the individual beliefs we hold about ourselves and the world around us. Beyond that, whether we are born into a pink or blue babygro holds some strong implications for how we will view life. We interpret things differently. The men in the study picked up on flirty behaviour even when it wasn't there, because we are fundamentally different. That's not a problem. In fact, it's why we bother with this whole messy mating process in the first place. Let's look at an example.

Jodie and Tom have fancied each other for months. Friends of friends, they've spent hours asking subtle questions like 'Can he cook?', 'Does she like rugby?' and 'Please, please, please tell me you've invited her to your birthday party.' They've both casually enquired about the other's relationship history. And finally, after months of agonising over whether 'passing by' someone's place of work is cute or creepy, listening to 'When will I see you again?' on repeat and obtaining each other's phone numbers via a cryptic chain of circles of friends, they go on a date.

She thinks he is funny, he thinks she is beautiful. He thinks she is sweet-natured, she thinks he is generous. In short, the beautiful flowers, swanky restaurant and ridiculously good wine provided a backdrop to the date they always hoped it would be. Then they linger in Tom's car at the end of the night. Tom says, 'I had a great time, should I call you?' Jodie pauses, looks thoughtful for a moment, and says, 'Yeah, sure, whatever. Thanks for tonight. See you soon.'

And then they never speak again.

So, what happened to Jodie and Tom? Why did their night transform from a date on cloud nine to the romantic scenario from hell? Well, because their inner dialogues and audio soundtrack ran alongside each other like this:

Tom thinks: She's brilliant, I definitely want to see her again. But I don't want her to think I'm rushing things, or all I care about is sex, so I won't suggest coffee.

Jodie thinks: I love him! He's amazing! I hope he wants to come in for coffee – I don't want the night to end.

Tom says: 'I had a great time, should I call you?'

Jodie thinks: Oh right, so he doesn't even want to come in! And he's trying to get rid of me with the 'I'll call you' line. I don't think so mate – two can play that game.

Jodie says: 'Yeah, sure, whatever. Thanks for tonight. See you soon.'

Tom thinks: Whatever?! Whatever?! That's not exactly enthusiastic, is it? She obviously didn't have as great a time as I did. Well, I'm not going to humiliate myself by pushing the issue. Clearly I'm not as much fun to be around as I thought.

Tom says: Nothing.

Jodie thinks: He's not exactly begging for a second date is he? And he hasn't tried to kiss me. I had better make my excuses and go.

Jodie says: Nothing.

Lights down, curtain up and the affair has come to a rather disappointing conclusion. The reasons behind Jodie and Tom's individual insecurities and inhibitions are unimportant. What is important is the fact that this scenario has thwarted a million relationships. If only it was all just as simple as finding somebody you like, discovering they like you too, meeting up, embracing this mutual interest and then floating off into the distance to begin your happily ever after. But it will never be this simple. From the moment you are born, the environment you develop in and the experiences you encounter colour your perception of the world. This can have dramatic and profound effects, long after you leave the family home or, indeed, a relationship. The experience you have and the schemas you develop can mean the difference between hearing: 'I'd like to see you again' and 'This was a disaster, but I'm trying to be polite.' It can be the difference between avoiding relationships and embracing them. The point is, we all have a history. And every time you initiate a new romantic relationship, this history comes into play and so does your potential partner's. Then you've got the added pressure from society telling you who and how you should be dating. No wonder it gets confusing.

The key to overcoming these perplexing 'guides' to new situations is to challenge them. Why assume a blatant compliment is a veiled insult? What evidence do you have for this? Why should you wait for him to call, just because your mum's always told you that only loose women make the first move? Learn to be active in the process, be a part of it, don't wait for it to happen to you. And enjoy it. The culture for fast-food, instant results and Botox lunch breaks means we expect high-speed connections in areas of our life beyond the internet. It's easy to start expecting a ready made relationship, but the fact is that the reason many relationships fail is because one or both parties judge the pace incorrectly.

Women have to stop worrying about results. You won't enjoy the race if all you can think about is the finishing line. Forget planning where the first date will take you. Use that energy to embrace it and enjoy it. Who cares if he wants kids and you don't when you haven't even ordered dessert? The key here is challenging preconceptions and expectations, understanding the difference between how men and women see dating, and learning to accept that although dating is often a fraught and anxious activity, it can also be great fun.

Men Should Remember:

- Do not be passive – state what you really want and what you are feeling.
- Be aware of what intimacy means to your dating partner.

Women Should Remember:

- Be assertive. Forget societal expectations or cultural training that discourages you from taking initiative. Make the first move if you want!
- Learn to enjoy the process and not just go for results.

Chapter 2

First Sex

The Kinsey reports still constitute one of the most important bodies of research we have on human sexual behaviour. Between 1938 and 1950, over 16,000 interviews were conducted with men and women in the United States investigating the moral boundaries they operated within, and their views on romantic relationships. Interviewees were questioned on biological, psychological and sociological responses to sex, love and the dating game. While the society in which we live may have changed, and many of us now hold entirely different morals to the generations before us, the biological and psychological sexual responses of men and women seem to exist as a stable constant. Many of the key gender differences the Kinsey reports unearthed in terms of sexual behaviour are still as true today as they were then.

So what did these interviews reveal? Well, for a start, a female pattern of sexual activity, whether that means masturbation, intercourse or fantasising tends to form an inconsistent pattern of peaks and troughs. A woman can go months without any sexual activity. On the other hand, when a man is not having sex with a partner, the frequency of masturbation increases. There appears to be a constant pattern of sexual activity, whichever form that activity takes. For a woman sexual drive seems to be more person-related than time-

related (Crowe, 2005). The 'right' time for a woman to have sex is often the time when she has found a partner who she can trust and feel a connection to. For a man the 'right' time can mean anything from finding a girl who is attractive/funny/drunk enough to realise it's been six months since the last time.

The research revealed that men are far more susceptible to stimulation. An attractive woman walking down the street can arouse a man to a point of physical readiness for sex. A woman is far less likely to get turned on by such a remote stimulus, and is far more responsive to physical touch and affection. Now that's not to say that a woman won't eventually reach the same state of arousal as a man. It just means that when she does, it is likely to be because she has responded to different cues, or has allowed herself to get in the mood.

The Kinsey research is still relevant in today's world because it goes some way to explain the massive discrepancies between male and female approaches to sex. Years on from Kinsey, in the 1980s, John Marshall Townsend interviewed over 200 people. He recorded male and female feedback which suggested that on one level nothing had changed. Women still attached more emotional importance to sex. Men still saw sex as just – well – sex.

And taking those findings back into the real world, let's look at Laura and Rob. They've been on six dates, each one a roaring success. Rob knows he fancies Laura: she's funny, beautiful and he's been ready to sleep with her since pretty much date one. No, in fact, he was ready to sleep with her the minute he met her. Despite his typically male urges, Laura has so far resisted his sexual advances. She likes Rob too. He's exactly what she's looking for in a partner, and she wants this one to turn into something serious. So, despite fancying the socks off him, she's holding back till she knows he is just as serious about her. Because their attitudes to sex and their sexual urges are so different, neither can quite get their head round the other's sexual schedule.

Rob might base much of his self-confidence on his sexual ability and feel Laura's reluctance to sleep with him is some kind of 'snub'. Maybe Laura feels it will scare Rob off if she expresses her fears that premature sex will ruin the relationship and prompt Rob to see her as 'easy'.

As exciting and intimate and relationship-enhancing as sex is, it also provides potential for a whole new set of communication breakdowns. Men and women view sex completely differently for a number of reasons, including the physiological factors the Kinsey studies identified, and this often makes it difficult to discuss sex with each other. We approach sexual encounters with our own gender-specific assortment of anxieties. So while you are panicking about whether the missionary position moulds your boobs into an odd shape, he'll be worrying about whether he's really doing the right thing down there. While he obsesses over the size of his penis, you'll be fretting over whether you should be shy and submissive or swinging from the chandeliers.

Again, we tend to hear incorrectly, as a result of our own schemas. When he says, 'Was that OK for you? Did you enjoy it?' She might hear, 'You could have been a bit more appreciative, you frigid bore, I nearly dozed off halfway through,' or something along those lines. And like most relationship hurdles, when we hit a communication barrier, there can be a number of negative consequences. For example, if a woman, through miscommunication with her partner, feels he views sex as a waste of time unless it culminates in orgasm, she may end up faking a response or avoiding physical encounters altogether, in case she 'lets her partner down'. A failure to convey your sexual needs to your partner can lead to frustration, anger and eventually resentment and avoidance of the sexual relationship altogether (Ford, 2005).

And before we even get to the stage where we are expressing our sexual needs to our partners, we have to cut through the social pressures and past experiences that colour our expectations of sex. Even before a couple makes it to the bedroom, they will have been individually exposed to a lifetime of social pressure, and most probably a handful of past sexual experiences. This will affect what we expect from sex, what we enjoy, or indeed feel comfortable with, and practical issues such as how long we wait before sleeping with a new partner. For example, society suggests, and reinforces the theory, that men see sex as far more important to their general well-being than women. Likewise, women are far more worried about when to elevate attraction to physical intimacy, and the reality is that more often than not, they are chiming in with society's clock and avoiding their own body clock.

In this chapter we examine the different ways men and women approach sex. We look at how this can lead to confusion, and the most common ways we run into trouble when it comes to communicating how we feel about what goes on behind closed doors (or behind open doors, or in aeroplane bathrooms, whatever you're into . . .) We'll look at society's impact in more detail and also look at the pressures that our individual schemas put on sexual relations and provide a glossary for the key communication errors that can occur once you decide to move your relationship into the bedroom.

What Sex Means to the Genders

It's not just that men and women seek sex differently, or talk about sex differently, or approach sex differently; they actually experience sex differently (Ofman, 2000). For a start, it has been argued that 'women aspire to psychological intimacy as a gateway to sex' whereas 'men aspire to sex as a gateway to the sense of closeness'. In other words, women want to experience a certain emotional closeness before sex, and men view sex as a route to this closeness. Men are generally expected to be assertive seekers of sex and to value sexual frequency and variety; women, on the other hand, are expected to be sexual gatekeepers, recipients of men's attention, and expected to value sex only as part of committed, romantic relationships (DeLameter, 1987; Levant, 1997). Numerous scholars have observed differences such as this. In other words, men seek sex for the sake of sex, women view it as both an accompaniment to a strong relationship and a method of securing that relationship in the first place.

So, let's go back to the six-second statistic. Apparently, alongside all that daydreaming about cars and football results men also manage to squeeze in some sex-related musing. Every six seconds, allegedly. Statistics such as this help reinforce the stereotype that men are far more pre-occupied with sex than women and, as we've seen through evolutionary theory and a process of socialisation, often this stereotype rings true. Men and women also differ on issues such as frequency, timing and quality of sex. Men in general seem to hold more permissive attitudes toward sex, to desire a greater variety of sexual partners and behaviours, and to seek sexual sensations more frequently than women do. These issues usually bear strong symbolic meanings (Beck, 1988) and so, for a man 'having sex when I want it' may represent being loved and desired.

And then there's the legendary one-night stand. By definition, one-night stands involve maximum excitement and minimum commitment. Unsurprisingly, men are far more interested in them than women. This is probably because they're far better at separating sex and emotion than women. So after a brief, post-nightclub experience, while the man is likely to scratch that notch in his bedpost, then move on without a second thought, the women may well be left wondering what their encounter 'means' or 'where it will go from here'. Women are found to be more likely to incorporate emotional intimacy and commitment into their sexual scripts (Reiss, 1986; Simon and Gagnon, 1986). Conversely male sexuality is more dominated by the casual-sex script (Marsiglio, 1988; Reed and Weinberg, 1984). Again, this takes us back to the Kinsey research: it stands to reason that men are likely to have a more simplistic view of sex – after all, their inclinations are far more basic than a woman's. Where a man might see a good-looking girl and find he suddenly has to fashion a pillow over his lap, your average woman will clock a model-type man and observe, 'Yes, he's hot. So what?'

Research conducted with college students supported this interpret-ation. Emotional involvement was viewed as a prerequisite for engaging in sexual intercourse by more women than men. Men tend to be more focused, logical and independent when it comes to sex, whereas women are more inclined towards discussion, emotional attachment and tend to rely on support (Crowe, 2005). So when it comes to sex, men see themselves as lone rangers, single-mindedly pursuing a clear, and uncomplicated objective. Meanwhile, for women, the pathway to sex often resembles an emotional roller coaster, with a few girly pit stops for advice and support.

Why we Tend to Approach Sex Differently

Sexuality is considered an integral part of personality (Leiblum, 2002). Therefore, it is shaped by cultural, biological and socialisation processes. Certain aspects of sexuality are physiological, so they're dictated by our bodies rather than our minds, but aspects such as what should arouse us and what constitutes sexual behaviour are learned – they are a product of the environment we live in and the lessons we learn. To understand how and why women and men approach sex gender-specifically, we just need to look at this combination of biology and environment.

Social and Cultural Differences

As we have established, men and women learn a great deal about relationships in childhood and adolescence. Much of this information comes from our family background. It is in our childhood home that we begin to learn what it means to be a boy or a girl, how adult relationships work and how our gender determines where we fit in to all of this. Our parents are largely responsible for providing gender-specific role models, and providing guidelines to acceptable and expected behaviour. In fact, parents influence sexual beliefs, opinions and attitudes more than peers, school or the media (Joffe and Franca-Koh, 2001).

Research suggests that a child's communication with their mother about sex can serve as a significant predictor of initiation of sexual relations, contraceptive use and pregnancy (Pick and Palos, 1995). In addition, those individuals whose parents conveyed unhealthy messages about sex (the belief that sex is a sin or dirty) were most likely to feel sexual guilt (Propper and Brown, 1986). Moreover, exposure to non-verbal sexual communication such as maternal sexual affection towards a spouse was a significant predictor of two specific attitudes in women: a) speaking more affectionately to men, b) being the more assertive partner in sexual encounters (Koblinsky and Palmeter, 1984). Young men who grew up in a family where the father was sensitive and caring to the needs and wishes of the mother, sexual and non-sexual, were more likely to go on to have similar happy, healthy sexual relationships with women.

So our parents lay the first building blocks in establishing our thoughts and feelings about sex and sexuality. As we grow and enter into teenage years, we spend a good deal of time not only developing the requisite social skills, but also discovering our own and our friends' sexuality. The values and beliefs developed in the teenage years about the opposite sex are often carried into adulthood with little modification. Thus, people enter sexual relationships with some real misconceptions about sexuality and the role of sex in a relationship. And we're not just talking about playground myths like 'You can't get pregnant if you're standing up' and 'If you have a bath with a boy you'll get pregnant.' Oh no. Despite moving past their posturing, proud adolescence, many grown men still fear that anything that borders on sensitivity will be interpreted as being somehow 'unmasculine' and thus represent inappropriate behaviour for a 'real' man. Undoubtedly, fooled by a few fumbling first encounters, women believe the only part of intimacy that matters to men is the sexual intercourse part. Some couples never really get beyond these misconceptions.

In terms of a wider societal impact, sex is one of those hot topics that undergoes an image change with each generation. The way your mother feels about sexual etiquette is likely to be hugely different from your set of sexual dos and don'ts. Equally, views on sex vary from culture to culture. What will send you running for the hills (OK, the bathroom) if attempted in the bedroom, may well be considered a sexual norm elsewhere. These societal prescriptions become integral to our process of learning how to 'be' male or female through observing the examples around us. Gender roles and gender-type expectations have direct implications for men and women's differential attitudes to sexual behaviour. Recent reviews have shown that men are expected to take proactive roles – being more assertive, independent and dominant – while women are expected to be more relationship-orientated, selfless and submissive. Such expectations encourage and foster role-consistent behaviour. Eventually, we behave this way, because we know it is expected of us. For example, if women are expected to be relationship-orientated, then they may also be expected to disapprove of and avoid sexual behaviours that are perceived threatening to relationships, such as casual sex, sex on the first date and early recreational sex (Alexander and Fisher, 2003). On the other hand, these behaviours are freely accepted, and even encouraged when exhibited by a man, because they fall in line with his perceived sexual personality type.

Traditional gender-role expectations also prescribe women to be more sexually naive, and men to be more direct and assertive about their sexual needs (Byers, 1996). Men are expected to be more instrumental and to communicate their sexual needs and desires far more freely. The sexual revolution that occurred between 1950 and 1970 made steps to shift these views a little, but sex stories and sexual bravado were still seen as the domain of young, virile men. It wasn't really until the generation of gender equalisation (born between 1957 and 1973) that the ideas of the sexual revolution came to be realised (Jong, Escoffier, McDarrah, 2003). Information and experiences became acceptable for both genders; although, admittedly, talking openly about sex was still seen as a masculine trait.

Today, women are witnessing an increasing acceptance of the idea of sexual equality and their right to seek their own modes of sexual expression and fulfilment. There is a general shift towards a higher permissiveness and acceptance of female sexuality. Probably the most significant change is in the reported incidence of premarital sex (Williams, 1987). Sex before marriage is slowly being seen as the norm rather than as living in sin. Indeed, many women today will argue that the sexual component of a relationship is as important as any other, and an area that should certainly be encountered and embraced as a couple, before entering into the commitment of marriage.

Despite these ground-breaking shifts in social morals, deviations from socially expected behaviours can still have different consequences for men and women. Men's potency or sexual orientation is more likely to be questioned if they display unusual or excessive behaviour, while women risk being labelled as 'sluts' (Alexander and Fisher, 2003). In other words, men are far more likely to have their sexuality discussed, if they fail to display sufficient evidence of an aggressive pursuit of sex or, conversely, a penchant for traditionally female pastimes. The first 'insult' that opposing fans levelled at sarong-wearing footballer David Beckham was 'gay'. For women, criticism is likely to take a different form. A woman who is seen to be open to the idea of casual sex or has multiple partners, puts herself in the firing line for descriptions such as 'slag' or 'slut'. Societal judgements tend to be harsher for sexually permissive women than men. It is important to take into consideration the possibility that our sexual behaviour is susceptible to these judgements and may result in inhibition or denial of sexual urges.

In general we can see that society tells us that men are more sexual than women. This allows them greater sexual freedom when it comes to quantity. Women are far more focused on the quality side of things, associating physical intimacy with emotional closeness and commitment, largely due to society's declarations that these are the qualities they should be hankering after. Women continue to perceive the combination of love and sex as the best one, although certain studies suggest that some men are also beginning to agree (Haavio-Mannila et al., 2002). But as a general rule, the stereotyping of the socialisation process determines the different ways we approach sex. For women, the politics of when they should let a man have his 'wicked way', what he and the rest of society will think of her if she does, and how it will affect their future relationship means that the move from a platonic to a sexual relationship is often fraught with worry and anxiety. It's no wonder men approach sex with a far more relaxed attitude, and the ability to see it as just a rather enjoyable little 'hobby', so different are the social expectations they have to contend with.

Physiological Differences

We've established that external influences play a part in how we feel about sex, but Mother Nature is also extremely instrumental in determining our part in physical relationships. Not only are there a host of psychological differences between men and women, but our physiological structures and processes are also entirely different. The genetic basis of human behaviour places sex hormones centre stage in the determination of sex-related behaviour. In addition to stimulating the development of male and female reproductive systems, they also stimulate differences in brain physiology and functioning, which then go on to produce different, gender-defined sexual behaviour (Edley and Wetherell, 1995). Several studies have outlined general physiological differences between men and women when it comes to the bedroom. These include variations in sexual drive and desire, in sexual arousal and in orgasm.

Sexual Drive and Desire

The desire to be involved in sexual activity is felt strongly by both genders. However, as Kinsey suggested, in males there is a biologically driven sexual urge which creates the desire for sex at roughly equal intervals (Crowe, 2005). This is largely down to testosterone, the testes-secreted hormone that stimulates masculinisation. Basically, this is the hormone responsible for all those wonderful little facets of masculinity that make men, men. It stimulates the growth of facial, underarm and pubic hair, muscular development, changes to the male voice, alterations to the male hairline and genital growth. Testosterone also affects male sexual behaviour by interacting directly with the nervous system. Without testosterone, sperm production ceases and, sooner or later, so does sexual potency (Carlson, 1998). So, it's pretty important.

In females, sex drive operates on a variable basis. Sexual behaviour of most female mammals is controlled by the ovarian hormones oestradiol and progesterone. These hormones not only influence sexual maturation – i.e. development of breasts and female genitalia – but also the willingness and the ability to mate (Carlson, 1998). In many animal species, the female is unresponsive to sexual activity most of the time and becomes responsive at the time of oestrus (Crowe, 2005). In humans, the ability to mate is not controlled by ovarian hormones and the human female is potentially responsive most of the time. However, this responsiveness varies with circumstances. So where we have established that male sex drive occurs at regular intervals, in a pulsing pattern of desire, female sex drive is less predictable, occurring at sporadic intervals, and dependent on different influences. For example, in many women there is a time of increased interest in sex at a certain point in the menstrual cycle.

Sexual Arousal

Sexual arousal involves all five senses; however, touch is probably the most important for both men and women, closely followed by visual stimulation. Certain areas of the body are thought to be particularly sensitive to sexual arousal – for example, in females the clitoris or breast, in men the penis or mouth (Williams, 1987). Despite this, almost any area of the body can have erotic potential as individual preferences differ.

Men and women are aroused in different ways. In men, sexual arousal is based on the erection of the penis, while in women sexual arousal is felt as wetness in the vagina with some enlargement of the clitoris and a general feeling of increased bodily sensitivity to touch (Crowe, 2005). Consequently sexual arousal for women is much more salient than for men. Evolutionary psychologists attribute sex differences to evolved biological dispositions of men and women developing over time due to their likelihood of maximising reproductive success (Buss and Schmidt, 1993). In other words, our sexual responses have developed in order to give us the best chance of fulfilling the ultimate evolutionary goal – reproduction and the continuation of the species.

Orgasm

In men, orgasm is accompanied by ejaculation, in addition to a sense of extreme pleasure. They can achieve climax within three minutes of starting intercourse. This means that for most men, the challenge is delaying orgasm for as long as possible. For women, orgasm is important but the most important part of the sexual experience is the emotional response of her partner (Crowe, 2005). She needs to feel a sense of trust; an increased bond with her partner will often heighten a woman's enjoyment of sex. Whereas for men, the process of orgasm is an almost guaranteed, auto-matic response, women often need to learn how to orgasm. As a woman learns about the responsiveness of her body she becomes more adept at stimulating and facilitating it. With practice she becomes less inhibited and more willing to give herself over to the experience. Orgasm really isn't the be-all and end-all to women in the way it is to men – many women find it just too difficult to achieve orgasm at all, while some are quite satisfied with non-orgasmic sex. They value the emotional intimacy and closeness that the sex brings without worrying about climax (Crowe, 2005). This flies in the face of the unrealistic 'ideal' of two lovers experiencing an earth-moving simultaneous orgasm.

So we've established a few basic facts. Firstly, and perhaps most obviously, men and women are built entirely differently. The actual physical experience of sex is different for the genders. We are stimulated by different things, we enjoy different things, and once we reach fulfilment, we experience completely different orgasms. Secondly, not only do our physical structures determine our sexual experience, but our psychological make up also plays a part, and this part of the equation is heavily influenced by the social context we live in. Armed with these facts, it's clear to see how sex could mean (at least) two different things to men and women. Confusion seems almost inevitable. For example, in a study that investigated whether men and women attach similar meanings to touch applied to equivalent body areas, findings suggested that there were fundamental differences in the meanings attached (Unger, 1979). What a man considers to be a friendly pat on the shoulder may be interpreted as a sexual signal by a woman. A woman greeting a colleague with an air kiss after office hours could easily transform itself into 'Hang on a minute! Beneath that cool, collected professional facade she actually fancies the pants off me!' once filtered through a male translation process.

Equally, imagine Paul and Jane. They've been on a couple of fab dates – a good movie with the right mix of gripping love story and occasional gratuitous car chase and a restaurant that allowed adequate under-the-table opportunity for a little footsie. Now Paul is going in for the kill and has asked Jane round to watch a DVD. Here's how the conversation goes:

Paul says: 'I was thinking we could have a quiet one tonight? I'll cook for us and hire a DVD.'

Paul means: 'I'm ready to step this up a level physically, and that's not going to happen in another lovely restaurant. Let's get some "alone time".'

Jane hears: 'I feel comfortable enough to just "chill out" with you. This is turning into something serious . . .'

Jane says: 'That sounds lovely, I'll bring some wine – looking forward to it.'

Jane means: 'Great idea. I like you too, and I'm looking forward to coming round to yours and finding out even more about you.'

Paul hears: 'Excellent, I'm so up for this. Can't wait for you to ravish me later, you stallion.'

Let's skip ahead to the date. Dinner has been eaten, the wine is flowing and the DVD is on. Paul's mind is awash with ways to divert Jane (who is curled up and sprawled across him) from the screen and into the bedroom. You see, what has happened here is Paul has taken Jane's affection as a sign she is ready for sexual intimacy when, in fact, all it means is that she enjoys feeling close to him. Cue some massive misunderstandings and a rather long, lonely night for Paul.

Where do we Go from Here?

The example above illustrates just one of the many ways difficulties can arise. Sexual discussion can still be seen as taboo, but communication really is the only way to crack these misunderstandings. Gaining a clearer understanding of the other's point of view will certainly untangle any misconceptions or fallacies in one's thinking. By making sure one understands what the opposite sex means, he or she can change the way he or she behaves and consequently avoid any misunderstandings. Here are some 'terms' that have become sources of great sexual misunderstandings between opposite genders:

Foreplay

What it means for a man	*What it means for a woman*
The necessary, if inconvenient, warm-up a woman requires for the main event.	An essential part of the love-making experience that, for some women, is actually more important than penetration.

What both sexes should remember

First of all, men who cuddle and kiss their partners and know how to enjoy sensitive foreplay will often find their partners will not only enjoy sexual intercourse more, but also reach orgasm more often. Most women need prolonged stimulation in order to reach a complete arousal, and foreplay will provide them with the required stimulation. The sexual response may be elicited by a wide variety of stimuli. However, stimuli which may be arousing to some individuals may be neutral or aversive to others. As the individual matures the sexual response is likely to be elicited by direct stimulation of body parts and by erotic situations (Williams, 1987).

WOMEN: When you say 'no' make sure that *is* what you want. When you say 'yes' be absolutely sure you know what you are agreeing to. Remember, you have the right to change your mind, but make sure you communicate that to your partner. When you set limits on sexual activity, and your partner ignores them, act immediately. Very firmly tell him what you object to and what you want him to stop doing. If he ignores your wishes do not worry about being polite – get angry, or yell for help.

MEN: Communicate, ask her and let her decide without feeling pressure. If she is not sure what she wants then back off, even if you are hugging or kissing this doesn't necessarily mean she wants sex. So keep communication active throughout so you can read what she wants from the situation. Do not assume that sexy clothes, a flirtatious smile, kissing or touching are an invitation to sex.

Penetration

What it means for a man	What it means for a woman
Regardless of how concerned he is with his woman's needs, penetration is generally the main event.	Just one way of making love, alongside options including oral sex, cuddling, etc., etc. Another part of the process.

What both sexes should remember

According to evolutionary psychology, sex is about procreation and that means penetration.

WOMEN: Communicate the things you like and dislike in your sexual relationship. Let your partner know if you are sexually aroused and when you are ready for penetration. It is in this kind of situation that communication is very important. Try to be clear and open.

MEN: Clear things up if you are getting mixed messages. Ask her directly what she wants. There is a difference between a woman being turned on and a woman being ready for penetration. Don't confuse the two, wait for the right moment. Respect your partner's limits. Do not pressure her to have sex by bullying, cajoling, threatening, forcing or by making her feel guilty.

Orgasm

What it means for a man	What it means for a woman
The whole point of sex. An inevitable conclusion that is usually impossible to delay or avoid once it is imminent.	A fantastic moment, but not the be-all and end-all. If it happens, then great. If not, then you still enjoy the intimacy of the whole experience.

What both sexes should remember

This is it. The final straight. For both sexes, orgasm results in a feeling of pleasure. The recent emphasis on orgasm, especially female, carries with it some masculine bias. In other words, orgasm is often seen in a very masculine way as the goal rather than a fantastic product of a rather enjoyable process. Concentration on the sometimes elusive female orgasm places maximum pressure on both partners. He must make her climax because of his masculine image and she has to climax or one of them is at fault (Unger, 1979).

WOMEN: For men, it is a penis-driven event with the most important part being a good orgasm. He needs to feel confident. Stoke that confidence by telling him openly how much you enjoy it, or how much he is satisfying you.

MEN: For women, it is an issue of intimacy. She needs to feel trust to become relaxed and let go. Ask your partner how she feels and learn if she needs extra stimulation. Do not feel pressure for her to achieve orgasm along with you.

Afterplay

What it means for a man
Afterplay? What afterplay?

What it means for a woman
That lovely cuddly phase after you've done the business. You've just shared an intimate experience and you want to bask in the glow.

What both sexes should remember

The classic male 'roll over and fall asleep' is a negative afterplay stereotype and one that should be avoided at all costs. In fact, afterplay can be just as exciting and stimulating as foreplay.

WOMEN: This is a good time to show your partner how much you enjoyed sex with him. Be explicit about what you liked. Be smooth and tender. Affection works for men as well as it works for you. Don't expect him to read your mind – if you loved that new thing he just tried, tell him.

MEN: Sex means emotional intimacy for women, consequently it is important that you give your partner lots of stroking, cuddling, kissing and hair smoothing after the action is over. Pay attention to her needs and discover areas of the body that can add to her pleasure. Remember her body doesn't have the same switch-off period yours does after orgasm, so make the most of it and concentrate on her.

Why is all of this necessary? Simply put, sex is a really important part of any relationship, and getting it right can do wonders for your success as a couple. The joy of an intimate sexual partnership can help overcome many general problems just as a poor sexual relationship can harm an otherwise good relationship (Ford, 2005). The key to good sex is good communication. Communication is an important factor in eroticism as it initiates and advances sexual intimacy (Ferroni and Taffee, 1997). It mainly refers to the process of self-disclosing your sexual likes and dislikes to your partner. This ability facilitates closeness and intimacy, while it allows partners to freely negotiate a mutually and maximally enjoyable sexual encounter (Cupach and Metts, 1991).

Research has suggested that sexual self-disclosure is important to a positive sexual relationship. In other words, we need to tell our partners how we feel about sex, and what we want from it. In particular, women find talking about their dislikes especially hard (Herold and Way, 1988). Additionally, it has been found that women tend to self-disclose if they are in satisfying and affectionate relationships but they also perceive sexual self-disclosure to be reciprocal. So, the closer the relationship, the happier we are to talk about our sexual needs and wants, but we want it to be a two-way feedback process. The problem with this is that men are also often unwilling to talk about what feels good to them, and aren't great at asking women what feels good to them either, possibly in fear of shattering the myth of the magnificent, intuitive male lover.

Talking about sex with one's partner is about revealing sexual desires, preferences, fears and standards. Sharing this information promotes not only intimacy but satisfaction as well. CBT can help as it unites two important elements: 'thinking' and 'doing'. Understanding why a problem has arisen is particularly helpful. According to CBT, one needs to look at a person's thinking patterns and motives underlying their behaviour. It is quite true that when we interact with others we rarely have time to mull over all the evidence in order to deduce a person's real thoughts and feelings (Beck, 1988). People usually depend on their observations, which are coloured by their unique deeply held beliefs. This is especially true when we try to draw conclusions for the opposite sex when, as we have already established, social learning conditions men and women so differently. Consequently, it is not surprising that both men and women make mistakes when it comes to interpreting the opposite sex.

Consider the following example, Kevin and Myra are both bankers, leading busy lives. They have been dating for a month – wining, dining and enjoying each other's company. Their first sexual encounter was good but definitely left room for a little improvement. Kevin loves the idea of Myra giving him oral sex and Myra loves the idea of Kevin being verbally expressive while lovemaking. Instead of communicating their needs and talking about them, each partner sticks to 'safe' territory, only subtly hinting at what they really want from the experience. So, afterwards, following a brief awkward spell, the dialogue below takes place:

> *Kevin says: 'Well, did you enjoy that?'*
> *Myra answers: 'Of course, I did.'*
> *Kevin means: 'I feel something's not quite right here. Is it me?'*
> *Myra means: 'Of course I do enjoy sex with you, but I wish you were less obsessed about oral!'*
> *Kevin hears: 'That was rubbish.'*
> *Myra hears: 'I only care about myself.'*

Instead of openly discussing their sexual encounter, they preferred to withdraw in fear of hurting each other's feelings. Their behaviour was largely influenced by their own understandings. The various guesses that went on were all wrong. If they were to check them out, they would find out their interpretations were primarily based on their own expectations, fears and internal states. By accepting everything that is said with their own skewed interpretation, they simply set up a cycle of confusion that means two things are likely to happen. Firstly, the chances of Myra embracing oral sex as Kevin wishes she would are fairly slim, as are the chances of Kevin communicating with Myra in the way she likes during sex. And secondly, this couple are on course to missing out on the strong, intimate bond that can develop through open, honest sexual communication.

Once people attach a meaning to an event they are likely to accept it as valid without further confirmation of its accuracy. Partners should check their mind-reading either by asking directly or by making further observations of their mate's behaviour. By doing so they can check the bias in their interpretations and correct their thinking. This technique helps one to be more accurate in knowing what one's partner is actually thinking and feeling so their interactions (sexual or non) can be more harmonious (Beck, 1988).

So maybe a woman will assume her new lover hates oral sex because he never initiates it. Each time they get intimate and he doesn't go down on her, she interprets this as further confirmation of her suspicions. Meanwhile, maybe her partner has developed the theory that it is she who hates the idea because she never suggests it, and he is scared of attempting something he thinks she doesn't like. Confusing stuff. The only way to get round this is for the individuals to challenge these assumptions, through verbal, or non-verbal communication.

Great lovers become great because they are willing to communicate comfortably with their partner. But raising the subject can be tricky. Sex is a fun, exciting, arousing business. But it can also be a particularly embarrassing business, especially when it comes to writing your sexual wish list for your partner, or putting him straight on that weird toe-sucking thing he thinks you love, (perhaps you've never had the guts to tell him that it actually makes your skin crawl).

Here are some tips on how to overcome this and initiate some productive sexual discussion with your partner:

- Sit comfortably with your partner,
- Verbalise your thoughts.
- If you have complaints put them in a positive frame, make them positive requests rather than negative criticisms.
- Use simple language.
- Try and tune in to what your partner is saying to you. Don't be defensive.

Interestingly, the ability to communicate needs and feelings during intimate sexual activity often helps build better communication skills in non-sexual areas as well, solidifying the relationship as a whole. Once you get into the habit of being honest about your requirements in the bedroom, you'll probably find it easier to communicate other needs to your partner. Let's be honest, asking him to refrain from smoking in your car will seem like a breeze compared to telling him you like being spanked.

Conclusion

Lisa and Louis have been seeing each other for a few weeks. They've mastered the art of great dating, they've laughed in the face of the awkward 'boyfriend–girlfriend' conversation and they've sailed through that first bout of 'friend-meeting'. In fact, they're feeling pretty pleased with themselves. The one area they are yet to reign supreme in is the bedroom. And so, after some careful deliberation during which Lisa has said 'I'm not ready just yet' meaning 'I don't want you to stop liking me if I sleep with you' and interpreted, incorrectly, by Louis as 'I'm not sure if I fancy you or not', they finally get down to it.

And that's where the problems begin. Louis is nervous. He really likes Lisa and he doesn't want to mess everything up by being the world's worst lover. In fact, he thinks, better to go straight for the kill and get it over with rather than take time over everything so she has even more opportunity to realise that his legs, but thankfully nothing else, have turned to jelly and his palms are clammy with nerves. Lisa interprets this as, 'I can't really be bothered with pleasing you, this is just sex to me.' Lisa is well aware of what would make the experience more pleasurable for her, but she is too nervous to convey this to her increasingly orgasm-focused partner. And she has begun to assume he's not that interested in what is good for her.

So Louis, assuming she is experiencing the same pleasure as he is, powers on and consequently falls asleep, satisfied that he and Lisa have got the first time out of the way and confident things will improve. Lisa lies awake for six hours wondering why he didn't care enough to consider her, then gets up, grabs her bag and leaves, feeling used, sad and determined to never call Louis again.

And this is the conclusion of Kinsey's research resonating long after it was conducted: women attach a deeper significance to sex. Louis has separated the sex and the relationship, assuming his bond with Lisa remains, even if the sex is something they need to work on. Lisa cannot separate the two and assumes the unsuccessful sexual experience is indicative of Louis' feelings and evidence that the relationship is also doomed to failure.

The joy of sex is well documented. It can enhance your general happiness and emotional well-being. There's nothing better than the feeling that the person whose arms you want to rush into (shortly before you rip all their clothes off and show them how much you've missed them in the last five minutes) wants exactly the same from you. The fact is when sex is good, it's really good. But to ensure it is, its important we clear the sexual communication lines with our partner, and that means learning to ignore, or even discard, the sexual myths and stereotypes we often place in the way of our real sexual needs.

Our upbringing, our physical make up and society all play a part in guiding us as to what sexual behaviour and expectations are appropriate. Which would be great, apart from the fact that some of the time these expectations are outdated, stifling or just downright incorrect. Take time to challenge your cognitions. Why do you think the way you do? How realistic is your thinking? Is there any evidence to suggest it might be wrong? If you challenge this theory and act against it, what is the worst that can happen?

Be clear with your partner. Accept they also have their own set of sexual prejudices which will affect the way they read your responses in the bedroom. They too will interpret you through a smokescreen of schemas, so communicate clearly and unashamedly. If you were in a business meeting and you were unsure of what your client was asking of you, you'd make sure you clarified it straight away. If you went to the hairdresser's, you'd want to make sure the stylist knew exactly what you wanted before she got gung-ho with the scissors. So exercise the same clarity of communication in your personal life, particularly when it comes to your sexual relationship. Embrace the fact that if you and your partner sometimes appear to be speaking different languages, at least this is the one area of your relationship where you can both let a little non-verbal communication do the talking.

Men Should Remember:

* Encourage your partner to talk to you about what she wants. And listen to the answer.
* Don't see orgasm as your ultimate goal. Focus more on making sure you and your partner enjoy the experience as much as possible.

Women Should Remember:

* Speak up. Don't fall prey to the myth that he should automatically know what you like and take the lead because he is a man.
* Be clear. If you mean 'no', then say 'no'. Try to avoid mixed signals.

Chapter 3

Meeting Parents and Friends

Mother-in-law jokes are as much a part of traditional family banter as embarrassing childhood photos and sibling spats. The image of a hen-pecked husband, bossed about and fussed over by his nightmarish mother-in-law is one most of us are familiar with. However, it seems that in reality the shoe may actually be on the other foot. In 1999, Dr Terri Apter conducted a research paper for the University of Cambridge. She interviewed thirty-four mothers- and fathers-in-law and thirty-two sons- and daughters-in-law for a report that was later presented at a British Psychological Society conference (Apter, 1999). Twelve families were also observed at occasions where both generations of the family were brought together.

Her results suggested that actually it is women who fall prey to in-law syndrome. Dr Apter found that many of the mothers expected their sons to do far less than their own husbands. While their husbands might be expected to muck in and help with the dishes or take out the rubbish, these menial tasks were deemed far too much of a chore for their precious sons, who were encouraged to put their feet up – in a clear demonstration of how they should be treated by their partners. In fact, Apter found that, in the presence of their mothers, many men reverted back to stone-age behaviour. She found that many women felt their mothers-in-law were unsupportive of their careers. Some *identified a tussle for status in the family home. And the mothers-in-law? They failed to understand why their sons' partners felt this way about them ...*

Dr Apter's research unveils some interesting points on family relationships including how the experience of dealing with a partner's family varies for men and women. Of course, within a romantic relationship, the most important bond is between the two individuals involved, but that bond is far from the only one that affects a relationship. Much as we may like to think that our other half's life began the day we waltzed into their lives, it just isn't true. Before us there was his mother – washing his socks, ironing his pants and cultivating that rather irritating tendency he has to leave both on the bathroom floor. There was his sister – fussing over him one minute, screaming at him to get out of her room before his Transformers suffered some serious damage the next. There was his schoolfriends – who still tease him about his somewhat sloppy football skills, and still have the ability to make him revert to a thirteen-year-old. And there were those girlfriends who have now made the transition from 'was an ex' to 'a friend'.

The reality is that whenever a new relationship begins, each partner brings a host of family and friends into the equation. Just as we all bring emotional history and relationship-related preconceptions with us when we start up with a new partner, we also bring a bevy of key characters whose opinions are important to us, and who usually have our best interests at heart. This is not a choice but a reality. And of course, as ever, being a man or a woman affects the way we perceive and address the challenges this presents. We know that men are less focused on the quality of interpersonal relationships, we know that women are more prone to analysis, and we know that women and men are socialised to interpret social situations differently.

There are a number of issues you and your partner will face before you even make the formal introductions. The first problem is timing. It's easy to avoid putting a name to your relationship while it is just the two of you existing in your own little world, with no need for definitions. But the minute you choose to introduce your new partner to the other important people in your life, they suddenly require a title. You can't really have 'This is Matt, my . . .' as an open-ended statement. Introducing your partner to your mum, neighbour or pet hamster is often interpreted as a less direct way of saying, 'I think you're going to feature heavily in my future, therefore I think it is important you meet those people who are also an important part of my life.' And for a lot of people, that's a little bit scary.

Then there are the 'what if they hate each other?' fears. Obviously your network of friends and family are hugely important to you. Equally, your new partner is important to you. Realistically, you want them both in your life for ever and ever and, more than that, you want them to grow fond of each other too. The problem is that when people care about us they, justifiably, have very high expectations of the cards life should deal us. Your boyfriend may not be the axe-wielding monster your mother seems to think he is, but more often than not, her warped view of him won't be related to who he really is; it will be tied up with who he isn't. Letting new members into a group can be stressful, and when we are stressed it is easier to develop a very clear-cut view of a situation where people are either victims or villains. Your mother's probably always had a very precise view of the man she envisaged you marrying and when you bring home your Prince Charming, and he doesn't quite match up her predictions, or wishes, it can be a bitter pill to swallow.

Then of course, there are the politics. Trying to feel involved and at home when you don't know things like where Grandpa always sits or what Auntie Jane said to Cousin Laura to make her cry at her mum's sister's anniversary party before Uncle Bob got drunk and pulled down the marquee, can really make you feel an outsider. Equally, if you suddenly find yourself getting dragged into his sister's friend's mum's anniversary party saga, you'll probably wish you were more of an outsider, and weren't suddenly expected to take a stance and have a view on every family flashpoint.

Such challenges can affect the life of the couple profoundly. The new partner can feel caught up in the family dynamics, or issues with friends.

This chapter is about developing your couple style, while still building and maintaining relations with each other's social-support networks. We will look at the processes of meeting friends and family through the eyes of a man and a woman, the challenges these processes present and how you and your partner can navigate your way through this absolute minefield by finding a common language.

Patterns of Interaction with Family

The structure of a family, and the traditions and routines it holds dear will be hugely influential in the way it accepts new members. So, if your boyfriend comes from a particularly involved family, where every member has a say in the choices of all of their relatives, or where the parents are particularly controlling, his parents may find it hard to accept that an external presence might have some claim on their son. This type of family is often upset when a member gets into a serious relationship and this can make it particularly difficult for the couple (Crowe, 2005). This kind of possessiveness means that is extremely difficult, but absolutely essential, for the couple to maintain their boundaries and establish which parts of their relationship they want to share with the family and which parts are strictly between them – whether that be your feelings about him discussing your argument with his mother, or making a rule that Saturday is a strict non-family day where you will devote time to each other, without interference.

For at least eighteen years, if not more, we are hugely dependent on our parents and the family we grow up in. People like to feel needed, so it can be a big deal for your family if they feel you are distancing yourself from them or that you are ceasing to need their love and care. A common fear parents have is that adult children will emotionally divorce them (McCarthy and McCarthy, 2004). This is a natural fear and entirely understandable, but needs to be acknowledged and addressed. However, some parents will completely refuse to accept that their children have grown up and are ready to live independently of them. According to systemic theory, families unconsciously try to keep things as they are. They have homeostatic and self-regulatory features. Changes create disruption and uncertainty in the system, which need to be dealt with if things are to move along (McGoldrick, 1980). The intensity of the situation will certainly overload the couple at times. Parents can put pressure on the new member or even resent her/him. Families work best when there is a sense of regularity and security, and any perceived threat to this can make members feel vulnerable.

Specifically, conflict indicates that the family is dealing with the struggle of separation while trying to maintain ties. This fear of losing a relationship with an individual can counteract the desire to see them live a happy independent life. The new partner feels caught up in the middle of the conflict and he/she is usually unaware of the dynamics. After all, nobody understands a family like those within it, and you might not be seeing the whole picture, especially if you are unfamiliar with the dynamic of the family. Also, in a worst-case scenario, a new partner might actually find themselves held responsible by their boyfriend or girlfriend for the inter-family issues. So, if a man has only started arguing with his mother since he introduced his new girlfriend to the family, he could easily start to associate her with the family unrest, and eventually resent her for the arguments. Some people allow their partners to handle their families or friends for them, while they become the innocent bystanders (McGoldrick, 1980). You can imagine the situation: you're spending another afternoon sharing fondant fancies and Earl Grey with his parents, swiftly sidestepping swipe after swipe from his mother about your hair, your job, your car and your family, and slowly realising that, to her, you will never be anything other then the cheap hussy who stole her baby from the nest. As you desperately attempt to use your eyebrows to silently communicate, 'If you don't jump in here and defend me, we're leaving' to your boyfriend, he shrugs with a dopey grin and goes back to the train set that he and his father have been tinkering with all afternoon. This is the scenario John and Alice find themselves in one Sunday afternoon. Later on they discuss the day's events . . .

Alice says: 'You and your dad were having fun today, weren't you?'

Alice means : 'Unlike me.'

John says: 'Yeah, it's great to see him. And Mum too.'

Alice says: 'Hmmm, sure.'

John hears: 'Not really.'

John says: 'What's that supposed to mean?'

Alice says: 'Well, you could have involved me a little more, or at least stuck up for me when your mother decided to launch into her character assassination.'

John hears: 'I hate your mother.'

John thinks: How dare she?! My mother invites her into her home and all Alice can do is be rude.

John says: 'Well perhaps you should make a little effort. My last girlfriend and mum were joined at the hip.'

Alice hears: 'My last girlfriend was better than you.'

And the conversation continues, gradually resulting in a climatic screaming match. The expectations, pressures and individual gendered interpretations of the situation results in a big fat mess. Being a woman, Alice over-analyses the undertones of the interaction with John's mum, and is ever-focused on how their relationship is defined. As a man, John fails to see the emotional intricacies and subtext of the relationship between the two women in his life and oversimplifies the problem, hurting Alice's feelings in the process. Nobody benefits when these destructive or awkward scenarios develop. In fact, these relationship dynamics simply act as buffers between individuals and rule out any genuine intimacy or affection, as well as making everything ten times harder for the partner who is stuck in the middle of both parties. Consequently, the task that each partner faces is that of maintaining both relationships without losing either.

How to Deal with Parents

According to CBT, the relevant core beliefs and assumptions one holds about relationships are particularly important in situations like dealing with parents (or friends, as we will see). Such situations can trigger these core beliefs and lead the person to perceive information in a biased way that tends to fit with and strengthen the beliefs, and in turn cause them to behave in ways that prevent them from challenging their beliefs (Flecknoe and Sanders, 2004). For example, a person who believes that 'if others do not like me then I am a terrible person' might avoid meeting the parents of his/her partner or selectively attend to experiences that support this belief. Hence, she or he may act in such a way as to make parents (or friends) more likely not to like them. Safran and Segal (1990) suggest that a person's interpersonal behaviour tends to invite, or pull, a predictable response from others.

Let's take Paul and Megan. Paul is an only child who feels he can never meet his parents' expectations. He's never been particularly close to them, and has avoided them more and more as he has gone through life, seeing them only on birthdays and at Christmas. Megan comes from a large close family where whoever shouts the loudest is the one that gets listened to, and family gatherings resemble badly organised football riots but with less violence and more shrieking. Megan loves the madness of an evening with her family and tries to see them at least once a week. Now, over the years, Paul has cultivated the schema: 'I am no good in social situations, people don't like me and I am hard to get on with.' So, when he meets Megan's family, his instinct is to remain detached and quiet – a tactic that works perfectly with his own family. Of course, this means he never really bonds with Megan's rowdy relatives and they find this hard to understand. Consequently, Paul feels even more isolated and uses his strained relationship with his girlfriend's family to confirm further his negative beliefs. Paul's history of family relationships and his feelings about them are massively influential in the way he connects, or fails to connect, with Megan's family. And so a self-fulfilling prophecy begins.

Overall, interactions with one's partner's parents evoke worries and concerns for everyone, largely because they tap into fears about acceptance and validation from others. These are common worries for many of us and they are not always irrational or inaccurate. Sometimes relationships with parents can be tense. Ultimately, the situation is an awkward one – just because you hit it off with your boyfriend after two glasses of wine and a caesar salad doesn't mean you and his mother will necessarily share the same instant bond. Realistically, you are trying to force a relationship, and that will always feel a little awkward to begin with. But the last thing you should be doing is ruminating for hours about what this means, and analysing exactly what it is about your behaviour, background or appearance that is preventing you from becoming best friends with his older sister. This won't alleviate the tension, and it won't make you feel any better. If anything it will simply make you feel more awkward. Clearly there is a gender flashpoint here we know women are more prone to this exhaustive analysis than men. For example, let's look at Lee and Sophie. They've been going out together for three months, and over the course of a week both arrange to meet the other's parents. Let's look first at the meeting between Sophie and Lee's mum:

> *Lee's mum says: 'So lovely to meet you – can I get you a drink?'*
> *Sophie thinks: Will she think badly of me if I say yes? Will it look like I've got a drink problem?*
> *Sophie says: 'Oh, yes – just a small glass of wine, thank you.'*
> *Lee's mum says: 'Medium or dry, dear?'*
> *Sophie thinks: Oh God, she's testing my wine knowledge – she obviously doesn't think I'm classy enough for her son.*

Even the simplest of questions evoke a bout of over-analysis and mild panic, as Sophie tries to second-guess the meaning behind every sentence.

Now we go to the first meeting between Lee and Sophie's dad:

> *Sophie's dad says: 'Can I get you a beer, mate?'*
> *Lee hears: 'Can I get you a beer, mate?'*
> *Lee says: 'That would be lovely, thanks a lot.'*

And so the differences between common male interaction and common female interaction become clear, as do the feelings of 'not good enough' that Dr Apter identified as commonly expressed by girlfriends in the presence of mothers-in-law.

If your problems with his family are more serious than a little tension here and there, this doesn't necessarily mean your relationship with your boyfriend is doomed from the start. It might mean you won't be sharing those idyllic holidays in Tuscany with the in-laws you had envisaged, but there are ways you can ensure your relationship can exist alongside your partner's relationship with his family. Although we have talked in great length about the advantages of confronting issues, an awkward family often calls for the opposite. If you are not expected to socialise with your partner's family on a regular basis, then the ability to bite your tongue and keep the peace should never be underestimated. Often it is better (or advisable) to keep the balance and be impartial when you meet the antagonistic party (Crowe, 2005). As birthdays, anniversaries, holidays (such as Christmas) are common occasions where families come together, below are some useful suggestions on how best to deal with these as they arise. These techniques can be used to help you cope with them more effectively and to maintain socially appropriate relationships (even with people you might not like).

Bite your Tongue

Everybody knows the difference between you saying your mother's a pain in the backside and somebody else saying your mother's a pain in the backside. No matter how many millions of names your partner uses to describe his family, there is little chance he will appreciate you expressing the same sentiments. Family is a strange thing – despite the rows and conflicts there is usually a strong survival instinct that teaches us to protect our loved ones from criticism. So you won't do your relationship any favours if you start to join in the slanging match. Remember nobody really understands a family other than the people who are actually within the family, so don't be drawn into assuming his parents are 100 per cent right, or 100 per cent wrong. Where possible, reserve judgement and stay out of it.

Don't be the Middle Man

You probably have enough contentious issues within your own family not to want to start playing referee to his family's disagreements. If the problem is that your partner cannot get his family to warm to or accept you, don't be tempted to get involved and act as mediator, member of the jury or head cheerleader. It simply isn't your responsibility and will only lead to conflict. One of the rules of family love is that you always forgive. You row, you sulk and then eventually you remember how much you care for each other and everything blows over, but you are not a part of the family and echoing, 'Yeah, I totally agree with your son. You are a moaning old dragon,' will stay on your record far longer than it will stay on the original perpetrator's. Let your partner deal with his own family.

Be on the Side of Reconciliation

In every family dispute there are three sides to the story: his side, their side and the truth. Detach yourself enough to look at the situation objectively, no matter how unreasonable you think his family are being. Supporting reconciliation is far more useful than vowing to support your partner's feelings, no matter how unjustified or unhelpful his family are. Equally, trying to take the family's side will never help your relationship in the long run, because your partner will feel that when the going gets tough, he can't rely on you to support him. Remain impartial, calm and focused on working things out.

The Two Most Important People

When you and your partner face external pressures, it is key that you keep looking inwards and remembering why it is that you are together. If his parents, his sister or his brothers continually place stress on your relationship, try to ensure the priority in each of your minds is looking after each other. That doesn't mean you have to take sides, or get involved. It just means you and your partner should work out ways to accept that life places pressure on relationships but you will always work through it if you think about each other first.

Be Realistic

Yes, we know that the dream is to find a partner whose family are the mirror image of your own, who has a mother who shares your dress size, taste in clothes and cooks a mean roast dinner, and a father who strikes the right note between dashing and sleazy, possibly looking like Robert Redford all the while. In this dream world, his sister becomes as close to you as your sister, and his brother asks you for dating advice and fashion recommendations. But, as we all know, dream worlds rarely bear much resemblance to the real world. Accept that you can't get on with everyone and that this isn't a sign you have failed in any way. The goal should be a situation that ensures everyone can at least get on even if you can't become the next Brady Bunch. Accept differences and maintain appropriate relationships that keep the peace.

Friends

Until the age of about four our family usually provides our entire social network, but as soon as we start spending time independently of parents – at nursery or school – we begin to build a new network that will play a huge part in who we turn out to be. From the first kid whose building blocks you kick over, to your first playground football team, to the group you go on your first holiday abroad with, our friends are massively important in who we become and how we think. Our friendships give us a sense of belonging, a sense of support that differs from that provided by our family and, usually, an endless supply of amusement. Although relationships with parents determine to a large extent our longer-term preferences, attitudes and values, during adolescence it is often relationships with friends that cause most concern and which preoccupy the thoughts of young people as they grow up (Shucksmith et al., 1993). In other words, while our parents often shape our deepest beliefs and values, it is our friendships we tend to put most effort into, and it is our friendships that shape our more temporary views of things such as romantic relationships, career moves and Kate Moss's latest outfit.

Friendships are based on a completely different set of structural relationships to those with parents. They are more symmetrical and involve sharing and exchange. They provide support and security; people can negotiate their emotional independence, exchange information, put beliefs and feelings into words and develop a new and different perspective of themselves. Friendships become important as they move to intimacy that includes the development of a more exclusive focus, a willingness to talk about oneself and to share problems and advice. Friends tell one another just about everything that is going on in each other's lives. Friends literally reason together in order to organise experience and to define themselves as persons (Shucksmith et al., 1993).

Potential Pressures of Dealing with Friends

Trying to include oneself in a friendship group is by no means a scenario we face for the first time when we meet a partner. All through life we have to navigate our way through social structures with the chief aim of feeling accepted, wanted and, at a most basic level, liked. Largely because most people appreciate exactly how much influence friends have on our decisions and feelings, there is usually a certain urgency in wanting a new partner's friends to feel positively about us. Friends can give out clear signals to each other both about style and about fundamental values and perspectives. Conformity is the price that has to be paid for approval and acceptance. The potential ways that friends can affect a couple are varied, as we shall see.

It is quite possible that at the start of a new relationship, the social group of each individual will not even enter the equation. The onus is on getting to know one another before making the fairly formal step of introducing each other to external parties. However, as the relationship progresses, both parties will want to share it with the important people in their lives, and this can create problems from the outset. People can have very different ideas about how intertwined their friends and their partner should be.

Take Nisha and Mark. They have been dating for six months, and are both in their late twenties. They met at a work social function, so their initial few weeks together involved meeting up for dinner, drinks, etc. – basically in situations where it was just the two of them. As they have grown closer, they have also got to know each other's friends, and here's where the problems started. Both Nisha and Mark have close groups of friends from early schooldays. Mark's friends place a heavy emphasis on meeting regularly in the local pub – regularly means every Friday and Saturday. Nisha meets her friends for lunch on Sundays, and it is not uncommon for the girls to bring their partners. Bringing a partner to one of the boys' gatherings would be akin to blasphemy. So Mark is more than happy to keep his relationship and his friends separate and see Nisha during the week. Conversely, Nisha thinks Mark should get more involved with her friends and devote more weekend time to her. It is easy to see how the two conflict. Mark doesn't understand Nisha's desire to have him ever-present when she meets her friends, just as she doesn't understand his reluctance to take her to his social gatherings. A typical conversation between the two goes a little something like this:

Nisha says: 'Do you know what you're doing at the weekend yet?'
Nisha means: 'I do hope you haven't jam-packed your schedule with "boys time" already.'
Mark says: 'Oh, probably just the usual.'
Nisha hears: 'No special plans, but I will of course be placing time with my friends above time with you.'
Nisha says: 'Great. I thought we could do something together – Jane's having a first birthday party for Oscar and she's invited you to come along with me.'
Mark hears: 'You spend enough time with the boys. This weekend you're coming to coo over babies and dream of what our lives will soon become.'
Mark says: 'No thanks, can't let the boys down.'
Nisha hears: 'But I can let you down.'

People can often have different ideas about the time a couple should spend with friends. Some people have close friendships while others maintain a distance. Some prefer socialising and others prefer less of a social life. Imbalances in terms of how isolated or sociable people think the new couple should be create pressures for partners because, with the inclusion of friends, the relationship takes the form of a triangle. There is another party to satisfy, which can create conflict between your friends and your relationship.

As happens with family members, friends may also displace their problems in dealing with each other on the intrusion of a new member. They may perceive the new girlfriend or boyfriend as no good for their friend, or their friend as having no taste. Close friendships can often set highly influential markers around acceptable and unacceptable behaviours. Those who are 'in' do not mix as frequently with those on the periphery of what is acceptable to the group (Shucksmith et al., 1993).

An added pressure comes from the fact that young men and women use and view friendships in quite different ways. For instance, as far as women are concerned, we can trace the development of friendships through an early adolescent period when emotional commitments are minimal and the focus of friendship is common activities. There is strong emphasis on loyalty and support. On the other hand, men's friendships rarely achieve the depth of intimacy of women's. Larger peer groups – the boys or the lads – often appear more important to them than individual friendships. According to research, young men describe their friends to researchers in terms similar to those used by adolescent girls – failing to see emotional support, closeness or security as important qualities of a friendship (Shucksmith et al., 1993). So, because our friendships take different forms and fulfil different functions it can be hard to communicate to our partner how they should fit in with the relationship. Once again, our gender-specific viewpoints preside over any debate.

How to Deal with Issues Deriving from Friends

Success in dealing with each other's friends results from successfully deciding the way you want your relationship to operate, and this will only come about through discussion and compromise. From day one, you both need to accept you are likely to have different ideas in terms of how often you see your friends and how closely they are involved in your relationship. Equally, you need to be ready to face the possibility that your friends may not bond with your partner quite as easily as you do, perhaps because they are particularly protective of you, or perhaps for the simple reason that strong shared bonds are difficult for a new person to infiltrate.

There also needs to be a period of acceptance for both parties where you acknowledge that although your friends are likely to have a huge influence over your opinions and actions as a child and as an adolescent, when you commit to a serious romantic relationship as an adult, you have a new influence in your life and a new commitment to honour. This doesn't mean you have to dump your friends and make your new partner the centre of your universe, but it might mean you need to work out ways to incorporate these two sides of your life. As with other differences between partners, it would be sensible to discuss the problem and come to some sort of compromise. A balance needs to be achieved so couples don't clash. A good idea is to set different nights of the week for social outings with friends and for staying home (Crowe, 2005). It is important to make time to nurture relationships and to go out and have fun with friends. Time management and organisation techniques can help here.

Having a positive outlook on the situation can help. If you're having problems bonding with your partner's friends, maybe that's because you're viewing them as a hindrance, people that get in the way of your relationship with your partner. Readjust your thinking and consider what getting to know them could actually add to your own life. Making new friends, showing interest in others and forming new bonds expands your horizons. Enrich your life by inviting others into it. Research shows that friendships can reduce stress and improve your overall health and sense of well-being. So building a network of supportive friendships can be vital not only to your relationship with your partner but to your own happiness. And of course, besides what a relationship can do for you personally, having a shared group of friends as a couple can enhance the time you spend together and increase understanding between the two of you. Don't think of it as a night out with his friends, think of it as a chance to find a new thing you enjoy doing together.

If you really find it difficult to establish these close bonds with your partner's social network, then the best, and least, thing you can do is work to achieve relationships that are viable and civil. This might mean a great deal of temporary compromise on your part, particularly if you really do not agree with his friends' morals, values or behaviour. But it is absolutely worth it if it cuts out long-term conflict. So, instead of agreeing to spend every single Saturday at the rugby club, getting increasingly irritated by the coarse humour, unlimited toilet jokes and wildly inaccurate animal impressions (or perhaps they're just natural mannerisms) until you finally explode and end up tipping a pint over somebody's head, why not just agree to drop him off at the club, have a quick drink with his friends and then leave him to it. If you can't make relationships work, then don't put yourself under the pressure of spending every minute with those people. Just work out ways you can make it work when you absolutely have to. It will mean the world to your partner, and work wonders for your relationship.

And don't fake it. Be yourself and be sincere. If you can't quite find common ground with somebody then make it your mission to find out as much about them as you can. The fact of the matter is that people like talking about themselves, so ask questions and make the individual feel important. Focus on their interests and any you have in common, rather than focusing too much on the tension between you. This will improve relations between you and them, and it might even help you to understand why it is you misunderstand each other. Don't overdo it. It's not the end for you and your partner if you can't make his best friends your best friends, so concentrate on getting on, and anything else will be a bonus.

Friends and Family – How not to do it

So, we've looked at some dos in building a relationship with the people who are most important to your partner, but what about the don'ts? In an article on the worst ways to handle conflict Elizabeth Scott (2006) has identified some pointers that will help you avoid the cardinal sins in friend and family bonding. If your behaviour is reflected through any of these tips, perhaps that's where you're going wrong.

Encouraging and Furthering Conflict

Constructive, calm discussion will be more effective and less damaging than fighting fire with fire and opting for conflict. An aggressive, volatile style will undoubtedly lead to further conflict, bucket loads of awkward tension and resentment long after the initial confrontation.

Being Defensive

Adopting a defensive attitude means your willingness to understand the other person's point of view is stunted. Defensive people work hard to accept responsibility that may contribute to the problem. This can create problems in the long run as issues go unresolved.

Being Right

In conflict, there is rarely a clear-cut right or wrong. Remember that people on both sides of any argument are likely to believe they are absolutely right, so the chances of agreeing are slim. Focus on reaching compromise and establishing a situation where everyone is happy (even if it means agreeing to disagree) rather than always 'being right'.

Trying to Win the Argument

Always remember this: winning the argument is futile if, in the process, you have managed to permanently damage relationships. While it is important to stick to your beliefs and stand up for yourself, sometimes keeping the peace and keeping the knowledge you are right to yourself can be far more powerful. If your aim is to win every battle, then you may well do so, but it won't do your personal relationships any favours.

Making Character Attacks

'You are a selfish old hag' sounds very different from 'I think your behaviour is a little inconsiderate.' Learn the difference between making a character assassination and criticising behaviour. People are more open to listening if it sounds as though you are making a judgement on one incident, or one aspect of their behaviour, as opposed to making a judgement on their personality as a whole. Consider the language you use carefully.

Forgetting to Listen

How many times have you started a sentence with, 'I just want to say this before you go mad ...' or, 'I know you'll hate this but ...'? Too often we pre-empt responses and assume we know exactly what is going to happen in a given situation and as a result we stop listening and only hear our inner dialogue. This inevitably means people are less likely to actually listen to you. Never underestimate the importance of properly listening to somebody rather than simply acknowledging that they are talking.

Conclusion

Johnny and Leonie have been seeing each other for two months, and they've decided it's time to bite the bullet and 'do the parent thing'. So Leonie suggests Johnny's parents come over to her flat for dinner one night. She starts planning the million ways she will wow them with her culinary genius and charming dinner-party wit. The food is ready, the aperitifs are served and she asks Johnny to give her a hand serving up. And then it happens. Mother-in-law syndrome strikes and Johnny's mum pipes up, 'Oh no, dear, let him relax and enjoy his meal. Blimey – in my day, I've fed sixteen hungry mouths all in one go. I don't know – you modern career girls!'

Leonie stops in her tracks and waits for Johnny's response, knowing full well this could go one of two ways. Johnny might say, 'Thanks, Mum – you're right. Yes, come on, Leonie – hurry up, I'm starving' and risk the eternal wrath of his new girlfriend, or he might, heeding the lessons of this chapter, decide he can respect his mum and his relationship in one fell swoop. Consider the difference in response: 'Don't be silly, Mum, you've always brought me up to help around the home and I'm not going to start forgetting that now! Leonie's spent ages cooking a great meal – I'll go and bring it in for us.' Mum flattered and girlfriend calmed in one go – a great demonstration of the fact that whatever is going on round us, we still have a part to play in mediating the interaction and ensure everyone feels respected.

Dr Apter's research identified a new strand to the mother-in-law story. She found that contrary to decades of jokes from men, women often have the worst time bonding with their partner's family – in particular their partner's mother. As women increasingly juggle families with careers, many of them find the older generation unsympathetic or unwilling to support their choices. The feelings this evokes boil down to the basic premise of any interaction with people that are important to your partner – feeling 'good enough'. You love your partner and it follows you want the people he loves to love you too; that applies to his mother, his father or his very best mate. The real issue here is making relationships work and balancing the expectations you and your partner may have of what exactly that means and how the relationship should take shape.

When dealing with any relationship issue it is important to acknowledge and respect each other's boundaries. Just because you limit your family occasions to Christmas and birthdays doesn't mean your new partner will be used to the same routine. Our families, our friends, the things we see, the people we come across and the relationships we encounter all contribute to our own individual set of boundaries. Our boundaries determine what we feel comfortable with and how we want our life to be. All through life we must assess how flexible we are with our boundaries, which ones we should stick to resolutely and which ones we can com-promise. This is never more the case than when negotiating the set up of a new relationship. Our friends and family are hugely influential in our lives, so we are likely to have some very strong feelings about how closely they should know our partner and how much time we want to spend with them.

Failure in a relationship does not necessarily have to be catastrophic. There is a real need for interpersonal skills in situations like these, especially when a conflict is involved. For example, tolerance, understanding, negotiating or making distinctions about productive or unproductive worry over relationships can all be important for managing such interactions (Crowe, 2005). Using the same skills and common sense in your bond with your partner's family as those you use in your relationship with him is a good place to start.

The real key here is accepting that your partner's boundaries and expectations will be different from yours. That doesn't make anyone wrong or right, but it does mean a little negotiation will be in order. Establish a routine and a structure that works for both of you. Make sure both your boundaries are being respected. Where the conflict doesn't involve you, stay detached and impartial. Where the conflict does involve you, make an effort to create a situation that is at least bearable, if not beneficial, for everyone involved. If your partner is important to you, then his friends and family should also be important to you, not least because they form a huge part of the reasons that he became the person you love so much. Take the time to build bonds with them, encourage your partner to do the same with your loved ones, and you should be able to establish a couple style that will laugh in the face of all those mother-in-law jokes.

Men Should Remember:

- As much as you should be loyal to your friends and family, you also have a responsibility to protect your relationship. Don't let your partner feel like your last priority.
- Accept that you and your partner will have different experiences of meeting each other's friends and families, and that some of these

differences will simply be down to her being a woman and you being a man.

Women Should Remember:

- Don't worry about whether or not his mum will become your best friend. What will be, will be – take each day as it comes.
- Accept that we can't get along with everyone. As long as the involved parties can be civil and respectful that shouldn't be a problem.

Chapter 4

Emotional Unavailability

In September 2001, Dr Moira Maguire and Dr Paul Cavendish unveiled the findings of a research project looking into the experience of crying for men and for women. To get to the bottom of the matter, they interviewed thirty men and fifty-seven women, testing their responses against a scale known as the Adult Crying Inventory.

Much research in this field has suggested that women cry more than men; in fact, this is accepted as a widely acknowledged truth. The point of this study was to establish exactly why this is the case. Maguire and Cavendish found that although the immediate experience of crying, the mechanism of tears and sobbing was very similar for men and women – the triggers for this mechanism, and the aftermath of a good cry were very different.

While there was evidence that men and women are equally likely to cry over experiences such as bereavement, a relationship breakdown or some other personal loss, there were some very specific differences between common male and female reasons for crying. Men were more likely than women to cry as a result of positive feelings (for example, at his team winning the World Cup – no surprises there then). On the other hand, women were more likely to cry as a result of conflict with others, or because of feelings of personal inadequacy.

When women cry, they tend to feel a range of emotions, including fear, self-pity, powerlessness, anger and frustration. Women also reported more reasons for stopping crying and were more likely to stop as a result of being comforted.

Crying is such a basic primal instinct it seems strange that men and women should experience it so differently. After all, whichever way you look at it, sad is sad. Happy is happy. Seriously hacked off is seriously hacked off. No? Well, no, because, like every other facet of your relationship, your partner and you are likely to experience emotions completely differently. As we've seen, men are less open to talking about their emotions and less responsive to proactive attempts to encourage them to do so or provide comfort. So what implications does this have for your relationship, and how can you work with a partner who seems to restrict emotional intimacy?

Relationships are devices that provide the opportunity for our basic emotional needs for care, love and safety to be met (Crowe, 2005). Relationships can also protect us from loneliness and improve our emotional and physical well-being. Most of us, deep down, feel the need to be listened to, understood and validated by another human. Relating to somebody we feel connected to and in tune with is important to us. Consequently, satisfying intimate relationships represent an important source of happiness. So, despite the stress they sometimes evoke, relationships provide a wealth of the key ingredients we require to be happy shiny people. Potentially . . .

Unfortunately, this isn't always the case; not all relationships are satisfying. While all humans share the same basic needs, each differs in the degree to which they can have them met by others or the degree to which they can meet them in others. For various reasons, some people may actually avoid making these connections, or expressing feelings of intimacy. In this situation, emotions – in all their manifestations – become a source of threat, and the possibility of experiencing, showing, talking about, or eliciting emotions in others induces a sense of vulnerability. This fear of emotional intimacy can restrict the development of new relationships. We nurture and further new relationships by opening ourselves up to people, and by sharing our emotions with them, consequently, when we are emotionally unavailable, developing intimate relationships becomes almost impossible.

So, we've established that emotional intimacy provides the foundation for romantic relationships. Accordingly, in order to have healthy, happy relationships, we need to learn how to be at ease with sharing emotions, and find ways to be comfortable being intimate with a partner. However, we have also learnt that men and women experience and deal with emotions entirely differently, so how do we marry the shared need to connect with others emotionally and the very different ways men and women go about this? This chapter will conceptualise the emotional unavailability that some individuals demonstrate. We'll look at how men and women Interpret intimacy and, specifically, emotional intelligence, and how the two develop. Finally, we'll look at ways you and your partner can find some emotional middle ground.

What Intimacy Means

Officially, intimacy represents 'an Interpersonal, shared, affective experience, which is manifested in various forms throughout the lifespan' (Williams et al., 2001). It is the ability to fuse one's identity with that of another person without the fear of losing it. Once individuals have established a mutual attraction, they begin to develop an interdependent relationship by increasing their mutual involvement. They develop a high degree of connection and closeness. Intimacy involves willingness to share, mutual trust and commitment. It represents the need for close contact, mutual disclosure and sharing one's world with another. According to Reis and Patrick (1996) interactions are considered to be intimate when the following three features are evident:

Caring: the feeling we are loved and cared for.
Understanding: the feeling somebody views you similarly to the way you view yourself.
Validation: the communication of acceptance, acknowledgement and support for each other's points of view.

The development of intimacy comprises cognitive, behavioural and inter-personal components. In order to be truly intimate, one must be both available and willing to be vulnerable. Each person will have a different emotional outlook, determined by his or her past experiences. As with any aspect of relationships, our past experiences have a massive influence on our future encounters, and negative memories can prohibit us from sharing ourselves fully with a partner, possibly through fear of rejection. In this situation, a common behaviour will be to attempt to move away from the possibility of intimacy. Our bad experiences of allowing people to get close to us, can mean that in the future we reject opportunities for intimacy. We might do this through creating distance in relationships, displaying high levels of emotional withdrawal, changing the subject when emotions are discussed, or being less effective in providing our partner with comfort and emotional support (Street, 1994). In other words, when we feel uneasy with emotional intimacy, we will often avoid moments where we're expected to relate on an emotional level and even withdraw to a point where, actually, we fail to meet the needs of our partner. None of which is hugely useful within an adult romantic relationship.

Unlike duvet-sharing, reasonable shoe prices and the importance of games where men run around after balls, research has indicated that when it comes to intimacy, men and women view the topic fairly similarly. There appears to be a general consensus on what constitutes intimacy and males and females tend to agree on what the characteristics of intimacy are (Epstein and Baucom, 2003). However, there are some gender differences in the ways men and women seek intimacy. A couple may demonstrate intimacy in several different ways, including the way they relate to one another sexually. But this chapter will focus particularly on emotional intimacy and how that affects male–female communication.

Sharing emotions and encouraging closeness are things that women tend to do more readily then men. As I said earlier, it is commonly accepted that women cry more than men and Maguire and Cavendish also found that women have a far greater number of triggers for crying. In general, women are keener to communicate feelings and they prefer to talk about issues close to their heart – for example, families and friends. They tend to value and engage in mutual self-disclosure in close relationships (Epstein and Baucom, 2003). And when it comes sex, emotional bonds play an important part in female experience. Female sexual responsiveness and satisfaction is closely related to intimacy, whereas for men the link is more biological. Men, being right-brain-competent, manage better in tasks such as maths, physics and engineering (Crowe, 2005). Consequently, they tend to prefer sharing activities and interests rather than feelings as a means of achieving intimacy. This doesn't mean they find a feisty bout of quantum physics sexy, it just means they are more comfortable discussing practical things, such as the sports club, than what their deepest, darkest insecurities are. Inevitably we are more likely to achieve closeness when both parties are comfortable and at ease. For women, talking about past relationships may help them feel that they are making emotional progress with their partner and, in turn, make them more inclined to relax with men physically. It's easy to see how confusion can occur.

As we have established, women are socialised (and biologically pre-disposed) to be emotionally expressive, nurturing and to direct their achievement through affiliation with others while, conversely, men are socialised to be emotionally inhibited, assertive, and independent (Kimberling and Ouimette, 2002). These two entirely different social models provide ample ammunition for gender conflict. Consider the following example of Paul and Nova. Nova complains that she doesn't feel their relationship has reached a sufficient level of emotional intimacy. So, the following dialogue ensues:

Paul suggests: 'Well, why don't we do something together? Let's go hiking.'
Nova replies: 'I like hiking, but we never get to talk.'
She meant: 'I don't think that will help us connect. I wish he would just take me out for dinner.'
Paul heard: 'She just hates hiking.'
He meant: 'When we go hiking together, I feel really close to you.'

Both Paul and Nova want to connect, but they have different ways of feeling close to each other. For Paul, undertaking an activity he loves with the woman he loves is the perfect way to spend time together. He probably enjoys the practical, goal-focused idea of embarking on a physical challenge with Nova, and feels that sharing time and sharing an activity is a route to increased intimacy. On the other hand, Nova feels that to grow closer emotionally, they actually need to talk about emotions. Neither party are right or wrong, they just approach the situation in their own gender-specific ways.

Further problems arise between partners when there is an incompatibility in each other's intimacy needs. The key to intimate relationships is the sharing of deeply personal information and emotion; it goes beyond simply spending time together, and this exchange must be reciprocal. For example, one partner may have a strong need for affiliation but not a strong need for intimacy and this might produce confusion or even discord (Epstein and Baucom, 2003).

Let's look at Tony and Alison who have been seeing each other for a couple of months. Tony has an active social life, spending the majority of his time with friends, and partaking in a number of sports within various clubs. Alison was attracted to his outgoing manner and his ability to connect with people. She wants a committed and intimate relationship and she assumes Tony wants the same. She has interpreted Tony's social behaviour and outgoing social skills as evidence that he also enjoys forging close bonds. So, she makes efforts to increase their level of intimacy by trying to connect emotionally with him via romantic walks in the parks, candlelit dinners for two and sharing sessions every morning in bed. She has recently started to realise Tony is resisting her efforts, and actually avoiding a deep romantic connection. So Alison concludes Tony isn't interested in a serious relationship.

Let's see what Tony is thinking here. He loves making new connections, but sees intimacy as something that develops slowly and perceives Alison as 'too pushy and demanding'. How could she expect to know so much about his inner workings when they are just at the 'getting to know you' stage of their relationship? Ironically, the relationship will flounder not because they don't want the same things but because they want them at different paces and expect them to flourish in different ways. As we will go on to see, it's hard to create or force intimacy, and by letting the relationship develop at a natural pace it's likely the couple would have become more intimate naturally.

The Experience of Emotional Unavailability

Avoidance of emotional unavailability represents a fear of experiencing and/or expressing feelings and, consequently, a fear of closeness or intimacy. It refers to the incapacity to take the chance to connect with another person by sharing true intimacy. Hence some people become financially or socially successful yet retain a deep sense of isolation because their fear means they fail to develop intimate connections with others.

Emotional unavailability is, in essence, when someone lacks what we call emotional intelligence. The term refers to 'a type of social intelligence that involves the ability to monitor one's own and others' emotions, to discriminate among them, and to use the information to guide one's thinking and actions' (Mayer and Salovey, 1993). We may learn or develop emotional intelligence in the same way that we may learn or develop any other skill, or it may be an emotional stage we go through simply as a result of other experiences and feelings. It is possible that emotionally unavailable behaviour can be demonstrated by someone who has previously shown great emotional intelligence, but who is going through a particularly hard time or a major life change.

Showing effective emotional intelligence involves abilities that may be categorised into five domains:

Self-awareness: observing yourself and recognising your feelings.
Managing emotions: Handling feelings appropriately; realising what is behind a feeling; finding ways to handle fears and anxieties, anger and sadness.
Motivating oneself: channelling emotions in the service of a goal;

85

emotional self-control; delaying gratification and stifling impulses. Knowing how to control and respond to emotions.
Empathy: sensitivity to others' feelings and concerns. The ability to see their perspective and appreciate the differences in how people feel about things.
Handling relationships: managing emotions in others. This incorporates social competence and social skills.

In other words, we can describe emotional intelligence as the ability to recognise, experience, manage and communicate emotions. More specifically, self-awareness, empathy and the ability to handle relationships (interpersonal intelligence) are essential *emotional skills* and demonstration of them contributes to a successful relationship. People who have not fully developed these skills may find it difficult to recognise and embrace these emotions in themselves and in others. Instead, they will probably disengage from emotional attachment in a variety of ways, perhaps using humour or preoccupation as avoidance tactics. In turn, they will be perceived by their prospective partner, or indeed their current partner, as emotionally unavailable, avoidant or immature. This will obviously create a massive hurdle for the development of a romantic relationship, where intimacy, closeness and trust are key.

So, where does this leave you if you find yourself encountering a relationship with somebody who is emotionally unavailable? Attempting to grow close to someone with an active fear of opening up can be relentlessly frustrating and often very painful. Usually in this situation, the more you try to penetrate the inner layers of somebody who has a distinct fear of being exposed, the more they will close up and resist your efforts. People who experience emotional attachment difficulties may find these difficulties reflected in their treatment of their partner – they may become cold, dismissive, or even cruel. Some cases demonstrate a tendency to use alcohol or drugs to mask their inability to connect. People also employ distraction and, in some cases, downright denial of their emotional issues. Throughout our lives, a number of factors can play a part in encouraging us to deny feelings that are negative, inappropriate or shameful – due to our early education or our religious upbringing. As humans we are designed to cope with positive and negative emotions, and in order to grow we must learn how to manage both. Influences which discourage our ability to deal with emotion in early life can have disastrous effects on our adult relationships. True emotional intelligence means we can recognise and cope with negative emotional input, as well as positive.

Key Cognitive Features of Emotional Unavailability

According to the cognitive model, this anxiety over sharing emotions and building intimate bonds is closely linked to inner themes of risk and danger. There is a genuine fear of vocalising thoughts, expectations and beliefs, and a fear of emotional arousal, which in turn leads to the stifling of feelings. For people who display these schemas, being asked to 'open up' is like being asked to enter an unknown and potentially dangerous territory (Butler and Surawy, 2004). Their inner beliefs tell them 'I can't go there', 'I mustn't let that happen', but they are not comfortable vocalising or explaining this inner dialogue; emotionally unavailable people will go out of their way to *avoid* saying what feels even slightly emotional.

Anxiety or fear of intimacy can be categorised into three distinctive kinds of thoughts:

1 The Meaning of Having Feelings

Emotionally avoidant people usually try to suppress their emotions because experiencing emotions leaves them feeling weak or vulnerable. Experiencing feelings may be seen as a catastrophe. Assumptions about the sort of person who experiences emotion, and how they do this, are often culturally influenced. For example, in many cultures the belief that 'Men should always be strong' and 'It is wrong to feel vulnerable if one is a man' are prevalent. This goes back to the 'big boys don't cry' lessons of childhood and continues through to the 'fear is weakness' mantra that many men demonstrate in later years. As we've seen from Cavendish and Maguire's research, crying is less likely to be a male response to feelings of fear, conflict or inadequacy; in fact, they are less likely to cry in general.

2 The Meaning of Expressing Feelings

Our thoughts about emotions and how they should be expressed are often related to how we feel others will react. For example, an individual might be restricted from expressing emotion by the following beliefs: 'If I let my boyfriend know how I truly feel, he will be upset', 'I will be rejected if I say I love you', 'If I open up, no one will like the real me' or 'No one cares about how I feel'. Our dominant fears in these situations are of displaying behaviours that will lead to rejection or humiliation. These fears are also linked to misconceptions such as: 'No one else seems to feel distressed' or 'Others can control themselves, so should I'. Finally, they may be linked to cultural beliefs that govern such behaviour, for example: 'Men should be able to hide their sadness', 'Women should be able to tolerate their pain' or 'It is wrong to tell your husband off'.

3 Confusion about Emotions

Being unable to label feelings or understand their significance often causes confusion and uncertainty and can provoke a wide variety of reactions. The subject may feel deeply unhappy, or as if something is missing from their life, without the faintest idea of why they feel this way. So, a person who feels depressed despite enjoying a healthy relationship, a thriving social life and a successful career, may avoid sharing these negative emotions because they simply don't know how to put them into words or present them in a coherent way. Feelings are often misattributed and, consequently, never fully addressed. So, after an argument with her boyfriend, a sad, angry woman might attribute her feelings to a physical symptom, for example a headache. Not only will this mean she does not confront her own emotional state directly, but it may also mean that she is uncomfortable dealing with others who do (Butler and Surawy, 2004).

Attachment Theory – How Emotional Intelligence Develops

Motivation for intimacy and attachment develops through early bonds with care givers. Attachment theory is a theoretical framework developed by Bowlby (1980) and proposes that the quality of early attachment is rooted in the history of interactions between the infant and the primary care taker and the degree to which the infant has learned to rely on the attachment figure as a source of security. According to this theory, the behavioural and emotional reactions that occur in a child's bond with his/her care giver are important as they lead to the development of internal working models or cognitive schemas. So we're back to those good old schemas again, the building blocks that make up our beliefs about the world and ourselves. They act as templates and they provide the basis for screening out and evaluating information that confronts the individual (Padesky, 1994). In simpler words, these are the lenses through which we view and make sense of our experiences. As we've already established, our schemas determine how we think, feel, act and relate to others.

Attachment theorists have described how individuals develop tendencies to behave in particular ways to elicit intimacy (Epstein and Baucom, 2003). Research has shown that warm and responsive parenting is expected to give rise to positive models of both the self and others, resulting in secure and fulfilling adult relationships. Individuals with secure attachment styles tend to meet their needs and be able to take care of the needs of their partners because they hold positive beliefs or schemas about themselves, the world and others. They have learnt to view themselves as worthy, safe, competent and loved. They perceive relationships as sources of satisfaction, where they can have their needs met. They are comfortable with others and feel safe. In other words if, as a child, you witness and observe happy, healthy relationships, you are more likely to go on to develop similarly happy romantic bonds.

On the other hand, unresponsive, distant or abusive parenting leads to insecure attachment styles. Such parents fail to meet a child's core needs for basic safety, connections to others (attention, love affection, empathy), autonomy and self-esteem (Young et al., 2003). The effect of such 'toxic' experiences is cumulative and leads to the development of maladaptive beliefs or schemas, which in turn leads to dysfunctional patterns of interactions and emotional regulation. An individual with an insecure attachment does not anticipate care-taking responses from others, and thereafter he/she will develop behaviours that can alienate or distance others (Epstein and Baucom, 2003).

In a nutshell, emotional avoidance or unavailability typically derives from (Butler and Surawy, 2004):

- **Early experiences:** for example, belonging to a family in which talking about feelings is not common or acceptable; painful or traumatic experiences that produce discomfort with feelings such as humiliation, criticism, betrayal, rejection, bullying, cruelty, etc.
- **Cultural factors:** determined for example by race, nationality, gender, age or religion. Such factors often influence the degree and type of emotional expression considered acceptable within a particular group.
- **Genetic or biological variation:** male versus female physiological differences, sensitivity to physiological arousal.

Relationships and how they are Plagued by Emotional Unavailability

As adults we enter intimate relationships with a ready made, well-established set of beliefs. We have already mentioned that many of these schemas develop from experiences in early family life and, in particular, the attachment styles we are exposed to. But our experiences in adult relationships also go on to affect our romantic futures and our beliefs about expressing emotion. A person's schemas not only affect how they think about relationships and behave, but they also influence how they respond emotionally within intimate relationships (Epstein and Baucom, 2003). So emotion-based schemas, however they are established, will inevitably influence our relationships throughout life. I'll explain how this occurs.

Throughout the life cycle our attachment styles are particularly important for close relationships and intricately related to relationship communication and satisfaction (Buunk, 2001). It is certainly known that romantic attraction is an automatic process that occurs immediately without awareness of the person involved. Nevertheless, research has shown that to some extent the chances of developing a romantic relationship with someone else are determined by the factors that are important in the development of affectionate bonds in our early life. Adult relationships, and in particular romantic relationships, share critical characteristics with our early relationships. Attachment theorists have proposed that both types of relationship can be conceptualised as attachment relationships (Shaver and Hazan, 1988). For example, in both types of relationships the individual seeks proximity and care, and loss is grieved. So, whether you are a four-year-old who has just fallen over and wants a hug and a plaster from Mummy, or a twenty-four-year-old who has flunked her first job interview and just wants a cup of tea and a hug from her boyfriend, the basic care needs are remarkably similar.

Let us look at some case examples of how our early development can stunt our emotional growth and plague our intimate relationships:

Product of the Past Syndrome

Lena is a thirty-five-year-old woman who suffered an abusive childhood. She finds it very difficult to trust others and has never had a long-term relationship with a man. She avoided dating until she went to university. In the first two years of university, she started going out with friends and doing drugs. Only then was she able to be intimate with men. The experience of sexual abuse by her stepfather damaged her trust in others and her capacity for intimacy with the opposite sex. She becomes angry and anxious with any man who seems to approach her romantically and finds it hard to challenge the belief that men are only out for sex when one asks her out on a date or pays her a compliment. Her basic belief is: men can't be trusted.

Never Good Enough Syndrome

Mike is a thirty-two-year-old high-flying city banker. He has been through a series of relationships, but none have lasted long. Every time he starts dating he gets carried away with the excitement that this one is 'the one'. But, despite this initial attraction, his relationships always end up in disappointment. He says the chemistry disappears early on and his partners always end up boring him. He feels intensely alone and shows a tendency to be demanding in his romantic relationships. Nothing a new partner has to offer is ever good enough for him. Mike finds it hard to challenge his belief that a woman will ever understand his needs. His basic belief is that: others are never good enough.

Rabbit in the Headlights Syndrome

Henry is a twenty-six-year-old teacher. He is a very good-looking chap with a big circle of friends. He is quite popular with women because he seems to be a genuinely sensitive guy. However, he has felt trapped in all his romantic relationships. He feels he is always striving to meet the needs of his partners and that, in doing this, he ends up missing out on some of the things that make him really happy. He is so easy-going and eager to please that he naturally gets on with his partners but this usually leads to his dates asking too much of him and assuming he will meet their needs. In turn, Henry finds it hard to challenge the belief that when his date makes a suggestion, she does not intend to control him or infringe on the lifestyle he loves so much. His basic belief is: a relationship will rob me of my autonomy.

Closed Book Syndrome

Myra is a twenty-nine-year-old lawyer. She is quite attractive, but often experiences difficulties in dating. She wants to be with someone but always finds her relationships end in disaster. She is open to falling in love but finds it much harder to get really close to someone. Her partners usually describe her as superficial. 'Everything has to be kept inside,' she thinks. Her parents have never really been affectionate and communication of emotions was a no-go area in her family. She finds it hard to let go of the belief that a partner will also find emotional expression inappropriate. Her basic belief is: if I show emotion, I will lose control.

In the above examples, the way schemas influence relationships is demonstrated through resultant behaviour. Often, our behaviour leads to outcomes that only strengthen our beliefs and enable us to continue fitting information into this biased view of reality. So, if Henry continues to believe that the women who come into his life want to change and make demands of him, he will initially probably bend over backwards to meet their every need, regardless of whether this is necessary or not. Even if the woman he has started dating doesn't mind whether they go out on Wednesday (when Henry plays tennis) or Thursday, Henry, through his past experiences and inbuilt schemas, will assume that, really, this woman wants to be a priority and will be unhappy unless he puts her first, and cancels tennis to see her on Wednesday. Eventually, Henry will start to resent these little unrequested sacrifices and the relationship will probably fail. This will only serve to reinforce Henry's belief that women want too much from him. Much of this thought process has probably occurred unbeknown to his partner, who would have been happy to slot into his life and honour the hobbies that are important to him. Henry's relationship beliefs lead him to behave in a certain way, which produces results that only reinforce his beliefs. So he is stuck in a vicious circle.

Thus, schemas render individuals prone to various emotional and behavioural reactions in their interactions with others. As also illustrated in the previous examples, a person with an insecure attachment may display hesitancy about getting close to others because of his/her earlier experiences of rejection, emotional disconnection or abuse. She/he might have learned that emotional needs are a sign of weakness or immaturity. So, Lena finds it hard to trust and build bonds with men, because her early childhood relationships didn't show her how to do this successfully. She has never been in an environment built on strong interpersonal attachments, so she is unsure how to build and maintain them.

Conversely, a person with secure attachment experiences is likely to have positive schemas about the self and others and therefore approaches relationships expecting closeness and intimacy. He/she may learn that emotional experience is validated and therefore important. Studies have documented that individuals with secure attachment styles cope with stress by seeking social support, whereas those with insecure attachment styles tend either to withdraw from their partners when stressed or be preoccupied with their partner's responsiveness (Simpson et al., 1992). Being around healthy, happy partnerships not only helps us to build good relationships, but also helps us cope within our relationship when things go wrong – when we are feeling down. Being able to show vulnerability, or inner pain to your partner is hugely important within a relationship, and we are more likely to be comfortable with this if we have developed secure attachment styles.

With respect to care-taking behaviour, securely attached men display more emotional support, reassurance and concern for their partner's well-being (Simpson et al., 1992). Their romantic relationships are characterised by trust, friendship, enjoyment, self-disclosure and collaborative problem-solving (Collins and Read, 1990). While insecurely attached men display an opposite pattern (Simpson et al., 1992). They often assert their own feelings and needs without adequate regard for those of their partners and are prone to engage in uncommitted sexual relationships (Simpson and Gangstead, 1991). Individuals with an insecure attachment style *do* have a need for emotional support but are concerned their partners may reject them while expressing such a need. So experiencing attachment difficulties doesn't mean an individual has different emotional needs from anyone else, it just means they are less able to respond to, or express these needs.

Coping with Emotional Unavailability

Closeness and intimacy are important buzzwords within a relationship, and they are also likely to be a source of conflict. As with any relationship, not feeling as though our emotional requirements are being met can produce a variety of responses ranging from frustration to despair. Emotional unavailability is likely to be one of the first big hurdles your relationship faces, and it plays havoc with the process of developing and cementing a new partnership.

CBT can be invaluable in terms of confronting emotional unavailability, not least because it encourages us to make the important link between our feelings and our behaviour. The first step is for each partner to be clear about what kind of emotional bond they expect or require within a relationship. Each person should be clear about what they need from their partner in order for the relationship to survive. This may involve reflecting on inner beliefs, as a method of establishing why they hold these expectations. CBT dictates that feelings and actions don't just occur – they are a direct result of our schema structures.

Sharing is an integral part of emotional communication and some-thing that should be practised with your partner. Individuals who avoid attachment will find this particularly difficult, so approach it slowly and progressively. Asking questions about your partner's feelings is only the first step; ensure you are explaining your own emotions, to create a feeling of a two-way interaction, rather than a one-way interrogation.

Asking empathetic questions can have two main results. Firstly, it will allow you to get a deeper understanding of your partner's emotions. Instead of asking, 'Why are you being such a moody idiot today?' it might be better to say, 'You seem a little distant today. Talk to me about how you're feeling.' A different approach is likely to produce more open results. Secondly, if you can provide a positive response when your partner does open up to you, then you can encourage further disclosure. So if you listen, and offer understanding when your partner shares something like, 'Sometimes I worry about getting close to you, because I'm scared you might hurt me or leave me', rather than flying into a rage, your partner is far more likely to offer you these kind of insights in the future.

And don't forget, this is about sharing. If you want to persuade your partner to confide in you, then make sure you confide in him too. If you feel more comfortable talking about emotional issues, then you can lead the way.

Conclusion

Emotional awareness is knowing when feelings are present in ourselves, and emotional literacy is when we understand those feelings and are capable of managing them or responding to them. In relationships it is important that we develop these skills for a number of reasons:

- Emotions alert us to what needs are not being met. For example, when we feel lonely our need for connection is not being met. When we feel rejected it is our need for acceptance that is being neglected. Emotions are the indicators of our inner states and they let us know when all is not right, so it helps if we can interpret and respond to them.
- Emotions enhance communication. Our facial expressions, for example, can convey a wide range of emotions. If we look sad or hurt, we are signalling to others that we need their help. If we are verbally skilled we will be able to express more of our emotional needs and thereby have a better chance of fulfilling them. If we are effective at listening to the emotional troubles of others, we are better able to help them feel understood, important and cared about.
- Emotions can help us connect with others. If we feel confident expressing our emotions, then we can let our partner know how we feel. This is likely to provoke reciprocal sharing, and the sharing of emotions is how we bond with people on a deeper level.

And when the emotional connections are a little faulty, there's the potential for a little awkward dialogue and a lot of misunderstanding.

Remember Henry? The commitmentphobe who's terrified that letting his guard down to a woman will give her a licence to lock him up and control his life? Let's look at his new relationship with Jenny. They've been dating for two months and, so far, it's going well. Jenny seems laid back and cool about things, and Henry has so far managed to stifle any claustrophobic urges until one day they happen to watch a documentary about orphaned children. Jenny is obviously moved, and an awkward silence descends. Until . . .

Henry says: 'Are you OK?'

Henry means: 'Are you crying? What's going on here?'

Jenny says: 'Sure. I just found that a little hard to watch — my parents both died when I was young and it just hit a nerve.'

Henry thinks: What's this documentary got to do with your life? I know that must have been hard for you, but this is totally unrelated. This is making me feel awkward. I don't know how to deal with your emotions and it makes me feel trapped.

Henry says: Nothing.

Jenny says: 'It's a long story . . . basically . . .'

Henry says: Nothing.

Jenny thinks: I'm opening up to you here, you could be a little more comforting. This is a big deal to me.

Jenny says: 'I'm sorry to burden you with this. How boring of me!'

Jenny thinks: I shouldn't have to apologise for my emotions.

Henry says: 'That's fine, don't worry.'

Henry thinks: Good. Can we go back to being normal now? That was weird.

Henry and Jenny don't understand each other's emotional standpoints. As we saw through Maguire and Cavendish's research, men and women have different emotional triggers. Henry doesn't understand Jenny's emotional trigger and his confused reaction reflects that. Equally, Jenny takes offence at his reaction because she doesn't understand his confusion. Had either of the pair exercised a little CBT, understood how their basic differences affected their viewpoints and therefore their reactions, they would be far closer to finding a common emotional language.

In conclusion, the happiest couples in the world are those who display understanding and empathy with one another's feelings and a willingness to appreciate each other's point of view. It is hard to elevate a new relationship to this level if there is a lack of emotional interaction. In fact, what differentiates our romantic relationships from the other bonds we build in our lives is how much of ourselves we share. We share ourselves physically with our partner in a way far beyond any other relationship. We often share our time with a romantic partner far more than with family or friends. In a healthy happy relationship, we share our inner feelings with a partner in a way that would be unusual in a family or platonic relationship.

In other words, sharing things with our partner that we wouldn't share with anyone else is one of the things that makes a relationship special, but for some people it's also the hardest thing to do. Overcoming emotional unavailability takes time, patience and tact. Go slowly, go surely, and don't expect anything of your partner that you aren't comfortable with yourself. If you want him to open up about past relationships, then try sharing with him first. If you don't think he's being honest about his feelings after a big row, then talk to him about yours, without the blame, the screaming and the swearing. Emotional bonding is a two-way thing, but once you get it right your relationship will be ready to progress to the next level.

Men Should Remember:

- Learning to talk about emotions will bring you closer to your partner and help you to understand them.
- Try to be sensitive. It might not be a big deal to you, but if it is to your partner then it is worth addressing.

Women Should Remember:

- Don't expect your man to react like a woman to sad, stressful or even happy situations.
- Don't interpret withdrawal as rejection. Give your partner space to deal with emotions in a way he feels comfortable with.

Chapter 5
Infidelity

In 2005, a group of researchers at Florida Atlantic University set about furthering the research that had previously been conducted into the way men and women respond to infidelity. They wanted to test the hypotheses that men are more upset about sexual infidelity than emotional infidelity and that women feel precisely the opposite. They also wanted to look within these hypotheses and examine how the relationship status of a man or a woman affects this response.

The researchers interviewed 236 undergraduates ranging from ages eighteen to seventy-four. The majority of the sample – 87 per cent – was married, but nearly 90 per cent reported that they had previously been in or were currently in a serious committed relationship. The subjects were asked a series of closed questions, ranging from 'What would upset you more? Imagining your partner enjoying sexual intercourse with another person or imagining your partner forming a deep emotional attachment to that person?' to 'What would upset you more? Your partner confiding things to another person they haven't confided to you, or your partner trying a sexual position with that person that you two haven't tried together?' The researchers developed a sexual jealousy score from the answers, enabling them to calculate their conclusions.

As previous research had suggested, there were far more men upset *by the physical aspects of infidelity and far more women distressed by the emotional aspects. In answer to the question regarding a new sexual position and confiding emotions, 33 per cent of men were more concerned with the sexual exploration, compared with less than 10 per cent of women. The researchers also found that whether they had been in a serious relationship or not, women were almost equally upset by emotional infidelity. On the other hand, men were far more likely to be upset by the emotional aspect if they had been in a serious relationship before.*

The subjects of the Florida Atlantic University project represented a typical snapshot of the range of feelings the mere mention of infidelity can evoke. Whichever way you look at it, infidelity is one of those hot topics everybody has an opinion about. What constitutes cheating? Is thinking about cheating as bad as committing the act? Does a kiss count? Have you been unfaithful the minute you fail to mention you are in a relationship? What is the best way to deal with infidelity? How many strikes do you get before you're out? Can a relationship ever recover from infidelity, emotional or physical? Can a leopard change his spots? There are a million ways of looking at cheating, what it comprises and how it should be dealt with, but one fact remains: infidelity, be it emotional or sexual, knows no rival when it comes to disrupting marital or other committed relationships and is still one of the most common grounds for divorce (Crowe, 2005). In other words, cheating is still one of the big players when it comes to relationship strife.

By the term infidelity, we refer to a sexual-emotional episode(s) of varying duration and intensity involving two people, when either or both are married or in a committed relationship (Lefrancois, 1990). Affairs by definition are hidden and secretive. As often as you read about happy, harmonious harems headed by men with smug grins and long beards, or ecstatically content couples who delight in the joys of an open relationship, occurrences are rarely openly tolerated. Extramarital sex is the most commonly cited cause of divorce cross-culturally (Betzig, 1989). A review of research on infidelity indicates that about 55 per cent of married men and 45 per cent of women have affairs (Scarf, 1987). By looking at the statistics this suggests that about 70 per cent of marriages experience an affair at some point. Rather depressingly, it appears you're about as likely to have an affair as you are to remain faithful. The statistics aren't great. And whereas affairs have previously been seen as the domain of men with lipstick on their collar, it has been found that the incidence of adultery has become almost as common among women as it has among men, even if, as research such as that conducted at Florida Atlantic University suggests, men and women still view infidelity completely differently.

The psychological sequel of infidelity is often dramatic, painful and downright exhausting. Anguish, depression, anger, humiliation and betrayal are the most common emotional experiences of the partner of someone who has been unfaithful (Buus and Shackelford, 1997). Crucially, when it comes to the aftermath, the first casualty is trust. While the betrayal itself may (and probably will) evoke feelings of rejection and unleash the equivalent of a firing squad on your self-esteem, the depressing news is that the worst is yet to come. In other words, even if we can get our heads round the fact that our partner has committed physical betrayal, what often goes on to destroy a relationship is the fear that it may happen again and the behaviour this fear is likely to produce.

One of the common misconceptions about infidelity is that it is the first step in the downfall of an otherwise healthy relationship. Research shows that, in fact, an affair or a betrayal is more likely to be a symptom of existing problems, and a warning sign as opposed to a sudden and unexpected blow to the relationship. In other words, if a partner is cheating, it's likely there are already problems within the relationship. Essentially, affairs tend not to occur within a genuinely happy partnership so, rather than being a catalyst, they are usually an indicator of problems.

In this chapter, we look at why infidelity happens, how it happens and the good, bad and ugly implications it can have for your relationship. The researchers at Florida Atlantic University attributed the differences between male and female responses to infidelity to a variety of factors: from the possibility that a man might raise another man's child if he is a victim of a sexual infidelity, to the female fear of a loss of parental investment in her children if their father becomes emotionally disengaged. This chapter is about looking beyond these immediate responses and examining how a relationship carries on from these initial reactions.

We will look further at how these reactions vary between the genders, and adopt a CBT approach to moving a relationship on from infidelity. Maybe an infidelity is the end of your relationship, maybe it isn't. Either way, moving on is key. Whether you choose to hit the road or stand by your partner, you can only truly recover from an infidelity by addressing it, by working out what It means for you, your partner, your relationship and finally putting it behind you. CBT's realistic approach can be the perfect antidote to the high drama of an infidelity, and we'll look at exactly how it can be implemented in the event of a romantic betrayal.

Why it Happens

There are two universal truths when it comes to affairs. Firstly, whatever he or she tells you, affairs don't 'just happen'. They don't appear out of the blue. Secondly, affairs simply do not happen when a relationship is happy, well-founded and healthy. When both partners feel fulfilled by and content with their relationship, an affair is very, very unlikely. Research has identified specific relationship variables that are closely linked to infidelity and can help explain why it occurs in the first place:

Relationship Satisfaction

One of the most obvious explanations for infidelity is a change in the state of the relationship, or indeed a continuing lack of relationship quality. Research has shown infidelity is more common among women as a result of dissatisfaction with their marriage, possibly because men are more motivated to cheat by factors such as opportunity, rather than deep-seated, ongoing motivations. Marital satisfaction can be broken down into factors such as sexual satisfaction, quality of emotional support and the level of love and affection experienced in the relationship. In accordance with the research suggesting the sexual aspects of a relationship are more important to a man than a woman, female marital dissatisfaction usually centres on emotional issues, while male dissatisfaction focuses on sexual issues (Glass and Wright, 1985). However, in general, shortcomings in any of these areas make a relationship more susceptible to infidelity. In a study by Buus and Shackelford (1997) their findings show that sources of conflict such as complaints, jealousy, possessiveness, being condescending and sexual withholding are the most predictive. These patterns may reflect, for example, that men who are inordinately worried about their spouse's fidelity show high levels of jealousy and possessiveness and perhaps condescend in an effort to lower their wife's/partner's self-esteem.

Another consistent pattern is the link between spouses' complaints about their partner's sexualising of others or, in laymen's terms, flirting. Both men and women who complain their partners are inappropriately flirty report a higher likelihood of displaying the same overtly sexual behaviour, or even having one-night stands. This may reflect a kind of reciprocity or alternatively a guilty projection where an openly flirty person accuses their partner of sexualising others in a reflection of their own behaviour.

Ways of Coping

An alternative explanation is that an affair can operate as a coping mechanism to avoid facing an ending. For someone who finds it difficult to face an ending, having an affair provides the security of a new beginning that can protect against and obscure the consequences that a relationship ending provokes. It can provide distraction from any painful feelings one may have about finishing a relationship. Often what the avoider tries to do is to shift the responsibility for ending the relationship on to the other person (Hayman, 2001). In this instance, embarking upon an affair may provide a buffer against the pain of a relationship breakdown by providing the faithful partner with an excuse to end things, preventing the cheating party from having to initiate the break-up.

As we experience different romantic relationships, we navigate our way through the process of falling in and out of love, and as part of our learning process we must learn how to deal with both ends of the spectrum (Hayman, 2001). For example, one learns how he/she stops loving and being loved or how to cope with being left or leaving. These are valuable experiences allowing one to learn how to deal with disappointment and endings. If, however, a pattern emerges where each relationship simply ebbs into the next, with a brief overlap period of infidelity, we never fully accept or learn how to respond to endings. Our ability to face an ending head on and cope with the ensuing emotional disruption is linked to our emotional intelligence and, inevitably, back to our previous relationship experiences. Constantly turning to cheating as a method of avoiding endings is a sign we have not developed this ability.

Family of Origin

Infidelity is intricately linked to family patterns. Just like problems with emotional unavailability, problems with commitment and even sexual issues also take cues from our early childhood experiences of relationships. According to many theorists, the roots of basic trust develop from a child's early experiences with their primary care givers. Whatever attitudes are developed out of these interactions, they are important for adult romantic relationships. Moreover, experiencing patterns of avoidance, betrayal, secrecy and seduction in one's family lays the groundwork for a habit of using infidelity as a coping mechanism later on in life. Research shows that being unfaithful is almost hereditary! Infidelity is more likely among those whose parents were unfaithful (Carnes, 1983). The relationships we observe as children teach us how to conduct ourselves within a relationship. If we grow up in an atmosphere where Mummy is continuously coming to terms with Daddy's latest indiscretion, it is likely we will accept this relationship model as a 'norm', and go on to tolerate, initiate or even expect infidelity.

In their 2005 research, the Florida Atlantic University psychologists also linked back to Buss (1992) and supported his assertion that parents socialise children differently according to gender, which is why they respond to infidelity so differently. He suggested that it is in the reproductive interests of the parents to urge their daughters to treat all relationships the same because it will help her cultivate and grow them. Historically, a woman's success was based on her reproductive achievements since she wasn't expected to provide for herself financially. Keeping a breadwinning man was key. Conversely, a man could only be 'cuckolded' if he was tied to a committed relationship, investing in children. If a wife is engaging solely emotionally with another man, then there is no chance she will have children with him, duping her husband in the process.

Personality

There is a school of thought that states that certain personality types are more likely to cheat. For example, people who display low frustration tolerance, insecurity and narcissism are seen to be more prone to affairs (Buunk and van Driel, 1989). No empirical research has been conducted to prove these hypotheses. What has been reported in findings is that people who feel alienated from life are more prone to extramarital affairs (Buus and Shackelford, 1997). Interestingly, narcissism has also been highlighted as a strong predictor of susceptibility to infidelity. These findings support theories that conceptualise infidelity as a way to assuage a fragile ego and the need to bolster self-esteem (Buunk and van Driel, 1989). A person who displays genuine self-confidence and self-esteem is unlikely to turn to an affair as a means of validation. Conversely, if an individual has low self-esteem, the excitement and flattery of an affair might provide them with the ego-boost they so desperately require. Perhaps these theories could form the basis of some of our most common social stereotypes. Consider the egomaniac footballer, posing and posturing in his Gucci glasses and six-ton Jacob & Co watch, convinced he is the best-looking man on the planet and consistently reassuring himself of this fact by cheating on his wife with a series of girls who are principally kiss and tells waiting to happen.

Readiness

Readiness for an affair is also very important. In other words, for an infidelity to occur, we need to be welcoming of it and willing to cheat. When we perceive a relationship shift and take a turn for the worse, individuals often experience dissatisfaction and describe themselves as feeling fed up, restless and ready for change (Brown, 2001). Atwater (1982) indicates that for women there is a link between talking about affairs with someone who has been a participant in an affair and personal readiness. The researcher argues that for a woman, such discussions can provide a way to bridge the fantasy and the actuality of an affair. So, for example, Mary has been with her boyfriend for seven years. She's not sure if he's 'the one' but they're comfortable and everyone around them expects them to get married and settle down. Now, let's say Mary's best friend Laura cheats on her boyfriend. For Mary, listening to Laura's experiences helps bridge the gap between affairs as something other people do, and an option that could realistically be open to her. According to Atwater's theory, Laura's infidelity could help move Mary into a position of readiness for an affair.

Whatever the reasons, or motivations, it does appear that people who are open to cheating, or even anticipating cheating, will cheat. Equally, if we are not in the right mindset for infidelity, it won't happen.

How does Gender Come into it Then?

Gender differences appear repeatedly in studies on infidelity (Brown, 2001). Such differences manifest themselves in terms of justifications, expectations, reactions and outcomes. For a start, until recently, men were more likely to embark on affairs. You can see why. Aside from the fact that from an evolutionary point of view men have been primed to strive for quantity over quality when it comes to sex, in the early days of sexual equality, male breadwinners were also far more likely to come into contact with potential extramarital partners while their wives were often cooped up at home with children, knee-deep in potty training and finger-painting. However, over the last few decades, as women have moved into the workplace and begun to discuss sex and, indeed, engage in sexual activity more freely, the score sheet has levelled and the overall infidelity rates for men and women are looking more and more similar.

Research backs this up, concluding that certain types of affairs are more common for men and other types for women (Brown, 2001). If you've made it to this chapter, it should come as no surprise to you that, as with a million other relationship issues, for a man infidelity is likely to be all about sex. Studies on self-reported sexual attitudes and behaviour consistently indicate men are still more inclined than women to engage in sexual behaviour outside committed relationships and are less discriminating with regard to the quantity and/or quality of their sexual partners (Baumeister et al., 2001). Men have also been found to be more approving of casual sex and they report a greater number of sexual partners compared to women (Okami and Shackelford, 2001). It is no coincidence that for men marital dissatisfaction often focuses on the sexual aspect of the relationship, and that when men have affairs they tend to be sexually motivated. Emotional involvement comes later on, if at all. For women, just the opposite is true with emotional involvement preceding sexual involvement (Glass and Wright, 1985). Whereas men are likely to be attracted to an affair by sexual motivations, women are more likely to be attracted to the emotional connection first, although recent research has shown that dissatisfaction with sex *can* motivate both sexes to cheat. Women are more likely to be emotionally involved in an affair and a variety of studies have cited that married women become unfaithful because of their dissatisfaction with the emotional content of their marriage or their desire for an emotionally satisfying relationship (Brown, 2001). And as we've seen from the 2005 research from Florida, just as men are more likely to engage in sexual infidelity, they are also more likely to be upset by this kind of infidelity in their partner and women fall into a polar-opposite category – more distressed by emotional intimacy and more likely to enter into it.

Interestingly, women who are happy in their marriage are often oblivious to the possibility of infidelity, whereas for men, an affair or an extramarital encounter can arise simply by chance. Opportunity and prior justification are predictive of an affair for them (Glass and Wright, 1992)

Glass and Wright (1985) argue that men and women approach infidelity in a manner that parallels sex-role behaviours in premarital relationships. Females are expected to be emotionally but not sexually involved with a man. Conversely, the male role reflects sexual rather than emotional involvement. Yes, recent generations may have grown up with more equal rules of engagement when it comes to sexual morals and behaviour, but these basic stereotypes and behavioural expectations still ring true. Younger women may seize sexual opportunities with less guilt and more enthusiasm than their mothers and grandmothers, but research shows that women still see sex as a more emotional, significant experience than their male peers.

Even in contemporary society, a double standard still exists when it comes to infidelity. It is still more acceptable for a man to have a mistress, providing he is reasonably discreet about it. Women are more likely to be forgiving of a straying husband, while the same behaviour is less easily tolerated in women and indeed is often grounds for punishment or divorce (Brown, 2001). Research across cultures shows that a woman's infidelity is more likely to lead to divorce than a man's (Betzig, 1989). Men are socialised to be less willing to forgive their partner but able to excuse their own sexual affair(s) as justified, and without feeling too guilty about them. (Spanier and Margolis, 1983). Think about the way we talk about cheating men and women. Men are often berated for infidelity with cheeky, playful language: 'He's been a naughty boy', 'He's been playing away from home'. Male infidelity is often seen as mischievous but almost par for the course. Conversely, cheating women are rarely described as 'naughty' with the same tongue-in-cheek affection, rather they become 'loose' or 'fallen' and tarred with a social stigma that marks them out as disloyal, trashy and tainted.

The societal stigma surrounding a fallen woman can be linked back to our ancient ancestors. Prehistoric man was built to provide and produce. Full stop. Fulfilling both these aims meant slaying the biggest mammoth and laying the most women. It was as simple as that. Male promiscuity wasn't just accepted, it was essential to ensure the survival of the species, while the woman concentrated on raising the child she had carried for nine months, then got ready for the next one. There was no procreative advantage to a woman having multiple partners – after all, she could only bear one child at a time. While the society we live in may have changed, ancient sociological pressures and biological urges run deep, and they may still play a part in our expectations of gender-specific sexual behaviour.

Overall, research has shown that gender can influence how likely we are to cheat, and if we do, what form that betrayal will probably take. However, gender differences are most apparent in our individual responses to infidelity. Male infidelity is more accepted than female infidelity and is less likely to determine the end of a relationship. Relationship contexts such as marital, sexual and emotional dissatisfaction represent more universal predictors and are closely linked in both sexes to infidelity (Buus and Shackelford, 1997). In other words, although infidelity is likely to be viewed entirely differently for men and women, the factors that trigger it are often very similar.

Understanding the Meaning it has for Both of You

When an infidelity occurs a million different excuses can and will be given. Some are more plausible than others: 'I was drunk and stupid' is always slightly more believable than 'I slipped and fell on top of her.' For men, heading the top-ten get-out clauses is: 'It meant nothing, it was just sex.' As we've already established while sex may be 'just sex' for a man, the phrase doesn't even exist in the vocabulary of most women. For women, it is rarely 'just sex' because they tend to attach much more emotional meaning to the physical act. So, predictably, for women the most common excuse is: 'I couldn't help it, I fell in love with him, he made me feel special and I couldn't resist.'

Understanding the meaning of an affair makes it possible to unravel the real underlying issues. Infidelity is usually a symptom of an unhealthy relationship, so the real key to dealing with it is looking at the causes. According to systemic theory, the couple has a reciprocal set of behaviours which reflect the particular function of the affair. When a person cheats on their partner, they're not just cheating on them, they're usually covertly conveying one of a variety of messages. Each of the following messages reflects a particular meaning (Brown, 2001):

'I'll make you pay attention to me.'

This message is usually evident in couples who cannot talk about and resolve differences. Dissatisfactions are not aired and communication is limited in an effort to avoid conflict. This kind of affair is often a result of frustration combined with opportunity and is likely to be a quick fling as opposed to a long-term affair because, ultimately, its express purpose is to command attention. Like a naughty child smacking their sibling in an attempt to get Mum's attention, this kind of affair is designed to provoke.

'I feel uncomfortable needing you so much. Therefore, I will prove I can get my needs met elsewhere.'

This belief is linked to couples who have problems with intimacy. Both spouses fear letting down the barriers and becoming emotionally vulnerable. It is safer if a distance exists. For this type of couple, emotional connection is achieved through fighting and conflict. The affair provides that conflict and consequently allows both partners to distance themselves from their genuine intimidating emotions and protects them against hurt and disappointment.

'Fill me up.'

This belief is held by partners who are serial cheaters. Affairs provide ways of filling voids created by emotional emptiness. Partners who participate in affairs for this purpose are likely to cheat with a string of sexual partners and enter into a number of different relationships. They are looking for fulfilment and validation, and do not feel completed by their relationship. The message here is, 'You are not enough. This relationship is not enough. I need more.'

'I feel a duty to my partner, but I am in love with someone else.'

This is the underlying cry of individuals who remain in a relationship out of a sense of duty, in the name of doing the right thing. This type of affair often arises when an individual has denied their emotional needs. Often, the relationship feels empty and communication is limited to practical matters. The affair itself is a serious relationship that provides for the unmet emotional needs.

'Help me leave my partner.'

This emotion is often experienced by partners who slide into an affair as they think about ending their current relationship. These affairs act as trials for the individuals to see if he/she can make it on their own, or if they are still attractive to the opposite sex. At the deeper level, this belief also demonstrates a desire to avoid taking responsibility for ending the relationship.

Distinguishing among the various meanings is important as it can help estimate the prognosis of the marriage. Whether it is possible to rebuild a relationship after infidelity depends on those exact meanings. The future of your relationship will also be dependent on your emotional reaction to the indiscretion, and this is likely to be highly gender specific.

Feeling the Impact of Infidelity – as a Man and as a Woman

If you haven't grasped the concept that men and women experience and express emotions differently by this stage in the book, then quite frankly you haven't been paying attention! Infidelity, like every other relationship upheaval, will be experienced entirely differently by each sex. Of course there are similarities: that crushing moment when you realise that actually the blonde girl from work isn't just 'a girl from work' or the minute when the link between your girlfriend's new underwear and your best mate's smug grin become painfully clear. These times are universally distressing. The big thing about infidelity is that it shatters our comfort zone, and violates our expectations. Within a seemingly happy, healthy relationship we come to expect certain qualities and behaviour from our partner. We assume they are, and expect them to be honest, trustworthy, predictable, committed and respectful of our relationship (Epstein and Baucom, 2003). Infidelity violates these fundamental assumptions and that holds true for a man or a woman. Empirical evidence suggests there are no major gender differences regarding the emotional experiences that accompany the immediate aftermath of infidelity. The emotional suffering of women is no less than that of men, especially if the affair is accompanied by emotional involvement (Buus et al., 1992). Both sexes must deal with the pain and upheaval of facing up to blatant disruption of their comfort zone. However, there are a number of aspects of infidelity that evoke very different, gender-specific reactions.

When we discover a partner has been unfaithful, one of the first things we do is make an instant comparison between ourselves and the new object of our partner's affection. More often than not we base this assessment on the same factors we use as the foundation for our own self-esteem. So if we feel that much of our appeal as a mate arises from our physical appearance, an immediate question will be 'Is she prettier than me?' Likewise, if an individual feels one of her best traits is her sense of humour, she may well ask her partner, 'Does she make you laugh like I do?' When judging a potential mate, and indeed themselves, men are far more likely to envy social status (probably linking back to the value evolution places on provider potential) while women are more likely to focus on aesthetic qualities, because throughout history this is how women have been assessed and valued. Women are more likely to experience jealousy when confronted with a physically attractive rival, while a man will be more jealous if their rival is a socially dominant male. (Buunk and Dijkstra, 2004).

Just as our feelings about a rival are linked to our gender, our feelings about the type of infidelity also depend on our gender-specific viewpoint. Consider these two scenarios. Leila has been going out with her boyfriend Jack for two years, and things are beginning to go stale. They have stopped making time for each other, and the relationship has slipped into a tired, boring routine. Meanwhile, Jack is becoming steadily closer to a girl at his gym. They've had dinner a few times, and gradually he finds himself confiding to her his problems with Leila. No physical infidelity has occurred. On the other hand, after a Christmas party, Leila, high on festive spirit and red wine, finds herself passionately kissing a colleague. Now, these two 'infidelities' are completely different: Jack comforts himself with the fact he hasn't cheated because he hasn't actually laid a finger on his gym buddy; Leila tells herself that her indiscretion doesn't count because it didn't 'mean anything'. However, if both parties were to discover the whole truth about their partners' actions, they would be horrified. As a woman, Leila places far more importance on emotional intimacy than Jack. The fact that her boyfriend would confide in and connect with another woman, particularly when she feels so distant from him, would be the ultimate insult. As a man, Jack is unlikely to appreciate the impact of his intimate dinners, but would be furious to learn of Leila's seasonal snogging, because men attach far more importance to physical connections. Neither party is right or wrong, both are simply behaving as their gender dictates.

The fact that we classify and approach infidelity so differently makes it all the more difficult to recover from. When he says, 'But it was just a walk in the park!' she hears, 'I can't find the time or the energy to spend with you or invest in our emotional connection, but I feel so close to this other woman I love spending quality time alone with her,' even if he literally means, 'But it was just a walk in the park!' When she goes home from work and says, 'I love this new guy in personnel, he is sooo funny, he has the whole office in stitches,' he might well hear, 'This new guy is so popular and amusing, I love being around him, he's such an impressive man, so much better than you!' These misunderstandings occur every day, and the key to working through them is learning to accept that the way you interpret a situation is not always the most accurate one, more often than not it will be filtered by your own gender-specific schemas.

How to Move Forward

So which way do we go after an infidelity? Do we subscribe to the 'leopards can't change their spots' school of thought and kick our relationship to the curb? Or do we fall in with the 'everyone deserves a second chance' crew and at least try to forgive and forget? Discussions about cheating and infidelity will always provoke a range of responses and opinions. We all have a friend who operates on a 'one strike and you're out' basis, the hard, strong woman who won't stand for her partner so much as thinking about cheating before he's out the door. We can probably also all lay claim to a long-suffering pal who relentlessly slogs on with a serial cheater. We all have different views on infidelity and, just like everything else, these views are likely to be based on our own history. Some people will always believe that cheating/infidelity is an inherently unforgivable sin. Others will always place faith in rehabilitation; claiming that being unfaithful can occasionally be nothing more than a colossally senseless mistake and that a relationship can survive if both parties are motivated to get through it. And in a sense, both theories are right. And yet, neither of them really matters. After you have been cheated on, once the dust settles, and you've heard heated advice, or rather instructions, from your hairdresser, your best mate and your auntie's neighbour's dog-walker, ultimately the only person who counts is you. Moving on from infidelity is about establishing what *you* can live with. What will make *you* happy or unhappy? What do *you* need to carry on, either in the relationship, or on your own? The answer for most people is simple. To move on, we need to close chapters, we need to put a lid on things, we need to build a bridge over the past – we need, in a word, closure.

We need closure whatever our decision. It is equally important for couples who resolve their issues and for those who decide to separate (Brown, 2001). Think about it like a sumptuous seven-course meal in a fine restaurant. Before moving on to each course, a refreshing sorbet is offered to cleanse the pallet, removing the taste of the previous dish and preparing the taste buds for the next course. You see, you can think about closure as a fruity pink champagne sorbet, if you will. It's fine to go hurtling from dish to dish, from romantic episode to romantic episode without cleansing the traces of the last experience, but in order to enjoy the next course fully, we should close the door on the last dish. That might mean leaving your partner to tuck into his Duck à l'orange on his own while you grab a Big Mac elsewhere, or it might mean you 'cleanse' together, and settle down for the next course as a couple.

If you decide that the relationship is worth salvaging and should continue, there has to be some way in which both partners can accept what happened and the betrayed partner can forgive the indiscretion (Crowe, 2005). Here, the closure comes from knowing that you have confronted the affair, surveyed the damage, dealt with the trauma and learnt to trust again. This can and probably will be a long and arduous process. Trust is a valuable commodity and it takes time to rebuild it. Whatever the nature of the infidelity, from a one-night stand to a long-term affair, it is important you and your partner address the threat posed to the relationship. Be honest about how it has affected the trust between you. Acknowledge that it will take time to replenish itself and needs nurture, time and effort from both of you.

Without condoning or accepting infidelity, partners can attempt to put this trauma in perspective (Beck, 1988). If you decide that you want your relationship to continue then you need to face up to the real underlying issues and find ways to move forward. You can do this by dealing with what happened. Several factors might threaten this: some people choose to sweep the issues under the carpet; common distraction tactics include work pressures, members of the extended family and the care of children (Brown, 2001). But the fact is that major relationship rifts don't just sort themselves out. Here are some steps you can take to invest in the restructuring and rebuilding of your relationship:

Step 1 Acknowledge what Happened and Own your Share of Responsibility

Sounds obvious, right? Ever since we were at school we've been taught to own up to our actions and acknowledge when they are wrong. But its remarkable how an infidelity can find us running scared from accepting our part in the drama. If you were unfaithful to your partner, you probably lied at some point, you definitely acted dishonourably and you may have blatantly disregarded and disrespected your partner. The only way to move on from these hard, cold facts is to accept them. Admit to yourself and your partner that these relationship violations occurred. There's nothing harder than trying to forgive somebody who won't fully accept their guilt. Likewise, if you and your partner have been arguing for months, and the steady decline of the relationship led to an infidelity, then you probably need to assess your own behaviour too. Nobody's suggesting that a few rows justify a betrayal, but accepting your own involvement in the situation can help you understand it. Perhaps your partner felt shut out or isolated. This doesn't mean he has a right to cheat, but it may have implications for the way your relationship recovers and renews itself. Acknowledge this, accept your role in the proceedings, and be honest with yourself and with your partner.

After both parties have realistically assessed their behaviour, a plan of action will become clearer. It is easier to see the possible changes that will occur and examine how these changes will affect the relationship. For example, one way to move forward is to accept that the relationship can never be quite as trusting and intimate as it had been before the affair(s) (Crowe, 2005). However disappointing or discouraging this might be, perhaps it is a more realistic and balanced way to look at things, at least until you have had time to begin rebuilding these crucial relationship components.

Step 2 Make a Decision about What you can Live with

We've touched on this. Nobody knows you better than yourself. After spending twenty, thirty, forty years inside your body with your own set of schemas, tendencies and emotions, you should have a pretty good idea of what you can and can't tolerate within a relationship. You probably know what your own personal boundaries are.

It's easy to say 'I forgive you', but saying it is about as effective as saying 'you are healed' to a five-year-old with a bloody knee. The words mean nothing unless you've cleansed the wound, dealt with the pain and sealed it off. If you know, in your heart of hearts, that you will never be happy with somebody who was unfaithful to you, if you know deep down you will never forget, then you need to move on. Whatever the wrongs or rights of the situation, you and your partner deserve the best chance of happiness and if that can't be achieved through pursuing your relationship, then so be it. Don't flog a dead horse. If you know you will never recover from the infidelity, then get out, and get out now, before you replace optimism with cynicism and start despising weddings, spitting at happy couples in the street and smashing up Whitney Houston CDs.

It doesn't have to be over, though. If you have searched your soul and decided that, actually, you can move on from this, and you do want your relationship to work, then that's great and often well worth a shot. Many couples come to counselling after infidelity has been discovered, in order to make sure they are both equipped for the long haul. Each partner needs to think about whether it is possible to rebuild the trust in their relationship and make a well-considered decision about the viability of the partnership.

Step 3 Rebuilding Trust and Commitment

Making the decision whether to hit the road or stand by your man is the (relatively) easy part. Then comes the real hard work. If you decide you do want to salvage something from the infidelity wreckage and rebuild your relationship, you need to accept you have a long, occasionally painful and often frustrating task ahead of you. The words 'I forgive you' won't magic your relationship back to full fruitful health. Nope. Both partners need to devote themselves to the process of rebuilding trust and commitment, and it will take a while. But there are a few ways to aid the process:

Developing Reasonable Assumptions and Expectations

A significant step in helping a couple move forward is the development of a new set of assumptions about each other and the relationship (Epstein and Baucom, 2003). More specifically, the newly formed negative set of expectations each partner has of each other needs to be addressed and where possible challenged, in order for everyone to gain closure and regain emotional intimacy and trust. Beliefs such as, 'He is self-centred and only thinks of what he wants' or 'She isn't the caring person I thought she was' can only destroy a relationship if they are allowed to fester. One of the first corrective steps, therefore, is to re-frame the betrayed mate's perspective of the offending partner. A good question to ask yourself, in order to challenge the belief that the infidelity is the end of your relationship is, 'Is the offence really an unforgivable sin?' This challenge can actually help you to 'de-awfulise' or 'de-catastrophise' the event and encourage the process whereby you begin to understand the circumstances that led to infidelity (Beck, 1988). As you try to reason and understand the circumstances in which your partner crossed the line of fidelity, this can provide some new meanings. As with any aspect of cognitive therapy, the key is framing your thoughts and feelings in a sensible context. Don't accept your deepest fears as gospel, ask yourself how realistic they are. Does your partner drunkenly kissing some girl at his office party mean he thinks you're fat, hideous and unlovable? No. It probably means he was drunk, foolish and inconsiderate, but that isn't a realistic indication of how he views you. Challenge your thoughts, ask yourself if the infidelity renders your relationship irreparable and be prepared to do some honest soul-searching.

Developing Open Communication

A crucial step in this process is working towards establishing increasingly greater levels of honest and open communication. In fact, communication often represents the only foundation on which trust can be built (Brown, 2001). Some basic rules for breaking old patterns of miscommunication include:

- Stop blaming; try to challenge the self-defeating tendency to blame each other for whatever is wrong.
- Speak effectively about what you feel, want and think.
- Listen to your partner. You're not communicating with him or her unless you're listening to them and trying to appreciate what they tell you.
- Discuss issues even when its painful. Avoidance of conflict is not healthy and trying to keep the peace will never be as powerful as speaking up.
- Use humour if it feels natural. Learning to laugh at the often absurd drama of the situation can help you vent your frustrations, and remind you of the common ground you share.

Developing Trust

Rebuilding trust can only happen when you focus on the realities rather than the illusions or false fantasies about the relationship. It won't be an overnight miracle. You both need to learn to note issues early and discuss your problems so they don't become unspoken resentments that will undoubtedly cause conflict and tension (Brown, 2001). Don't be scared of disrupting the peace once you and your partner have started to move through the trauma of infidelity. It's far better to voice your concerns as they occur, rather than gradually build up a big knot of worry that's impossible to untangle once you decide to address it. If you feel untrusting, or suspicious, or insecure about the strength of your partner's commitment after an infidelity then express those emotions so you can confront, examine and work towards assuaging them.

You should both obtain realistic and reasonable expectations for the relationship and abandon any dreams of having it all or wanting guarantees of fidelity. Trust takes time, and it won't be rushed. If you want to rebuild your relationship, you need to rebuild it on a foundation of realistic expectations and prepare yourselves for a long, slow challenge.

Conclusion

In all its forms, from a fumble on the photocopier at a Christmas party to a carefully executed full-blown affair, infidelity is always a tricky issue to navigate. It can shake your relationship to its foundations and have disastrous implications for the emotional well-being of everyone involved. The scary thing is that an affair occurs in almost half of all relationships.

Let's look at Joanne and Tim. They've been going out for five years, but have experienced real problems within the last two. Joanne discovered Tim had slept with a work colleague, Lisa. They decided to work through things and put the infidelity behind them. Six months on, Tim casually mentions that he and Lisa met for dinner because she was feeling down about her mother being ill and just wanted someone to talk to. The following dialogue ensues:

> Joanne says: 'How could you do this to me? After all we've been through?!'
>
> Joanne means: 'I thought this was just about sex – I thought it was a stupid one-night stand.'
>
> Tim thinks: Why is she so mad? I haven't done anything wrong here. It's not like I slept with her again.
>
> Tim says: 'I didn't do anything, she just needed someone to talk to.'
>
> Joanne hears: 'I am this woman's emotional support, she relies on me and opens up to me. Not like you.'
>
> Joanne says: 'This is worse than sleeping with her, Tim. Why can't you see that?'
>
> Tim thinks: Don't be ridiculous.
>
> Tim says: 'Now you're being unreasonable, you're just determined to blame me for everything. Talking isn't cheating.'
>
> Joanne thinks: By being an emotional support to this woman, you are betraying me. You don't love me enough to make this work.
>
> Tim thinks: I can't do anything right. This is never going to work.

Regardless of who is the victim or the instigator of the affair, don't expect your partner to see things in exactly the same way you do. We've established that men and women experience infidelity in different ways and initiate it for different reasons. In this example, Tim and Joanne need to accept that a lack of cohesion between approaches to dealing with the affair doesn't always represent a lack of understanding, or mean their love is doomed to failure. You can work through this scenario by realising you experience it differently depending on your gender. Take time to understand your partner's viewpoint, and take biological and societal factors into consideration – understand the impact of gender on his/her behaviour, and factor that into your communications.

Be realistic and focused regarding closure. It might take weeks, months, years to get your relationship back to full strength after infidelity. Every day you need to make a conscious effort to put the affair behind you. Don't let it affect the relationship you have now. You basically have two choices: you can weather the storm, and wait for the next sunny day; or you can let the black cloud of betrayal shadow the rest of your relationship. If you go for the latter, you might as well pack it all in, because both of you will be far happier if you simply up and leave.

Finally, if you decide you can't live with the pain of the betrayal and, in order to move on, you actually need to leave the relationship then remember you need closure too. Don't internalise the affair. While it may be a reflection of your relationship, it probably isn't a direct reflection on you. Don't make it about you, because that could have worrying effects on your own self-esteem. Just because you choose to leave you partner, doesn't mean you don't need to confront the issue and gain closure, so make sure you dedicate some time and energy to moving on.

Infidelity is painful, heart breaking and potentially life changing, but it isn't the end of the world. Not only can relationships recover from an affair, they can actually gain from one. Any painful experience gives us a chance to learn about ourselves and a whole load of other useful stuff like love, life and relationships. So, whatever your decision, take what you can from the incident, address it and then move on. Know yourself, know what you can tolerate and ensure that your own emotional well-being is foremost in your mind. If that means smashing up those Whitney Houston records, then so be it . . .

Men Should Remember:

- Don't underestimate how important an emotional connection is – your girlfriend is just as likely to be upset by a chat in the pub as a full-on sexual affair
- Accept your way of moving on may be to forget about it and put it behind you. Your partner's way might be talking about it into the early hours.

Women Should Remember:

- Men and women see sex vastly differently – a physical encounter might mean nothing to you but the world to him.
- Be honest about what you can get over and what you can't.

Chapter 6
Moving in Together

The British Panel Household Survey has been running since 1991 and holds data from over 10,000 adults living in over 5,000 of the UK's households. In 2004, Dr Stephen Stansfeld led a team of researchers on a study that examined this data alongside the responses to a mental health questionnaire issued to over 4,000 of these adults – men and women. Essentially they matched mental health and well-being against living circumstances, and the results seem to clarify age-old wisdom on the differences between men and women.

Both sexes were found to benefit emotionally from long-term relationships – that is, both sexes displayed more robust mental health when in a committed relationship. However, men who married displayed significantly lower levels of mental health than those who chose just to live with their partner. Conversely, women did better emotionally if they married their partner rather than just cohabited. So, in short, everyone's happier when in a healthy relationship but we differ in the way we respond mentally to living with a partner. Getting married is beneficial to a woman's mental health, but actually detrimental to a man's when compared to cohabiting.

Ironically, single women were better off than single men. So, it's clear that men do have something to gain from being in a committed relationship – it's just that, for a man, being married isn't as emotionally beneficial as simply living with a partner. Ultimately, the research asserted that this is definitely a breeding ground for conflict.

As Stansfeld says: 'The difference in men and women in their reaction to cohabitation may be due to women wanting more security in a relationship. In cohabitation, there isn't as much security as implied by marriage.' With this he touches on the crux of the matter when it comes to sex differences in viewing marriage. Men and women view the idea of moving in together entirely differently. While women see these great relationship steps as a way of gaining stability, men are actually healthier and happier when they are less committed.

This explains why many women find it so hard to get their man past the first hurdle – living together feels like one step closer to marriage. Cohabitation is a major step for any relationship and it is becoming increasingly commonplace. You know you're pretty serious about each other. You've explored the depths of each other's personalities to unearth the good, the bad and the unmentionable (your singing and his hygiene habits, if forced to mention them), and you're almost totally sure he's the one you were dreaming of while enduring first loves, playground romances and, later, a string of demoralising dates. The next step? Thirty years ago, you would be picking out a bridal gown in virginal white quicker than you can say 'something borrowed, something blue'. The accepted process went like this: meet each other, court each other, get engaged, get married, move in, have children, happy ever after. Nowadays, committing to marriage before a period of cohabitation is virtually unheard of. There is a huge trend for testing the waters before jumping in hook, line and sinker.

In the past your mother's mother would have needed to find a well-to-do man to marry her sharpish so she ceased to be a financial burden on her father. With today's equality most women now fly the nest and become financially independent long before they even think about marriage. According to Prinz (1995) women's improved education and consequent increased economic independence have radically affected their position in the family and have influenced the trend of delaying marriage. Because a woman's financial status no longer depends on the man she marries, the pressure is off, and many women afford themselves the time to live with their partners before making the big commitment. However, research like Dr Stansfeld's suggests that women are still experiencing an emotional hangover from prehistoric times when women were dependent on their men, and that actually women are still on a one-way mission to tie down their man.

In any case, despite the rise of cohabitation, we haven't seen a whole generation shunning marriage, preferring instead to stick to being 'housemates'. Far from it. It's just that now cohabitation is seen as a taster for marriage. They say you never really know someone until you've lived with them, so living together has become the ultimate test for those who are planning marriage for the future. On the other hand, interestingly, American psychological research has indicated that the effect cohabitation has on marriage may actually be negative (Thomson and Colella, 1992). Everyone knows a couple who were blissfully happy until they moved in together, and the reality of shared living quarters proved too much for the relationship.

Whether you and your partner view living together as the next step before naming the date and picking the rings, or as an alternative to making the big commitment, or as an entirely separate issue from marriage, it is still a huge step in any relationship. Motives, expectations and actual experiences will vary for every individual and every relationship. In this chapter we look at all three of these aspects of imminent cohabitation. Why would you want to move in together? Do you share the same motives or do you have different reasons for wanting to live together? Do you view the experience as a prelude to marriage while he sees it as a long-term solution? What are your expectations? Are you dreaming of thrilling trips round Habitat and plush white furnishings while he is already planning his first boys night in – curry, beer and rubbish boy films included? How do you communicate these elements to each other in a sensitive and effective manner? This chapter is about considering moving in together, establishing the right decision for your relationship and maintaining open, honest communication throughout, even when it feels like you are speaking in your gender tongues.

Cohabiting – What's the Point?

Cohabiting before marriage has become hugely popular in recent years. Gone is the stigma of living in sin our parents' generation had to face. Throughout much of Europe and the US, the number of unmarried, cohabiting couples has increased and, as a lifestyle choice, it is far more widely accepted (Lefrancois, 1990).

Sharing a home can help couples enjoy the intimacy and closeness of marriage without the legal obligations. This can be an advantage for those couples who do not want a long-term commitment, and for those for whom marriage will never be an option (Lefrancois, 1990). Some people feel marriage acts as an unwanted and destructive pressure, because of the legal commitment to stay together. It is as if tension does not develop as long as one still has the option to terminate the relationship (McGoldrick, 1980). Some people are put off by the connotations of the terms husband and wife, preferring to live within a looser structure that carries less connotations. It is certainly true that there are couples who do not perceive moving in together as a trial for marriage but as an alternative to marriage. For them, living together outside wedlock can actually be seen as a rejection of the institution of marriage (Prinz, 1995).

However, research shows that, for most people, the first shared home is still the training ground for marriage. Cohabitation represents a transitional stage that is later transformed into a legal marriage (Prinz, 1995). But of course, from individual to individual, relationship to relationship, choosing that first flat together is far more complicated than simply signing up for a marital training course. Usually, there is a shared wish to spend more time together. Evolution and socialisation have moulded us into social beings who feel most secure when we are surrounded by a community, and many people feel protected by the commitment and security of living with a partner. Some couples move in together for financial or logistical reasons. And of course, as ever, these motives will be shaped by whether we are a woman or a man.

To examine the differences in the way the genders view cohabitation we don't need to look back to the prehistoric era when cavemen went out hunting while their womenfolk tended to the cave. We don't need to look back to the fifties where moving out of the family home was the sign a daughter had truly matured and was ready to face the big bad world. You only need to look back as far as your own childhood. To this day, many women remember playing with doll's houses, child-size mock kitchens and mini baking sets. And the boys? Were they baking scrumptious cakes made out of imaginary ingredients or putting a two-inch wooden family to bed? Oh no, far from it. Little boys were too busy running round the garden with Action Men or reading Superman comics. Who do Action Man and Superman live with? Who knows? Who cares where they rest their heads for the night when they share the combined power to combat any man (or any other plastic rival) bare-handed and fly round the world in a questionable pants–tights combo and still be taken seriously? When you switch back to the here and now, it's even clearer to see why men and women would view cohabitation differently. How many *home beautiful* type magazines are marketed to men? Think about your boyfriend's Hollywood heroes – would James Bond pop down to Sainsbury's to grab some toilet cleaner? Not unless there was a worldwide toilet-cleaner-conspiracy and he fancied the checkout girl (who would also be a Russian spy, obviously).

When a woman lives alone she is a spinster, when a man lives alone he is a bachelor. When you look at the facts its no wonder men view moving in together so differently to women. We've already established commitment is a rather scary concept for men, and evolution has taught them to secure the safety of the species by sowing their wild oats. So to him, moving in with a girlfriend can feel like tattooing 'Hands off, ladies! I'm spoken for!' on his forehead. Conversely, even in this age of sexual equality, women are encouraged to view settling down with a man as the ultimate goal – so, far from being a daunting prospect, cohabiting often feels like one step closer to the holy grail. As Dr Stansfeld's research shows, women are emotionally more healthy if they are in a more committed relationship, while men's mental health actually deteriorates as they move closer towards marriage.

Take Lisa and Jack, both in their late twenties. They've been together for two years, both paying ridiculously high rents on their respective London studio flats. Jack's lease is coming up for renewal, so Lisa suggests he should move into her flat. To Lisa, this is a natural progression. After all, they spend pretty much every night together anyway, so it seems illogical for her to spend half her time lugging her clothes, shoes, hair straighteners, toiletries, make-up, etc. to his every night and for him to spend the other half of the time wondering if there's a stray pair of boxers at Lisa's or if he's going to have to recycle whichever particular pair he has on that day. Lisa's fairly convinced that she and Jack will go the distance and eventually get married, so it makes perfect sense that they would take that next step and start sharing living space. When she suggests this to Jack, he goes strangely quiet and proceeds to spend the next six nights out with the boys. So, she takes it up with him:

Lisa says: 'Have you thought any more about what I said the other night about us moving in together?'

Lisa means: 'Why are you avoiding the issue? What's the big deal here?'

Jack hears: 'Nag, nag, nag. I've asked you about this already – give me an answer NOW. Are you going to move in and let me rule your life or not?'

Jack says: 'Why can't you just chill out? What will be, will be.'

Lisa hears: 'This isn't as serious for me as it is for you. I think you're more involved than I am.'

Lisa says: 'Oh for God's sake, Jack! When will you grow up? There's no point in this relationship if it's not going to move forward.'

Jack hears: 'Move in with me or it's over.'

Jack thinks: I won't be bullied into letting her make all my decisions. I'll put this off some more and deal with it next week. I'm going down the pub.

What's happening here is that Jack perceives a sudden threat to his independence. When Lisa says, 'If we're serious about each other, then what's the harm in taking the next step?' Jack hears, 'We need to move in so I can make sure you are mine for ever, and eventually cajole you into waltzing me down the aisle.' When Jack says, 'I'm not ready,' Lisa hears, 'I don't like you enough – someone else might be round the corner.' Now, of course, neither of these perceptions is correct, but the way we are socialised means Lisa is likely to feel more positively about these levels of commitment, and Jack is more likely to associate them with loss and restriction.

Great Expectations

We've looked at some of the reasons why individuals might want (or not want) to move in with their partners. Unfortunately, the potential for conflict doesn't end as soon as you've made that crucial initial decision. Oh no. Moving in with a partner is a big deal. So if a couple decides to bite the bullet and go for it, chances are they've both put a great deal of thought into it which means they've probably got very definite expectations about what house-sharing will be like. And while you're picturing candlelit dinner parties where you and selected other couples will be impeccably dressed and intelligently witty, he's already working out how he's going to get the average beer spillage from a usual Friday night out of those cream carpets.

Expectations are key. In this instance, the word 'expectation' refers to the beliefs a person holds about the characteristics an intimate relationship and one's partner should have, and they are used to evaluate whether the other's behaviour is acceptable and appropriate (Baucom et al., 1989). Our expectations shape our visions of how a situation will unfold, and once we encounter that situation they form the benchmark for how satisfied we are with it. Of course our happiness with our living set up doesn't just come from meeting our own expectations, it comes from harbouring expectations that are similar to those of our partner. As in the examples above, if you and your partner expect hugely different things from cohabitation, somewhere along the line, one or even both of you is likely to be let down.

Where do these expectations come from? We're all human beings, we all live in the same world, and we're all made in the same way. Why would two people of similar age with similar interests have such varying views on how a romantic love nest should operate? Well, there are a number of reasons. Rather unsurprisingly, the home you grew up in colours your view of how you would like your own home to be once you fly the family nest. Our expectations of domesticity are formed as children, from small issues such as whether or not you remove your shoes at the door, to how the inhabitants of a home communicate with one another. Our views on conflict resolution, division of labour and closeness are all shaped by our early experiences of living at home, and these experiences vary hugely. For example, some families are close-knit and place emphasis on emotional sharing and protectiveness. Children from these families learn to connect emotionally and to value their parents' opinions. In other families, children learn not to discuss differences and to avoid conflict altogether. In some other families, boys are not expected to be involved in helping with domestic chores, which are seen as women's work.

Culture also plays an important role in one's development of expectations. A Hindu, or South American or Muslim home has different features from a typical European home. Religious or traditional values are deeply ingrained and often passed on subconsciously to younger family members. Remember that our home is the first environment we familiarise ourselves with, so the lessons we learn here stick for life. For example, some people learn that nothing happens without the agreement of all the family members, while others discover that only one person makes the decisions. Some families are more traditional than others. They may follow the rule that housework is taken care of by solely the female, and women should be homemakers. Many boys in these families are not generally in the habit of helping with domestic chores (Crowe, 2005). Take Jon and Anita, who have just moved in together. Jon comes from a very traditional Greek family. His mother takes great pride in caring for her four sons and her husband, relishing the cooking, cleaning and fussing that this role entails. Anita was raised by her mother, an endlessly busy career-woman who returned to work as soon as her two kids were old enough to walk back from school on their own. The trouble here is that Anita has been taught by her upbringing that the best way to ensure you get fed and clean is to do it yourself, which is fine, except that Jon is left starving on the sofa waiting for someone to clear his lunch plate and make him some dinner. Take a look at the dialogue below:

Jon says: 'Hi, darling, what's for dinner?'

Anita thinks: Why are you asking me? You know where the kitchen is.

Anita says: 'I've been busy – I haven't thought about it.'

Jon thinks: She's too busy to make time for me. I thought that when a woman loved you, she would want to take care of you.

Jon says: 'Oh, I thought you would want to look after me now we've moved in together and you're the woman of the house!'

Anita hears: 'I expect you to run around after me.'

Anita says: 'You're not living with your mother now – you're an adult, Jon.'

Jon hears: 'I disagree with the way you were brought up, you big mummy's boy!'

Neither Jon nor Anita are right or wrong, but they will have to work on the fact that their vastly different family backgrounds have shaped different sets of expectations, and they need to find ways to communicate to get through these differences.

So our expectations shape our behaviour, and this is where the potential conflict arises, and where our gender-specific interpretations can lead us into trouble. The pressures and duties of everyday life mean you and your partner will have to deal with issues you have never come across before. If your boyfriend comes from a family where his mum dealt with the finances, but in your house your father always paid the bills, then you need to discuss how you compromise the expectations you may have of one another, hopefully before the utilities get cut off . . .

When we don't get this compromise right, the results can be disastrous. When a man says, 'But I want to go to the pub again, it's my life and I can do what I want,' his girlfriend might hear, 'I don't care if this upsets you, my commitment is to my friends, not to my home with you.' Equally when a woman says, 'Would you mind doing the washing-up tonight?' her boyfriend might hear, '——'. i.e. nothing, because he switched off the minute he realised he was being asked to perform a household chore and immediately reverted back to the thirteen-year-old who had to be bribed to wash his own hair, let alone the family's dishes.

Clearly there are elements of living together that need to be negotiated. These can range from practicalities – who does the cooking or who pays the bills – to more complex issues such as how to share time with parents or friends (Crowe, 2005). Decisions should be reached about how to use space, time and money. Moving in represents an important transition stage for the relationship, where new boundaries need to be established and communicated.

Moving In and Moving Forward: Communicate, Communicate, Communicate

No couple should despair if they are having problems adjusting to living with one another. Seeing your boyfriend four nights a week when you are waxed, tanned, in a good mood and wearing matching underwear is a whole different kettle of fish to seeing your boyfriend every time you want to chill out at home, every time you want to watch something particular on TV and every time you want to put on a face mask, your sloppiest pyjamas and watch embarrassing girl films. And really, that's just scratching the surface. Moving in together presents a raft of issues that, chances are, you would never have dreamt could cause a rift, but this doesn't mean you can't work through them. There are some simple steps you can take to ensure your relationship survives the stresses of playing house together.

Moving in with a partner means joining your lives together and forming a new household. It often confers rights and obligations with respect to family and friends, money, holidays, sexual behaviour, etc. The couple now finds themselves in the milieu of making decisions about absolutely everything, from who buys the coffee to who has which side of the bed. It is much better to confront the major issues through detailed conversations right from the start. Couples who do not plan these things in advance are at risk of running into conflict at a later date. A trap they can easily fall into is that of lack of communication. Because of romanticisation of the attraction when couples date, there is a tendency to idealise each other and avoid looking at the enormous and long-range difficulties of living with someone (McGoldrick, 1980). Romantic love can be fascinating, but the reality of living together will have a tough job of living up to the fantasy envisaged during those first flushes of new love, and when our expectations are dashed, and we begin arguing over the minutiae of living together, we can fall into the guilt–blame trap with our partner.

Accepting the realities of a situation isn't necessarily a bad thing. The loss of an idealistic situation can actually provide the opportunity to get to know each other as real people and develop your relationship in the process (Crowe, 2005). Consequently, if you want to clamber out of these situations and move on in your relationship, you need to learn to speak a language you can both understand. An analysis of the way you approach and speak about your relationship is very important in boosting your communication with your mate. Listening is far more powerful than assuming – as discussed earlier – so take the time. And when you listen, listen to everything. Don't filter out the elements that challenge negative beliefs you may have developed about your partner, yourself or your relationship. If a man comes home and says, 'Have you had a hard day? You look tired . . . I'm heading over to my mum's for dinner tonight, it's her birthday,' and his partner is subconsciously looking to reinforce beliefs that he is devoting less time and energy to the relationship, she may well hear, 'You look awful, I need to get out of the house to get away from you. See you later.' The concern that the partner has expressed, and the justification for leaving has been swept aside in the rush to confirm insecurities and concerns the woman may have.

To House-share or Not to House-share – How your Behaviour can Help the Process

A satisfying living relationship is based on understanding, respect and companionship. It is based on each partner listening to what is required by the other and working to fulfil these needs, and on each partner acknowledging and respecting the other's boundaries. It all sounds lovely, but is easier said than done. To help transform this ideal into a reality for you and your partner, it is useful if you can identify flashpoints within your relationship and look at how you can modify these situations when they occur. Therapy can be helpful, because it encourages couples to overcome deeply ingrained fears and change their behaviours. Here are some suggestions about adopting certain behaviours to help you improve communication within your relationship and aid your transition into cohabiting:

Showing Sensitivity

This is necessary at any stage of your relationship, but particularly when you are experiencing an important transition. As we've discussed, each individual is the sum of their collection of experiences and beliefs. Showing sensitivity means you are aware of this and take it into consideration when communicating with someone. This quality comes entirely naturally to some people; in others it must be cultivated (Beck, 1988).

Solution:
The answer to this one is a little investigation. Next time your partner says something like, 'I'm not ready to let you into my life to the point where we actually live together' then, before resorting to anger or insults, try and think where your partner's feelings are coming from. Perhaps his last girlfriend tried to control his life the minute they swapped door keys? Maybe his father left the family home when he was younger and he is anxious about letting anyone into his home, for fear they will leave too? Resist the temptation to assume 'My boyfriend won't let me move in

because he is selfish' and acknowledge these feelings are usually signs of hidden vulnerabilities or soft spots.

Showing Understanding

This is your ability to reflect on what your partner says to you. The easiest thing in the world is to react to a comment or situation as you immediately perceive it. Actually, the most useful thing in the world is being able to remove yourself from the situation and get a far more neutral view, or even better, to be able to empathise with your partner and appreciate why they feel the way they do. In romantic relationships, misinterpretation is the biggest cause of conflict and you can really address this if you can put your own interpretation aside and consider the possibility that actually your partner means something entirely different. So, if your partner says, 'I'm going out again tonight, I'll try not to wake you when I come in,' instead of hearing, 'I'll be late, I can't be bothered to see you,' make the effort to hear the sentiments intended, which are likely to be more like, 'I love living with you, but I need to maintain my relationships outside ours. However, I accept we live together and my actions will affect you, so I will try to be as quiet as I can if it is late when I come in.'

Solution:
The key is to look at both your partner's and your own automatic thoughts and examine them for bias. Analyse your feelings and ask yourself if they are entirely justified, or if they are influenced by factors unrelated to your partner's words or actions. A number of exercises will be outlined later to help you do this and consequently gain a greater degree of openness and empathy with each other.

Showing Companionship

This issue concerns the strength of your relationship. Can you and your partner be supportive of each other through thick and thin? Can you compromise when contentious issues arise? Companionship means you share your life with a partner who adds value to your life, and who you can depend on and trust, through good times and bad. Effective companionship cannot be developed when conflict is handled through the use of stonewalling, contempt, labelling each other and threats to leave (Leahy, 2005).

Solution:
When conflict arises, change your tack. Typically, we go into arguments with the aim of winning and arrive at a situation that resembles two bulls locking horns. A far more effective strategy involves changing the objective, so that you and your partner aren't actually battling to win the argument – you are working together to reach a compromise. Resolution, not retribution, should be the goal. You and your partner need to be able to discuss these issues without point-scoring. Winning an argument brings no satisfaction if it leaves your partner destroyed and your relationship in tatters. If you don't want to move in but your partner does, then don't make your aim to 'keep going until I get my way and my partner accepts that I will never move in with him'. Instead, your mission statement should be 'I recognise my partner and I have conflicting views on this, so we will keep discussing it until we reach a solution that addresses and fulfils both sets of needs, so we can support each other.'

Making Decisions

Decisions form a part of any relationship, from 'are we actually ready to live together?' to 'which worktop should the toaster go on?' The mark of a good relationship is a couple who can tackle each decision with diplomacy, understanding and willingness to compromise. Avoiding or ignoring decisions means you run the risk of running into dissatisfaction and resentment at a later date (Crowe, 2005). For example, if a couple's discussion over where they should live in order to meet both partners' commitments to their friends, family and career, usually ends up deteriorating into conflict, then one partner may well end up giving in for a quiet life, or the issue may be ignored until some poor estate agent bears witness to a world-war-three-type clash at their desk. Neither of these results constitutes an example of really dealing with a decision, and consequently neither partner will get that cosy feeling that comes from an amicably reached compromise.

Solution:
Making tricky decisions with your partner is like practising a sport. The more you do it, the easier it becomes. Once you both get into the routine of discussing issues, recognising each other's point of view and deciding on a clear path of action, it will become as much a part of your relationship as your sex life or Sunday morning fry-ups.

Keeping your Expectations Realistic

Life is not a Hollywood love story. Sure, you may well hope moving in with your other half is the blissful, relaxing, stress-free, even romantic experience you see on the big screen. You may well hope that unpacking takes all of five minutes before your partner whips up a romantic candlelit meal in your brand-new dining room, before whizzing through the washing-up and whisking you upstairs for a night of unbridled passion. You may well hope this is merely the prelude to a lifetime of nights in where you agree on what to watch and spring-cleaning operations where you both gleefully complete your chores. Go ahead, hope for all these things, but don't expect them. Be realistic about what living with your partner will be like. Many of the difficulties in your relationship will be ever-present even after you decide to move in together. Sharing a roof won't whitewash your relationship and make it perfect. That doesn't mean that you can't work through your difficulties, it just means you shouldn't expect cohabiting to solve them, or you will be disappointed.

Solution:
The aim should be to set your own realistic goals and to try to discuss them with your partner. It is important to consider whether your goals are similar to your partner's, and whether you have similar expectations – or you could run into problems as your future together progresses. Be careful not to

let wishful thinking or mind-reading get in the way of effective communication of your hopes and fears for your relationship. And ensure you communicate with your partner on how you see cohabiting working, to avoid your expectations being dashed once the boxes are unpacked and the three-piece suite is on it's way.

Conclusion

The option of moving in together has experienced a shift in meaning over the last few decades. Cohabiting with a partner has been transformed from an event that occurs after marriage to a prelude to the big day. The day-to-day stress of running a shared home and balancing two sets of domestic priorities gives most couples a good idea about whether or not they are ready to take the big step and tie the knot. Living together allows one to experience the intimacy and closeness of playing house without the commitment and legal obligation of marriage, but this doesn't mean that pre-marriage cohabitation is a walk in the park. Oh no.

Initially, you have to make the decision to move in together. As we've seen a thousand times, commitment often comes easier to women than men – partly due to their upbringing, partly due to pressure from society and partly due to frankly unhelpful role models such as James Bond and George Clooney! So women might have a tougher time convincing their man to share living space than vice versa. But what's really important is that you acknowledge and accept the reasons behind this. Realise that moving in may well have different connotations for you than it does for your partner and work out how to overcome these objections, rather than taking offence at the possible threat of delay to your plans of domestic bliss. Keep communicating throughout the decision-making process, and constantly remind yourself that you will communicate in different ways because you are different genders. 'I'm not ready yet, can we wait a while?' doesn't mean 'I never ever want to suffocate my bachelor lifestyle by living with you, you nagging old hag.' It probably means 'I'm anxious about whether we are ready and what this will mean for our relationship.'

If you only hear the words through your own filter, then you will miss the best bits.

For example, look at Nadine and Jake. They've been dating for two years and have started talking about moving in together. One night, they embark upon a debate that goes something like this:

> Nadine: 'Right, turn the TV off, I want us to start looking at sofas.'
> Jake: 'The football's on – let's talk about it later.'
> Nadine: 'Why don't you ever get more involved? Turn the TV off, Jake!'
> Jake: 'No! Stop nagging me!'
> Nadine: 'Don't make me feel like your mother! I'm so fed up with this.'
> Jake: 'Oh, I'm getting out of here.'

And imagine how differently the conversation could have gone if Jake had explained his feelings a little more and Nadine had dwelt less on hers:

> Nadine: 'Are you busy? Can we have a chat about your thoughts on what we do when my lease runs out?'
> Jake: 'Just watching the football, can we talk a little later? We do need to work something out.'

It is also important to be aware of putting your partner in a role they do not want to be in. No one wants to be the naughty child or the chastising mother, but by interacting in a way that minimises the person down to a specific behaviour we find ourselves shoved into roles we resent being in. And this only serves to escalate the problem. With a few simple changes to the opener, Nadine manages to change the tone from accusatory to light, she manages to make the discussion feel like a joint decision, not one she has made already, and she doesn't encroach on Jake's personal time, by simply enquiring rather than demanding. In return, Jake feels consulted not confronted and the conversation ends on a positive note.

And once you have made the decision to bite the bullet and sign that lease, then you need to keep a handle on a few things. Namely, singing to Barry Manilow in the toilet, shaving your legs in the kitchen sink and your wildly unrealistic expectations. You may come from a family that rivals The Waltons for inter-family relations, but remember that his experience of the family home may not be quite so happy, and he may well expect different things from your new living arrangement. Likewise, you may well be used to catering for one with dodgy microwave meals, but if your partner is used to being waited on hand and foot by his ever-fussing mother, then your expectations may clash somewhat. Everyone who lives with someone else must go through a period of adjustment, and just because you and your partner love each other and want to spend the rest of your lives together, this doesn't exclude you.

So, really you have two main challenges here: the decision and the period of adjustment. Two different hurdles, but one universal solution – keep talking. Nothing is so scary that it can't be ripped to a manageable size by a good long chat with your loved one. And beyond talking, make sure you listen – not to what you want to hear, not even to what your partner is actually saying (although that's a good start), but to what your partner is trying to say. Put yourself in their position, leave your own judgements at the door, and you and your partner are likely to develop a routine that will benefit your relationship long after the house-warming party.

Men Should Remember:

- Don't assume your partner is a mind-reader. Think about how it would feel to hear, 'I don't want to live with you' and explain yourself more comprehensively.
- Don't bottle up feelings of frustration or being trapped. Be honest and you and your partner will be better equipped to deal with your feelings.

Women Should Remember:

- Re-frame cohabitation for your man. Make it about intimacy and fun, not curfews and nagging.
- Learn to accept that sometimes what your man says is what he means. There's no deeper meaning, there's no hidden insult – it is what it is.

Chapter 7

Marriage

In 2004, Barbara Dafoe Whitehead and David Popenoe launched a study on behalf of Rutgers University to establish current attitudes within the modern family and specifically on male attitudes to marriage. The study examined a statistically representative national sample of 1,010 English-speaking heterosexual young men, aged twenty-five to thirty-four. The respondents were married, single and never married, divorced, widowed and separated and were questioned on their attitudes to relationships, cohabitation and marriage.

The researchers set out to establish which backgrounds and lifestyles were most likely to contribute to a young man becoming the marrying kind and, conversely, which factors would contribute to him becoming the non-marrying kind. Perhaps unsurprisingly, men who came from traditional backgrounds were more likely to embrace marriage and had positive feelings about marriage.

Dafoe Whitehead and Popenoe also identified a core of men resolutely opposed to the idea of marriage. These men weren't just against tying the knot, they were less likely to believe a partner to be telling the truth about previous relationships, they were more likely to fear divorce, more likely to say that single men have better sex lives than married men and more likely to agree that 'If you marry, your biggest concern would be losing your personal freedom.'

Of course, male attitudes to sex were also linked to age – most men had been married for the first time by the age of thirty. So does it stand to reason that past this age most men will have abandoned these notions and feel more positively about marriage and display increased readiness for the commitment? Well, actually no. Dafoe Whitehead and Popenoe found that a high percentage of over thirties still claimed that they wanted 'fun and freedom', over half said they weren't interested in getting married 'any time soon' and less than a quarter agreed that 'your most important goal is to get married'.

All this flies in the face of reason when you consider that research consistently shows that married men live far longer and are far healthier and happier than their single counterparts. Surely in this age of sexual equality and female liberation men can't still see marriage as a lifetime doomed to trips round IKEA with the ball and chain? Is it still such a big deal? The fact is that making the transition from boyfriend and girlfriend to man and wife is a huge step for any relationship. It is a defining, magical, thrilling, important step that bridges the gap between a serious relationship and a lifelong commitment. Marriage shifts the relationship from a private coupling to a formal joining of two families (McGoldrick, 1980) and furthermore it constitutes one of the most celebrated and widely recognised rituals or ceremonies in modern society. Suddenly your name begins with 'Mrs' and usually ends with something completely different from the name you were born to. It means you suddenly have to tick different boxes on all those forms you fill in. And it means that you make a solemn promise to share the good, the bad and the ugly with another person for the rest of your life.

Despite Dafoe Whitehead and Popenoe's findings on the reported reluctance of men to don a suit and buy a ring, marriage is as popular as ever. As society's standards of acceptability have shifted over the years, people are certainly in less of a rush to get married, but they definitely aren't abandoning the idea altogether. Previous generations were quick to condemn living in sin, but by 2006 cohabiting often formed the buffer between a committed relationship and marriage. While the ceremonial and traditional aspects of a wedding remain the same, the societal implications and even the legal implications of marrying or remaining unmarried have certainly lessened. Living together before marriage is fast becoming the norm, and the law is shifting to recognise unmarried partners in situations such as inheritance disputes. The career option is now a viable path for both genders, so many women are keen to pursue a career before they commit to a marriage. Overall, current statistics show that young people delay marriage due to educational and career aspirations and couples marry later in life. On average, men wait until they are thirty-six to say 'I do', while women wait until they are thirty-three years old. What is so striking, however, is the fact that the number of couples getting married has risen according to official figures. In England and Wales in 2004, there were 270,000 marriages,over 15,000 more than in the 2002 figure the Office for National Statistics reported. The fact is, marriage is still seen as something to aspire to, a goal, and a natural progression for most couples.

Despite this, marriage still represents a point of contention and an issue for concern within many relationships and, as we've seen, particularly for a number of men. Some couples worry that a white dress, a big party (oh, and a couple of rings and some legally binding bits of paper) will have a detrimental effect on the relationship. After all, if everything seems to be going well, why risk ruining things with such a dramatic change? Some couples experience a huge imbalance in each partner's expectations of when, why and how marriage should be considered. Why are women always seen as desperate to Jimmy Choo it down the aisle? Why do weddings create so much stress when they are supposed to be such joyful occasions? These are a few of the issues this chapter will cover. Firstly, a framework for viewing the transition to marriage as a psycho-social process will be presented, followed by a summary of how one's views on marriage affects the choice to commit or not. We will also examine how the two genders differ in the way they approach and discuss marriage. As ever, being male or female plays a very specific role in the way you will feel and talk about marriage. This chapter is about learning the difference between 'I do', 'I will' and 'Darling, please can you stop nagging me about tying the knot'. It is about learning how to frame marriage in a different light to that expressed by the subjects of the Dafoe Whitehead and Popenoe research project. And finally, it is about learning how to work with your partner to establish whether marriage really is the next step for your relationship.

What is Marriage?

Marriage is a committed relationship between two individuals recognised by civil authority and/or bound by religious beliefs. The defining element of marriage is that of commitment, and marriage represents the focal point of the entire ideology of family. According to sociologists Berger and Kellner (1964) getting married is viewed as a transition in which two individuals come together and redefine themselves in order to develop a new understanding of the world. Spouses are in a constant interplay making the marital relationship the most important social and personal bond in the life of the individual (Collard and Mansfield, 1994).

Hence marriage is, for most, the ultimate intimate relationship they voluntarily enter. It constitutes the same gravitas and often features similar stipulations to the relationships we share with our parents and siblings, in terms of the time spent together and the bonds we form. The key difference is that deciding to get married is usually a choice we make rather than a situation imposed upon us, which you could argue makes it even more of a serious commitment.

It's no wonder so many people choose to make this commitment. Society and the media sell marriage to us incredibly effectively. Marital relationships are portrayed in the media as sources of lifelong companionship, romance, support, sexual fulfilment commitment and individual well-being. Marriage is viewed as the best forum for meeting individual needs for affection, companionship, emotional and sexual intimacy (Halford et al., 1997). Partners, either expressly (through their vows) or indirectly (through their actions), pledge themselves to meet these needs.

For the past century, sociologists have assumed that marriage enhances psychological well-being. Studies have shown that being married can help protect individuals from life strains and provide a sense of security, meaningfulness and purpose (Horwitz et al., 1996). According to the classical sociological perspective, emphasis is placed on the functions marriage fulfils both for the individual and society. Not only is marriage supposed to provide some semblance of a safety net between you and the big bad world as you and your partner help each other through difficult times, but it also performs a role in society. This is particularly relevant with regards to having children. Marriage creates a solid legal structure for a family, and researchers believe the result of this is that the children are legitimised and socialised and the well-being of the adults is optimised (Collard and Mansfield, 1994). Not only does marriage define the legal responsibilities of each parent but it nails down the roles of each partner as mother and wife, father and husband. In this respect, marriage can be seen as a type of concrete that sets your relationship in stone and provides a universally recognised family structure.

Marriage – the Research

Akin to most major life transitions, a fair amount of research has been conducted in the field of marriage. It can be useful to refer to this to help identify some of the factors that can influence whether and when we decide we are ready for it. Unsurprisingly, many theorists have identified the length of the relationship as a key factor. It is clear that after a relationship has lasted a certain duration marriage is seen, if not by the individuals involved, then by those around them, as the next logical step. Research has also identified the level of commitment, the amount of conflict and the decisiveness of each partner as strong indicators of readiness for marriage. Interestingly, research also shows that the course of a relationship is influenced more by male than by female desires and concerns (Erber and Gilmour, 1994). In other words, if a man asserts he wants to get married, the couple are more likely to make it down the aisle than if the woman is the one who wants to tie the knot.

It has been revealed that people often decide to marry shortly after some distressing event such as illness, death of a parent or after other traumatic loss (McGoldrick, 1980). This could possibly be attributed to the natural desire for security and comfort in the face of loss or grief. It could also be attributed to the way that trauma or loss can encourage us to take greater risks, adopting the maxim that life's too short. In addition to this, a sudden desire to marry can also be linked to feelings of loneliness or a longing to have a child. (Erber and Gilmour, 1994).

Perhaps rather predictably, the feeling that we have found 'the one' is also a key factor in whether or not we feel we are ready to marry. This is a two-way street. Mate selection is generally viewed as a commitment process characterised by both partners developing a consensus that marriage is mutually desired (Erber and Gilmour 1994). There is evidence that a form of assertive mating takes place. People tend to select mates who share similar characteristics to themselves. Marital partners have been found to resemble each other in level of physical attractiveness, socio-cultural factors and values.

Marital adjustment has proven to be more difficult when any of the following are true (McGoldrick, 1980):

- The couple marries shortly after a significant loss.
- The wish to distance oneself from one's family is the initial reason for marrying.
- Family as well as socio-economic backgrounds of each spouse are significantly different.
- The couple marries before age twenty or after age thirty.
- The couple marries after an acquaintanceship of less than six months or more than three years of engagement.
- Either spouse has a poor relationship with his/her siblings or parents.
- Marital patterns in either extended family are unstable.

Research has also supported the idea that the way we view marriage is largely down to our first-hand experiences of witnessing the failures or successes of marriages around us. Dafoe Whitehead and Popenoe identified family background as a key factor in whether a man could be described as the marrying or the non-marrying kind. Family attitudes and myths about marriage filter down from generation to generation and this can make the transition easier, or harder, depending on your personal experience (McGoldrick, 1980). The most immediate and direct experience of marriage most of us witness is that of our parents. In the same way that if we are taught our ABC as a child we are more likely to turn into good spellers, if we observe and learn from a good marriage we are more likely to go on to form a good marriage ourselves, partly because our feelings about marriage are likely to be more positive and, consequently, we will be more relaxed and less anxious about it.

Consider the case of John and Marisa who have lived together for four years. They are both in their early thirties. John is absolutely certain that Marissa is the woman he wants to marry, and he has made this clear to her many times. However, Marissa grew up in a household barely held together by her parents who essentially hated each other. Her father was controlling, her mother weak. When they finally divorced, once Marissa had grown up and moved out, both denounced the partnership as the worst mistake of their lives. Now, years on, they are both still bitter about the time they spent together, and are unable to move on. Marissa is hugely happy within her relationship, but her first-hand experience of marriage means it is a concept she feels very negatively about. John's parents are still happily married. So it's clear to see how this couple differ in terms of their views on marriage – understandably so. It's also clear to see how this will affect their discussion of the issue:

> John says: 'I can't wait for the day I can walk you down the aisle.'
> John means: 'I love you and wish you would be a little more open-minded about this.'
> Marisa hears: 'You're just not committed to this relationship! To me, our relationship will only be complete once we are married, nothing else is good enough.'
> Marisa thinks: Why won't you drop this? I love you but I've told you I'm not interested in marriage. You know I think it'll only end in tears.

Consequently,

> *Marisa says: 'So we can spend the next forty years of our lives making each other miserable?'*
> *John hears: 'I just don't care enough about you to make that kind of commitment. I'm sure marrying you will be a disaster.'*

These differences highlight the need for open communication. Couples need to appreciate that the decision to marry isn't as simple as 'I love you' or 'I don't love you'. Research has proven that a whole host of factors come into play. Recognising the role your background, your upbringing and the events in your life play on your readiness for marriage is really important. And all this before you've even begun to look at the issues that arise just because he is a man and you are a woman . . .

A Tale of Two Genders

The story of any married couple is always the tale of two people. Although they may experience the same events, the reality for each partner may well be different. And these differences are likely to be a result of our gender-specific traits and emotional tendencies, as well as a result of the expectations that society places on us based purely on whether we are male or female. Marriage represents a highly gendered institution. Men are still expected to be the main provider or breadwinner and the anchor of the family in the outside world. Meanwhile, women are still expected to adopt a more submissive role as housewife and be the anchor of the family internally. In their study, Mansfield and Collard (1988) found that when men were asked the question 'Do you think there will ever be a time when you cease work for a while?' their answers were related to their work – for example, being made redundant, being sacked or retiring. Women answered in terms of the possibility of childbirth and childcare. These findings reflect on the economic and social pressures men feel to remain in work and support their family, and the duty women feel to their homes and children, above the duty they feel to their careers.

Within the romantic relationship, before we even begin to look at parental roles, research has shown that men and women view things vastly differently. It has been found that women have stronger influence on the maintenance of a marital relationship and are more sensitive to problems in the relationship (Heaton and Blake, 1999). We know that women are more emotionally in tune than men, and this means they are more likely to pick up on problems, to worry about them, to discuss them (with friends, hairdressers and basically whoever else will listen) and to confront them. Meanwhile the man in the relationship may well be oblivious to the fact that anything is actually wrong. So this can cause conflict from the word go.

A look at the characteristics of single and unmarried individuals of both sexes is also revealing. Research shows that a differential relationship exists between marriage and gender with variables relating to economic and social achievement. Higher levels of intelligence, education and occupation are associated with singlehood in women. Conversely, singlehood in men is associated with poor interpersonal relationships with parents and siblings (Unger, 1979). Successful women are far less likely to marry than their male counterparts. Undoubtedly, this links back to the age-old stereotypes of men as the dynamic, successful providers and women as carers and nurturers who stay at home and raise children. Clearly, men who adhere to this societal expectation are more likely to marry than women who challenge the stereotype and occupy the typically male role.

Research has also shown that women who marry early usually display low levels of self-esteem. At the other end of the spectrum, women with good self-esteem are likely to date more and enter into fewer serious relationships. This can probably be attributed to the fact that validation from others is usually the first crutch we look for when we don't value ourselves particularly highly. If we feel confident and assured of our self-worth, then not only are we less likely to rely on anyone else for security or self-assurance, but we are also likely to have higher expectations about what we expect from a relationship. As a good education and fulfilling career play a large part in the development of self-confidence, the research concludes that it seems education and career-related opportunities provide women with a chance to develop concepts about psychological freedom as well as increased scope for independent living (Unger, 1979). They are therefore likely to be in less of a rush to get married, and happier to be alone.

This is great for them but apparently not for the rest of society. The social stigma attached to being a single woman is infinitely more negative than the glamorous image single men enjoy. While the word 'bachelor' conjures up images of independence, hedonism and carefree living, the word 'spinster' is steeped in loneliness, sadness and a sense of rejection. Compare Bridget Jones to James Bond. When men remain single, it is seen as a choice, or even a lucky escape from marriage as they revel in the freedom and fun that the men in Dafoe Whitehead and Popenoe's study talked of. When women remain single it is seen as an imposed reality, usually as a result of some innate psychological flaw, in line with the orthodox view that being able to form long-term, intimate, committed relationships is an indicator of emotional maturity and of a healthy personality. Now, as we've seen, this is rarely true; in fact research dictates that healthy, emotionally sound women are actually less likely to settle down. It is therefore a stereotype. Unmarried women are still more susceptible than men to social judgements about their motives or chances of getting married. This emphasis on marriage as the ultimate goal requires women to have a plausible reason for their singlehood (Unger, 1979). Hence women are pressurised to care more about marriage and, as a result, usually end up investing more in the idea than men.

Research also shows that a marriage is also more strongly related to home-life satisfaction for women compared to men. This difference may be attributed to gender differences in the psychological purpose of marriage. Males usually have more instrumental gains from marriage (in the form of services, for example housekeeping). Females, who have fewer alternatives, may invest more emotionally in their marital roles (Denmark and Paludi, 1993). And obviously this is a recipe for conflict.

So marriage is yet another area likely to create tension between a couple, not least because of the way our gender affects the way we see it, and the way our environment conditions us to feel about tying the knot. As highlighted by the responses of the subjects in the Dafoe Whitehead and Popenoe study, for men, marriage is often associated with what they are losing – fun and freedom. Conversely, further research shows that women are taught to associate marriage with what they can gain. Men are socialised to feel that walking down the aisle constitutes kissing goodbye to the freedom of single life, whereas woman are conditioned to feel that marriage is a box to be ticked as soon as possible, so they can get on with the business of making and raising babies within a socially accepted family infrastructure. Of course these stereotypes don't apply to every couple; in fact, they probably apply to very few couples in today's world of increasing sexual equality. But they can go some way to explaining why couples see marriage so differently.

Consider the case of Tom and Angie, who are both in their early thirties. After living together for five years, both of them are struggling with deciding on the next step. Angie wants to get married, and has made this blatantly clear to Tom, who feels exactly the opposite. As far as Tom is concerned, marriage is an unnecessary formality that exists to make others happy – he doesn't want to march down the aisle just so Angie's mum can have a chance to get her wedding hat out of the closet. For him marriage is about fulfilling the expectations of others and he considers himself perfectly happy within his existing relationship with Angie. However, this isn't being communicated to Angie particularly successfully. She interprets his hesitance to pop the question as a sign that he doesn't love her enough, or that he doesn't picture her in his future. When Angie says, 'It would be so lovely to call you my husband!' Tom hears, 'But, everyone else is getting married! Why can't we?!' Likewise, when Tom says, 'Splashing out thousands of pounds on a big party and a piece of paper seems like a waste of money,' Angie hears, 'I'm not spending that money on you because I don't want to commit to you. Someone better might come along next week.' The key to untangling this 'he says, she says' mess is establishing the reality behind each partner's words. Once Angie articulates her real motivations behind wanting to get married: that she wants to demonstrate to Tom how committed she is to him, that she wants to provide a traditional home for their future children and that she is so proud of him that she wants to be recognised as 'his' in the most official way possible, Tom's defences will relax. Equally, once Tom explains that he feels so strongly about Angie he doesn't need a big ceremony to prove it, and that he wants to make a commitment too, but he doesn't feel comfortable making such an exhibition of it, Angie will feel secure and better prepared to negotiate. Once Angie and Tom begin to deal in truths rather than assumptions they are halfway to establishing a compromise.

Marriage – the Vital Ingredients

Now, of course, you and your partner love each other. You know you care about each other's welfare, you want to make each other happy, and you still get that little weird butterfly thing in your tummy when he phones. But is that enough to build a marriage on? Well, quite frankly, no. While love and genuine affection are key ingredients for a happy marriage, it takes a little more than that. Love and affection provide you with the incentive so often needed to overcome differences and work through problems, but, ultimately, they aren't enough on their own. Cognitive behavioural thera-pists have identified the other factors that contribute to a successful marriage. They are particularly useful if you are deciding whether or not you are ready to don a long frock and step down the aisle. As you read through these key points, evaluate how closely they reflect your relation-ship and compare the way your partner deals with and feels about these factors, compared to your own feelings and behaviour. This can be really useful, not because you have to abandon the relationship if you feel it doesn't tick all the boxes, but because it can help you identify areas you and your partner could work on.

Commitment

This one encapsulates the idea that you are in the marriage for the long haul, whatever happens, and whatever issues you have to face as a couple. Beliefs Beck (1998) identified as a good indication of true commitment include: 'If we have troubles in our marriage, I will work on them with my spouse'; 'I will not withdraw/isolate/leave my spouse when things get difficult'; 'We will stay together in good and bad times'. In other words, you and your partner assume responsibility for each other's happiness, come what may. Commitment represents reliability and provides a sense of security for both partners. It means we know what to expect from our partners and that we can rely on them.

Problems with commitment can manifest themselves in a number of ways: being vigilant or watchful of your partner's flaws, expressing fear of being permanently trapped, looking for an 'out' of the relationship, avoiding emotional intimacy, not making the effort to ensure the growth of the relationship, showing lack of affection, being critical of your partner. Beliefs associated with these behaviours range from: 'If I distance myself from my partner I am less likely to get hurt' to 'I cannot be dependent, I must not make myself vulnerable'. People who hold these beliefs are usually fearful they will be hurt or rejected – the failure to commit is usually a reason that their commitment will not be returned. These schemas are often established through relationship memories from childhood. By trying to avoid being hurt, these schemas actually set up a vicious cycle of reinforcing that exact fear by creating unstable relationships/marriages.

In general, the key thing you need to look out for when considering the level of commitment you and your partner display is whether you are equally committed to the relationship. If you believe you are not equally committed, establish why this might be, find ways to articulate these concerns and address them together. A marriage will not flourish if one partner embarks upon it half-heartedly, so, before you make the leap, you need to be sure your partner is ready to commit himself fully in the same way that you are.

Loyalty and Trust

When we talk about loyalty and trust, what we are really talking about is the premise that you are both dedicated to each other's best interests and neither of you will deliberately hurt the other. Beck (1998) found beliefs such as 'I can count on my partner', 'I place my partner's best interests first', 'When I need her/him, she/he is there for me', 'She/he is not going to purposefully hurt me' as good indicators of loyalty and trust. According to these beliefs the person experiences a solid sense of trust, which can provide a sense of security and reliability. Holding these beliefs allows partners to be at ease with each other, rather than constantly suspecting ulterior motives or bad intentions.

The opposite of these beliefs means that either partner will be unable to make a total commitment or will display a lack of responsibility for their actions. It might mean they are unwilling to make sacrifices, or are looking for an escape route, or are even unfaithful. Again, you need to ask yourself whether you and your partner display any of this behaviour. Just like commitment, trust and loyalty are reciprocal qualities and are only truly in existence if both partners devote themselves to ensuring that they are key qualities of the relationship.

Cooperation

Finally, can you and your partner work together? Have you identified joint objectives and planned a clear solution that will meet these objectives? Beliefs that demonstrate that you have, include: 'We will work together and jointly decide on important issues', 'Each one of us takes responsibility for things within the relationship', 'We will coordinate as best as we can what we do'. These beliefs involve the willingness to deal with conflicts and difficult situations. In a marriage that displays a great deal of cooperation, differences can be accepted and resolved.

Where there is a lack of cooperation within a relationship, this may be a result of partners acting in a way that could be described as egocentric, self-centred and dismissive. It may mean that you and your partner ignore each other's decisions and wishes, to a point where you could even become deceitful.

Think hard about this one. Do you and your partner have shared goals? Does he want the same as you want for yourself? Do you both want the same in terms of where you live, whether you have children and how many? Couples who share united goals and work together to achieve them have a far greater chance of going the distance.

So, How do you Know you're Ready to Make the Transition?

The transition to marriage for a couple is dependent on the discrepancy of their meanings. It is important your views on the meaning of getting married are similar.

Failure to appreciate differences in meaning can make the transition extremely difficult. It often leads to getting stuck rather than getting married. Communication usually becomes obscured by the need to enforce what one wants (to marry or not). In such situations both partners need to step back and reflect on their meanings. The reluctant partner needs to think what they are fearful of. They need to ask themselves what is colouring their view. Perhaps their family experiences were bad, their parents were divorced and they therefore find it hard to commit; or maybe their family have expectations of what a successful marriage is. Such issues should be addressed and resolved early on.

An important clue that you and your partner are possibly ready to make the transition is the development of a 'couple style', which is comfortable and functional for both of you. Here are some indicators that can actually help you determine whether or not you and your partner have developed and settled into a style that lends itself to a long and happy marriage:

Spending Quality Couple Time

Remember those days when you and your partner actually 'did' things? At the beginning of a relationship, the focus is usually on finding activities you both enjoy and using them to get to know one another. As the relationship solidifies and becomes more reliable, this quality time often gets neglected. After all, if you live together then you already spend enough time with each other, right? Wrong. There is a huge difference between sharing another TV dinner in silence and actually enjoying each other's company. Quality couple time means sharing activities. It means feeling close and nurturing your relationship. Quality couple time involves sitting together, sharing concerns, discussing your dream house or what you would do if you won the lottery, taking days off to do things together and sharing hopes, ideas and feelings.

When we are ready to marry, the lure of the 'singles' scene' doesn't shine quite so brightly. Instead, we gain our pleasure from time with our partner and appreciate the benefits of a trusting, committed relationship with one person as opposed to a jam-packed schedule, chock-a-block with dates with a list of candidates. One well-documented variable of marital satisfaction is high rates of positivity in marital interaction. Happily satisfied couples spend time together, do mutually enjoyable tasks/activities together and behave more positively toward each other (Halford et al., 1997).

Being Intimate

In a happy, healthy relationship, emotional and sexual intimacy play key roles. Emotional intimacy means you and your partner know and understand each other's personalities – you are aware of and sensitive to each other's hopes, dreams and anxieties. And you are comfortable divulging your inner thoughts to one another. Equally, sexual intimacy means that you and your partner are happy and comfortable confiding your feelings about sex, your fantasies and your insecurities. A healthy sexual bond is crucial to a long and happy marriage, and should never be underestimated in terms of importance.

Do you and your partner feel entirely comfortable with each other? Are there things you don't feel you can share with each other? A successful 'couple style' will incorporate emotional and physical intimacy or, at least, recognise how important they are, and work towards achieving them.

Feeling Loved

Loving someone is one thing. Feeling, indeed knowing, they love you is just as important. When we feel loved and secure within a relationship we are comfortable being ourselves and revealing the good, bad and ugly aspects of our personalities. Within a good 'couple style' both partners will be well aware that their other half knows them inside out and still loves them. This security is important because it allows us to be open, honest and vulnerable.

Feeling loved is what will get you and your partner through the bad times. Remember there are no perfect marriages or perfect people. All people and all marriages have weaknesses and vulnerabilities (McCarthy and McCarthy, 2004). In the eye of the storm, knowing your partner loves you unconditionally will protect you, strengthen you and, eventually, carry you through.

Holding Positive and Realistic Expectations About Marriage

There are two key things here. Firstly, remember the old adage that you reap what you sow. The more you put into your marriage, the more you stand to gain. If your husband-to-be trudges down the aisle moaning about his loss of freedom, and pandering to the stereotypes of men as commitmentphobes who are cruelly deprived and restricted by marriage, then it doesn't bode particularly well for your marriage. Go into your marriage with a positive outlook, and remember the decision to tie the knot should be a positive one shared by both partners. Be excited, be enthusiastic, and enjoy it.

Secondly, you should be realistic. Before you trot into church you and your partner should face the reality of wedded life head on. Recognise that hearts, flowers and fantastic sex often come as part of a package that also includes frustration, conflict and compromise. That's not to say your marriage won't be everything you dreamed it would, it just means you have to accept the rough with the smooth. Marriages can be hard work, but as long as you accept this from the start you should have no problems addressing the various challenges that may be thrown at you.

Making Plans for the Future

Lastly, do you and your partner have the same dreams for the future? Do you trust each other to work at achieving and realising these dreams? When you commit to a marriage, you commit to a shared future, so it's rather important you establish whether you actually want the same things from life. Issues such as children, and where you live may be easy to ignore when you don't foresee them arising for another ten years, but it is impossible to build a happy, healthy marriage on false expectations.

Be honest right from the start about what you want from your marriage and encourage your partner to do the same. Then ensure that you are both committed to transforming these aspirations into a shared reality. The way your partner behaves should help you ascertain whether or not you can trust him or her to make this commitment. If either of you have a habit for talking the talk and then failing to walk the walk, the chances of you dedicating yourselves to these lifetime goals are slim. Be aware of this, and work on it.

Conclusion

Let's look at Zara and Max, who are both in their late twenties. Ever since Zara was little, she dreamed of being a bride and a wife. She and Max have been together for four years and both are absolutely convinced they have found 'the one'. Zara is ready to stop dreaming about dresses and ready to start getting fitted for one, in between booking churches, organising table plans and picking bridesmaids, while Max still sees himself as the independent young man about town he was as a youngster, albeit with a beautiful girlfriend he loves dearly. Max knows Zara is ready to settle down, due to the endless bridal magazines left lying around, the surreptitious lingering by jewellers' windows and the endless badgering by her mother. But to Max, marriage means he has well and truly said goodbye to his youth. He's heard the tales about how women rule the roost once they are wearing a wedding band, and, essentially, he's running scared. Our self-concept (the way we see and value ourselves) may take some time to incorporate a new role, like husband or wife.

Of course, he's never actually asked Zara why she wants to get married. He assumes it is so she can chain him to the iron, ban him from seeing his friends and bombard him with forty years of chat about soft furnishings, childcare theories and dinner parties. When she says, 'You'd look so gorgeous in a morning suit,' he hears, 'I can't wait to get you down the aisle and under my thumb.' As you may have guessed, the reality for Zara is rather different. She herself leads an active social life, and the last thing she wants is to chain Max down and restrict him. The problem is she's struggling against twenty-six years of social conditioning that have taught Max to feel marriage is a sacrifice rather than a positive choice. She is battling against the feelings of the scores of men in the Dafoe Whitehead and Popenoe's study who felt that marriage represented a threat to 'personal freedom' and that single men experienced far superior sex lives to married men. The words 'husband' and 'wife' carry burdensome meanings and bring conceptions of heavy responsibilities that are not imposed by living together (McGoldrick, 1980). The challenge here is for Zara to reframe marriage for her boyfriend. She needs to explain very clearly what marriage means to her, and what it doesn't, so he can see the many positives that come from being man and wife. Equally, Max needs to articulate his fears and concerns about marriage so Zara can understand his reluctance and allay these anxieties.

Right now, couples are freer than ever before to dictate the path of their own relationship. Societal expectations, while still in operation, have relaxed; consequently, many people are choosing to live together for a while before jumping into marriage, and this often acts as a useful trial before making a more serious commitment. Gender roles have shifted slightly, accommodating a woman's right to a career and recognising the value of an involved father in the home. While this societal shift provides each individual with greater flexibility to establish a structure that works for their relationship, it also means the potential for conflict within that relationship has increased tenfold because the rules are unclear. Forty years ago, if you liked somebody and began courting them you were pretty much married off to them in the minds of everybody else, and these expectations set very clear guidelines for when this was expected to happen, how it was supposed to happen and exactly when you were supposed to start producing babies. Now the guidelines have blurred, and each couple takes responsibility for the future of their relationship, a can of worms has been opened, and marriage often becomes a breeding ground for conflict and misunderstanding.

Much of this is down to the way we are socialised as men and women, and, specifically, how we are taught to regard marriage. Once again, we can see how our own gender-specific schemas can turn 'Let's wait another year' into 'I'm never marrying you, I'm just biding my time until someone better comes along', and how 'I can't wait to marry you' can become 'I can't wait to have even more control over you'. As with most situations, the answer lies in battling through these gender tongues and working out what the genuine emotions are behind the words being used. Dafoe Whitehead and Popenoe identified men as marrying or non-marrying but they also took the measure of accepting that the non-marrying men would probably become the marrying type someday. When your man is ready to take this step will be down to a number of factors. Indeed, when *you* are ready to take the step will also be down to a number of factors. All you can do is be honest with your partner, be genuine about your motivations and be realistic about the best decision for your relationship. Study the factors that contribute to a happy marriage, and measure your partner's expectations for the future against your own – then you should be on your way to ascertaining whether this decision-making process ends in 'I do', 'I will . . . but not just yet' or 'Never going to happen'.

Men Should Remember:

- Don't be a victim of years of social stereotyping that tells you that marrying your partner will restrict your lifestyle or threaten your freedom. Go with your own feelings.
- Don't assume your partner wants to marry you for one reason or another. Talk to her. Establish her motivations.

Women Should Remember:

- Don't see marriage as the ultimate goal. View a happy, healthy relationship where both of you feel loved and secure as the objective.
- Remember that 'not yet' doesn't mean 'I don't love you enough'.

Chapter 8

First-Time Parenting

I n the late nineties, a group of researchers in Germany set out to establish the way male and female responsibilities shifted after the birth of a couple's first child. They studied 175 expectant couples, focusing on three things: the mothers, the fathers and the relationship between the couple. Half the couples were first-time parents, the other half were expecting an additional child. The couples were surveyed and observed from the beginning of the pregnancy to beyond the birth – some for as long as eighteen months after. Both partners were measured by a set of criteria including: extent of professional work; division of labour, attributions for the onset of pregnancy, emotional reaction to pregnancy and desirability of pregnancy.

In these modern days of equal opportunity you would be forgiven for assuming that criteria such as professional work and division of labour would reveal strikingly different results to the families of yester year. Obviously, women are still the only ones able to incubate and deliver a baby, but the increase in the number of career-women and rise of the house husband, in addition to improved legislation for working mums, must surely have had a dramatic impact on the way men and women adjust to a new arrival in the family. The results beg to differ. After all that hard work to get the female of the species some equal footing in the world, it seems that childbirth actually reverts us back to being dedicated housewives with business-hungry, breadwinning husbands.

The research by Kalicki, Fthenakis, Peitz and Engfer in 1998 showed that the transition to parenthood realigns gender roles within the home. Women find themselves assuming responsibility for household jobs and childcare, and men find themselves doing less around the house and spending more time at work. The researchers used their findings as evidence that childbirth is one of the reasons that gender stereotypes and societal expectations prevail. Even couples with a particularly modern, equal relationship dynamic found themselves reverting to traditional roles once a new arrival burst onto the scene. In essence, the research showed that parenthood has very different implications for men and women, and these implications are apparently unrelated to the couple themselves; they are reasonably universal.

Despite the evident lack of change in gender roles for parents over the last few hundred years, there are some changes that have occurred in our society regarding parenthood. A few million years ago you wouldn't have had any choice about certain matters. As soon as you were physically able, you were a one-woman baby factory, and objections about careers, independence and chocolate footprints on sofas were futile. Nature dictated our basic instinct, our very reason for being was to reproduce, and when you look at the facts that basic instinct still stands. After all, if everyone decided that iPods and health farms were far more fun than nappies and breast pumps and gave up childbearing altogether, after a while the human population would start to feel like a rather quiet group to belong to. Essentially, our species relies on reproduction, and will only continue to thrive if an adequate proportion of the population continue to parent. Statistics show that more than 85 per cent of couples have children whether biological, adopted or step-children (McCarthy and McCarthy, 2004).

But that doesn't make it easy. Oh no. As natural as the urge to create a mini-me is, childrearing is far from easy work. From conception to, well, for ever, being a parent brings as many stresses and pressures as it does joys and wonders. As we've learnt from previous chapters, anything that evokes guilt, stress or absolute exhaustion is likely to place pressure on a couple and, what's more, both partners will experience and express those feelings in completely different ways to each other. As the research by Kalicki et al. shows, we also have entirely different experiences of parenthood, depending on gender and the expectations it labels us with. So why do we do it in the first place?

Aside from the irresistible physiological instincts, the decision to have a child is, for most people, an emotional choice. The primary emotional reason that a couple chooses to have a child is to experience the process of childbirth, participate in parenting and watch the child grow into a person (McCarthy and McCarthy, 2004). Parenthood is seen as one of the key life stages, and many people claim they would feel 'incomplete' were they unable to have children. We see children as a natural extension of ourselves as individuals, and usually as an extension of our relationship.

Children provide an amazing security in that their lives overlap with their parents' lifespans and then continue into the future. When we have children, we know we have contributed to the continuation of our family. Children are the difference between a couple and a family. They are the difference between a two-way bond and a multi-layered structure. Children bring fun, youth and amusement to a family. Children often bring out the best in people, and having children allows us to experience an entirely different set of emotions, and feel a specific sense of pride, love and responsibility that is seldom felt in any other human relationship. Parents of all social and cultural environments report feelings of creativity, accomplishment and competence from the experience of having and rearing children.

However lovely all this sounds, the chances are that when your baby has splattergunned the kitchen with apple purée for the fourteenth time in one morning, or your two-year-old still hasn't grasped that a full potty does not constitute a great hat, the wonders of parenting are easy to forget. And let's not forget, serious academic research suggests you'll be the one clearing up the purée or, worse, the contents of the potty. When you and your partner haven't as much as air-kissed in ten months because your little boy has taken up permanent nocturnal residence in your bed, the joys of a three-person family might seem a little idealistic. When your relationship is feeling a ten-ton pressure because of a person who weighs less than a few bags of sugar, parenthood can be lonely, frustrating and downright miserable, particularly when the one person you would expect to understand – your partner – feels a million miles away, because they are going through an entirely different process.

In this chapter, we will discuss the process of becoming a parent as it relates to changes in the couple relationship and how each of you deals with the process according to gender. This isn't the guide to good parenting – think of it as 'A Guide to Help Your Relationship Survive Parenting' or 'A Guide to Why "Not another nappy!"' Doesn't Necessarily Mean "Get me out of here"!' Early in the chapter we present a framework for viewing the transition to parenthood as a process, focusing in particular on the impact becoming a parent can have on your relationship. The bulk of the chapter centres on summarising findings on how marriages change with parenthood, examining differences among genders in how their lifestyle becomes redefined by virtue of parenthood, linking the ways wives and husbands initially assume their roles as care givers, and probing how they come to feel about each other and the marriage. Parenthood is a project, and it can be all-consuming, but it should always work alongside the ongoing project of ensuring your relationship survives the ride.

The Choice to Have a Child

OK, so we've touched on a few of the reasons couples decide to have children – evolution, the desire to create an image of oneself and continue the family, a longing to partake in one of life's greatest challenges – but the fact is that an individual's motivations are likely to consist of a number of these objectives, and empirical research shows that when examining motives for childrearing there is a great deal of individual variation (Unger, 1979) Each individual's motives are entirely different. What's more, these differences are likely to be related to gender. The table below looks at some of the key reasons that women and men choose to have children:

Women

- experiencing love life's fuller meaning
- opportunity for personal growth
- stimulation and feeling of pride
- to make someone in one's own image
- experiencing the birth process

Men

- having fun – to do and enjoy things with the child
- experiencing love life's fuller meaning
- to make someone in one's own image
- partnership benefits
- desire to be needed and loved

Gender-related reasons for having children.

Our reasons for not procreating also link back to whether we are male or female. If men are reticent about the pitter patter of tiny feet, it tends to be because they feel apprehensive about early, inevitable consequences of conception – pregnancy and childbirth. On the other hand, women who shun or delay motherhood tend to do so because they are more concerned about the long-term pressures of childrearing. This makes sense when you look at the research by Kalicki et al. suggesting that it is the women who take the lion share of the childrearing responsibility.

Remember that the single easiest part of having a child is conception. The moment that egg is fertilised is often completely out of your control and for many couples entirely effortless, but, from that point onwards, you'll never have it that easy again. Rather than strengthening the marital bond, the stress that accompanies the arrival of a child can actually sever the bond (McCarthy and McCarthy, 2004). A baby dramatically changes your lives and your relationship. Hence, it is important to be able to distinguish the motives for having a child and examine them carefully.

You should both acknowledge together that the decision about whether to have children represents a choice rather than the expected thing to do. Both of you need to consider and explore carefully your attitudes, feelings, goals, values and life circumstances. Ideally, having a child should be a mature, joint decision that validates the stability of your marriage; a decision that must be based on healthy motivations rather than on factors such as saving a shaky marriage, pressure from family and friends, or an attempt to prove something to one's partner, etc. (McCarthy and McCarthy, 2004).

How Children Affect the Relationship

So, you're sailing along just fine. You and your partner have just got used to each other; you've found your dream home; you've accepted his unhygienic habits; he's accepted and embraced your somewhat emotional dramatics. And then suddenly, you welcome your new housemate – a four-kilo energy drainer who puts you both to shame in your respective specialisms. Hygiene? This new creature ensures you are up to your wrists in human waste more times than you care to count each and every day. As for emotional dramatics, for someone whose every whim, potential need or slight discomfort is catered to at a moment's notice, your new little friend makes a hell of a lot of noise. And all of this without the slightest acknowledgement of normal working hours or standard meal times. The joys of having a baby are clear, but the agonies can be overwhelming. Having your first child represents a transition to the next stage in the life cycle, and there's no guarantee it will be a smooth transition.

Despite the fact that most couples report the arrival of their children as a source of great satisfaction (Crowe, 2005), as we've already remarked, children can also be a source of great stress. Rather sadly, research shows that the arrival of children generally causes deterioration in the quality of a marital relationship. Introducing a new member into your family means you will be tired, concerned, more restricted and you will probably have a lot less money. (It's amazing how much children cost even before they can drive, shop or eat solids.) These factors add up to a melee of potential triggers for relationship discontentment. With the arrival of the first child, contentment drops and stress increases. Studies on marital satisfaction over the life span reveal a U-shaped relationship between satisfaction and time period, with satisfaction being lowest when children are young. If we go back to the German research from the nineties it's easy to see why there may be inter-marital discontent: women automatically shift to take more domestic responsibility, and men adopt more responsibility for keeping the family going through his career. Any conversation between the sexes will be in two different dialogues. Let's look at Mark and Lisa. They've been together for four years and just had their first child. One night Mark goes to the pub after work and returns late, and drunk.

Mark says: 'Hello, darling! Have you missed me?! I missed you!'

Mark thinks: God, it felt good to spend a little time away from the house, and away from work tonight. Even if the room is spinning and I feel a little ill . . .

Lisa thinks: How dare you?! I've been slaving away clearing up after your child and you've been boozing down the pub!

Lisa says: 'Great! I'm going to bed.'

Mark hears: 'I'm not happy unless you're unhappy. Because I'm tired you should be too – I resent you having fun.'

Mark says: 'Oh, don't be so boring. Aren't I allowed one night away from the house?'

Lisa thinks: Don't make me feel like your mother. I need some support, and I need some acknowledgement of the work I do around this house.

Lisa says: 'Oh go to bed, Mark. You idiot.'

Despite the common spats that parenting can evoke, it isn't all bad news. A longitudinal study of newly weds explored the impact of parenthood on marriage (McHale, 1985). Couples who became parents during the first year of marriage were compared with couples who remained childless during the year. Data was collected from each couple two months after the wedding and again about a year later. Surveys focusing on the behavioural properties of marriage (amount of companionship, sex roles and so on) were conducted with each couple. The results confirmed earlier research showing that the transition to parenthood affects companionship and marital role patterns, but no evidence was found to support the idea that parenthood is associated with a decline in the partners' love for one another. So at least we can ascertain that while parenthood might mean you spend less time together or bicker more, it is unlikely to have any effect on perhaps the most important thing – your love for one another.

Despite this promising evidence, it is clear that, even if only for a temporary period, parenthood can have a detrimental effect on your relationship with your partner. The problem is that bringing a child into the world creates a whole new role for each partner to fulfil. Suddenly you are not just a girlfriend or a wife – you are a mother, which is a full-time carer. This role is so all-encompassing it can take over and detract from your role as a romantic partner. This appears to be more prevalent among women than men, who obviously experience the physical transition of mother-hood, and, as we've seen, tend to be more heavily involved in the baby's care after the father returns to work.

Traditionally and historically, men and women have very different roles. The traditional male role does not promote care taking and nurturing of children (McCarthy and McCarthy, 2004). Belsky et al. (1985) found that the negative impact of children mainly affects women and does so within the first six months of the child's life. Ruble et al. (1988) present findings that indicate a woman's negative feelings are linked to violated expect-ations about who does what at home: they reported doing more housework or child care than they expected initially. This is also a time when depression is likely to occur. The effect of this may be to blame her partner for not sharing responsibilities, and the outcome can often, not surprisingly, be a deterioration of their feelings for each other. So further to Kalicki et al.'s findings that showed the roles we assume when we become parents, this further research suggests that these roles can have a negative effect on the relationship.

As with any relationship stumbling block, a major communication barrier often arises from the simple fact that you and your partner are different genders and experience things differently. So next we look at the gender-specific reactions to parenting.

Implications of Parenting on Genders

Females

OK, so there's one big fat obvious difference here. As involved as a man wants to be in the parenting process, there's one job that is strictly the job of a woman: physiologically, at least, a man's work is completed after conception. Women carry the baby for nine months, and at the end of those nine months, it is they who give birth. Without dramatic scientific advances, no amount of parenting books or antenatal classes look likely to change that. So from day one women have a different experience of pregnancy to men and, inevitably, are likely to experience a vastly more dramatic transition period. After the birth of the child, women are likely to play a bigger part in the baby's initial development. Even in this age of equality, the idea that women are naturally the primary care takers prevails. Very few families are run by house husbands, and research shows that even when both parents work, the mother still spends more time with her children than the father. Women, even if employed, spend about seventy hours a week with their children, compared to the thirty hours that is typical of fathers.

Equality may well have touched many areas of modern society, but when it comes to childcare, tradition and biology dictate that women are less likely to pursue their careers after having children than their male partner. Hence, for women, two major adjustments need to be made simultaneously: giving up an occupation and assuming the role of mother for the first time (Unger, 1979). Relinquishing a career is a traumatic enough change on its own. As is having a baby. When you consider many women tackle both transitions literally within months of each other, it is unsurprising that this usually represents a particularly stressful period in a woman's life.

Research and anecdotal evidence demonstrates that a common feature of motherhood is guilt, however you choose to parent. Mothers who choose to stay at home often feel alone, overwhelmed by the constant attention children require and desperate for adult company.

They complain of feeling isolated and burdened by responsibility (McCarthy and McCarthy, 2004), and often end up feeling guilty about these negative emotions. Equally, mothers who choose to pursue their careers and return to work usually worry they are not spending enough time with their children. This concern is compounded by the constant media coverage of women who 'have it all'. You know the ones – the city high-flier who makes millions a day and gets home in time to stir dinner, serve it up, change nappies and wipe snot, presumably before cracking into a bout of rigorous and earth-shaking sex with her equally successful husband. These women are news stories because they are such rarities, but when you're struggling to dress yourself in the morning, let alone your screaming child, it's easy to feel as though you just aren't making the grade.

Let's look at Mena and James. They met at work, when they were both with the same investment bank. Five years on, they are married and proud parents of a three-month-old daughter. Mena has given up work, and her only adult company during daylight hours is James' opinionated mother, who appears to have, rather annoyingly, assumed the persona of super-gran. James leaves for work one morning:

James says: 'God, today's going to be a nightmare – I've got three meetings, a new business pitch and a company lunch.'

Mena thinks: That would be my idea of heaven at the moment. At least you aren't stuck at home with a little baby and an old lady.

Mena says: 'You're lucky – it must be great to still feel important.'

James says: 'Lucky? I'm exhausted! At least you get to sit around all day with my mum running around after you.'

Mena hears: 'You're lazy and my mother does all the work anyway. I don't appreciate you and I don't know how much work you do for our new family.'

Mena says: 'Your mother's an absolute pain. And don't you dare call me "lucky" – this is the most draining thing I've ever done in my life and I could do with some support.'

The problem here is not that either partner is being particularly unreasonable. Mena is adjusting to the fact that her role in life has completely changed and she feels isolated and uneasy. Consequently, she is oversensitive to James' comments. On the other side of the coin, James envies the time Mena gets to spend with their daughter and is perhaps guilty of underestimating how much hard work this entails. Neither partner is wrong, they are just having trouble adapting to their new roles and the expectations placed upon them.

Pregnancy and childbirth are turning points in a woman's life, especially with a first child. Among the biggest life changes reported by women are lack of privacy, sleep deprivation, reduced couple time, less energy to be sexual, cutting of social contacts, chronic tiredness/exhaustion, decline of standards for housekeeping and personal appearance. For example, extensive confinement is experienced when she breast feeds the baby. Some women also have problems with their body image and report feeling less attractive. Regaining sexual desire is also gradual and its functioning variable.

So, let's be honest about this, empirical research (as well as every mother's personal experience) suggests that pregnancy is a time of mixed emotions for most women. Joy and excitement combine with anxiety, stress and occasionally depression (Walker, 2002). Which of these states predominates varies between women and across different stages of pregnancy. Depression during pregnancy is less common than anxiety, but there is growing evidence that predicts post-natal depression (Green, 1998) and it has emerged as a common occurrence and an important issue. Studies suggest that 8–15 per cent of new mothers are affected by post-natal depression and many others experience depressive symptoms that are milder or less enduring in nature (Feeney et al., 2003). A depressed mood is usually accompanied by other problems such as extreme fatigue, feelings of guilt, disturbances in sleep and appetite. Collectively, these problems have serious implications for women's well-being, for couple relationships and for childcare (Murray and Cooper, 1997).

The reactions of family members and the levels of resources available can have profound effects on the experience of parenting for women. For example, women whose partners are unsupportive have poorer well-being than those with supportive families (Collins et al., 1993). Longitudinal studies have reported higher rates of post-natal depression when husbands are perceived as uncaring or overcontrolling (Feeney et al., 2003).

Males

The role of the father has come under scrutiny in recent years. Historically, everything was fairly clear-cut. Being a father meant dragging home a cow big enough to feed your family for a week. It meant making sure the cupboards were stocked and your brood was sheltered and clothed. And that was about it. Touchy-feely paternal bonding was considered rather unnecessary. This societal gender model worked beautifully alongside the typical female place in the family: the woman churned out babies and then stayed at home to recover and raise their offspring. The majority of parent–child interaction was down to the mother. Before schools and nurseries, teaching and learning also fell to the female remit. Men's interest in undertaking parent roles was inhibited by the belief that caring for children was ultimately women's work (Burgess and Ruxton, 1996). This led to many men developing little or no interest in caring for children and viewing it as a task that they felt offered them little status or reward (Lewis, 1996).

However, as equality has shifted, society's expectations of typical gender roles and the role of the father, in fact what it means to be a man, has adapted. Just as women have marched their way onto battlefields and into boardrooms, men have entered previously off-limit domains. The rise of the 'new man' has encouraged men to be more sensitive and demonstrative about their emotions, and this has allowed them to embrace the paternal experience in a far more emotionally involved way. As ever, the role models we are surrounded by play a part in our development and endless newspaper pictures of Jude Law having a kickabout in the park with his little ones, or David Beckham posing for another photoshoot with Posh and the junior Beckhams only serve to reinforce the idea that fathers should be taking an active role in their children's development.

Many men are keen to be closer to their children than their own father was to them. They do want to be involved in their children's upbringing (Burgess and Ruxton, 1996). A recent European survey revealed that more than 85 per cent of both men and women think men should be involved in bringing up children from an early age. It is now well established that men can be competent care takers. Research shows that heightened paternal participation increases marital satisfaction and men develop socially and psychologically through participant fathering. (Burgess and Ruxton, 1996). Male attitudes and behaviour seem to be gradually changing.

A male's major parenting complaint is lack of time and skill, as well as absence of peer and family support for the father role (McCarthy and McCarthy, 2004). Surprisingly, many men also suffer from role strain in trying to balance work with family. Expectations of them becoming involved fathers are growing; and due to women's continuing employment they are asked to take greater responsibility for childcare (Burgess and Ruxton, 1996). The message is that men should play a bigger role at home, and indeed many of them want to. Let's look at John and Amy – their son Cameron is four months old. Amy is going away for her first weekend without the baby and leaving him with John. The following dialogue ensues:

Amy says: 'Do you know where the bottle teats are kept? Are you going to remember to change his nappies? You will remember to buy some more cough mixture, won't you?'

John thinks: Relax, woman! Everything will be fine!

John says: 'I'll work it out – don't worry. How hard can it be?!'

Amy hears: 'Looking after a baby is easy. If you can do it, it must be . . .'

Amy says: 'It's not as easy as it looks, John! He's our son, and I expect you to get this right or I won't be able to relax!'

John hears: 'You're not up to the job of caring for your own son, you useless man!'

So John feels isolated, undervalued and out of his depth. Where women are expected to be naturals at caring for a child, John feels that being a man means everyone expects him to cock up. Clearly, the prospect of facing parenting as a man presents its own challenges.

How to Cope Together As a Parent Team

The majority of serious, committed couples decide to have a baby sooner or later. Since you want to have a child, how then can you approach parenting in a beneficial, positive manner? Often, couples behave in an adversarial manner when they most need to be a team. It may take a fair amount of time, discussion and mutual understanding to work through parenting (Crowe, 2005). The goal should be a consensus reached through compromise and communication, rather than a battle of wills where both parents simply strive to replicate their own family backgrounds.

It is now established that men can be competent care takers of children. Research has actually revealed that the parenting styles of mothers and fathers within couples are remarkably similar. Where fathering differs from mothering, this is more strongly associated with situation than with gender (Lewis, 1996). As soon as men assume similar levels of responsibility to mothers for young children, parenting approaches generally become indistinguishable (Gbrich, 1987).

Being a good parental and marital team is reciprocally reinforced. There is a positive correlation between being a good couple and being good parents (McCarthy and McCarthy, 2004). Actually maintaining a balance between the two roles enhances each person's psychological well-being and quality of life. Some useful ideas to consider and employ are the following:

Communicate What you Need from Each Other

When we're tired and under pressure, the temptation is to blame our partners, or take it out on them. When the baby has dirtied the day's eighteenth nappy, or when we've survived on half an hour's sleep a night, we often take our exhaustion or frustration out on those close to us – and who could possibly be closer than the person you live with and are raising a child with? Steer yourself away from snappy sarcasm and criticism, as this will inevitably cause both partners to become defensive and possibly begin to resent one another, and it will inevitably escalate disagreements (Epstein and Baucom, 2003). Note the difference between: 'Oh, it's all right for you, you're leading the life of luxury. I wish I could sleep all night and then swan off to the office all day like you do, instead of being cooped up in the house with your screaming child' and 'I appreciate the time you spend working to provide security for the family, but I think we need to look at ways you could help me with the baby more, and I will look at ways I can make your busy life easier.'

Learn to Support Each Other

Whatever else happens, remember that as well as being parents, you are a couple, and the health and happiness of your relationship has a direct impact on the welfare of your child. Being the world's most conscientious, caring, devoted mother is great, but not if it comes at the expense of a happy loving home. Talk about things that are nothing to do with the children. Remember life BC (before children), re-live memories, laugh at his latest CD purchase, slag off the newsreader's suit – anything that means you are reinforcing the bond that existed between you before you even dreamt of having babies. Challenge beliefs like, 'Responsible parents should always put their child's needs first.' Remember your needs are just as important, and a sure-fire way of producing happy children is surrounding them with a happy adult relationship model. Work together, and ensure both of you takes responsibility for tasks and acknowledge and reinforce the other's contributions and domains (McCarthy and McCarthy, 2004).

Manage Work Demands

Many would argue that raising children is a full-time vocation in itself. So rocking up for a nine to five every day, and running a household at the same time can seem like mission impossible. Work has a habit of encroaching on time that could otherwise be spent with your family. Work demands can create conflicts between the couple about the investment and relative time in their parenting and their relationship (Haddock et al., 2001). If one of the partners believes the other works too much, it can be easy to attribute this, often incorrectly, to a lack of concern for or commitment to the family.

Reinforce Father's Involvement

Men should be actively encouraged to become involved in the child-rearing and learn to share parental responsibility. A wife who encourages and reinforces how integral and important the father's involvement in parenting is builds a sense of him playing an active role. Encouragement and reinforcement for what he is doing well and constructive suggestions for change make all the difference (McCarthy and McCarthy, 2004). A good idea is to attend antenatal examinations and parent-training courses.

Share Everyday Tasks and Responsibilities

Of course, the rest of the house doesn't grind to a halt once a new inhabitant enters. Dishes won't start washing themselves, bills won't pay themselves and the hoover is sadly unlikely to start navigating its own way round the house. Remember that despite the plethora of extra jobs your baby introduces to your family's daily routine, there will still be a number of non-baby-related chores to attend to. Establish a scheme where both of you take responsibility for your fair share of baby watching, and your fair share of general household duties. This way, you can avoid either partner feeling overwhelmed, and ensure you both get equal time to be a parent, and equal time to be an adult, without the unwanted distraction of an occasionally screaming child.

Stop Comparing Yourselves to Others

When it comes to baby raising, there are no hard and fast rules. There is no such thing as a perfect family or a perfect mother. Everybody makes mistakes, everybody feels frustrated, angry and exhausted at times. Remember that the friend of yours with the perfectly behaved toddler, and the seemingly baby-sick-proof white jeans isn't really as perfect as she appears and, besides, this has absolutely no bearing on or relation to your competence as a mother. If you're looking for someone who is doing a better job than you, you will always find someone, but your assessment won't necessarily be accurate. Work with your partner to establish your personal parenting goals, and work to them, not to some impossible standard set by some Hollywood movie star who knocks out ten films a year (and, incidentally, probably has just as many nannies and au pairs). Work out what's important to you and set your own goals.

Adopt Realistic Expectations about Parenting

This is important. From the word go you and your partner need to be realistic about what parenthood entails. Just as you might not look radiant and glowing the minute after you've screamed and sworn your newborn into the world after six hours of labour, your baby might not sleep through the night until he turns three. Your life will change and, ultimately, your baby's needs will be more urgent and more specific than yours so be flexible and prepared to abandon plans and work to your baby's whim. Accept that parenting will place a great strain on you, and be ready to support each other. If you prepare for vomit and sleepless nights, you're more likely to enjoy the experience than be shocked and overwhelmed by it.

Ask for Support from Extended Family

Everybody loves a new baby. A newborn is like a sign above your door saying, 'Please feel free to pop round any time you like and antagonise and excite the baby I have spent three hours trying to cajole and soothe to sleep. Oh, and while you're at it, make sure you give me absolutely no warning, just to make sure I have no chance of changing out of my pyjamas by the time you arrive.' Extended families can be a blessing. Grannies and grandpas can be fantastic babysitters, and just the answer to providing you and your partner with a little alone time. Make the most of them, in order to reduce some of the pressure you will inevitably be feeling. But always be clear that while they may have a wealth of experience with children, you are the parent here, and the responsibility and authority lies with you. Certainly ask for advice, but make sure you aren't pushed into parenting in a way that differs from the values you and your partner hold dear. Be strong, stand by each other and do what you believe is best for your baby.

Conclusion

No one ever said it would be easy. Having children is hugely rewarding, massively fulfilling and genuinely exciting. But it is also wrought with anxiety, guilt and absolute exhaustion. When you have a baby, you are making a lifelong commitment that doesn't have an opt-out clause. For at least eighteen years you are responsible for the choices, the development and the happiness of another human being. That's a huge responsibility, and one that usually works best when shared with someone else. The traditional evolutionary model of a mother, a father and a baby developed for a reason that reaches beyond the biological necessities. However, the expectations this traditional model places upon us can evoke feelings of stress, guilt and inferiority. While the role of woman in society has changed, it appears the role of mother has been frozen in time. The German research by Kalincki et al. demonstrated than upon becoming a mother many women find themselves assuming responsibility for traditional female tasks such as cooking, cleaning and keeping the house in immaculate order while their partners slip into the traditional breadwinner mode. As we've seen, any differentiator between men and women is likely to cause conflict and misunderstanding, so this division of labour can be a serious flashpoint for many couples.

The key to ensuring your relationship is enhanced rather than destroyed by parenthood is in accepting your roles and lives have changed. The answer is in appreciating what a huge upheaval this is for both of you individually and for your relationship as a whole. Ultimately, the solution is in letting this understanding and appreciation filter through to the way you communicate with one another. Remember Mena and James who were having difficulties adapting to the expectations their new roles placed upon them? Mena missed her hectic career and James was slightly envious of the amount of time Mena was able to spend at home with their daughter. Imagine how differently their dialogue could have gone:

James says: 'God, today's going to be a nightmare – I've got three meetings, a new business pitch and a company lunch.'

Mena thinks: God, I miss being busy – I love my daughter, but I enjoyed feeling busy and needed at work.

Mena says: 'God, I miss being busy – I love my daughter, but I enjoyed feeling busy and needed at work.'

James hears: 'God, I miss being busy – I love my daughter, but I enjoyed feeling busy and needed at work.'

James thinks: I can see where she's coming from, but the grass is always greener – I feel jealous about how much time she gets to spend with our daughter.

James says: 'Sometimes I wish we could swap jobs – you get to spend so much quality time with the baby. Sometimes I worry I'm missing out.'

Mena hears: 'Sometimes I worry I'm missing out.'

Mena says: 'Why don't you take some time off next week? I'll book some lunches with friends and some days at the health spa and you can spend some time with your daughter.'

By articulating what they actually mean and accepting the pressures each other are under, Mena and James move closer to a mutually accept-able solution. They manage to tackle the male–female translation barrier by saying what they actually mean and hearing things correctly, rather than using sniping and sarcasm to communicate.

Having a new baby can introduce a new dimension to your relationship with your partner. The shared pride and joint endeavour a child represents can deepen your bond, and help you see one another in a completely new light. Just as a happy relationship is good for a child to be born into, the benefits are reciprocal, and a baby can refresh and strengthen a happy relationship. Remember you and your partner will experience parenting in completely different ways; keep the communication channels open to navigate your way through these differences. Before you both became parents, you were boyfriend and girlfriend, or husband and wife, and your commitment to these roles is just as important as your commitment to your newborn. Becoming a mother doesn't deprive you of being a girlfriend, wife, lover or friend, and staying true to these roles will do wonders for your emotional well-being. Work with your partner, be realistic about the stresses and strains of parenthood, and the rest should look after itself.

Men Should Remember:

- This is a big change for you, but your partner is the one bearing the physical toll of childbirth. Communicate your appreciation and accept the resultant stress of the process may impinge upon the way she communicates with you.
- If you feel left out, undervalued or inexperienced, then voice those concerns. Communication is key to working through this with your partner.

Women Should Remember:

- Don't resent your partner because he hasn't been through the same physical change as you; recognise this is a huge transition for him too.
- Accept and take into consideration the fact that your hormones may well be affecting the way you interpret and process conversations with your partner.

Chapter 9

Separation

In 2002, a group of researchers from the Francis Marion University in America presented the findings from their latest research project to the annual convention of the American Psychological Society in New Orleans. Jordan, Shriner, Proot, Bledsoe and Mahoney were well aware of the wealth of research that focused on the reasons romantic relationships end and wanted to look closely at the process that followed and the way individuals felt about that process. Consequently their research focused predominantly on the descriptors used by those experiencing a break-up. The researchers interviewed over one hundred undergraduates, male and female, asking for an open-ended description of their last relationship break-up.

The results were grouped into a number of criteria and analysed. Some interesting findings emerged when responses were compared across genders. When men initiated a break-up, they saw it as a joint decision – a collaborative action – but when they were the dumpees, as it were, they saw it as the sole responsibility of their partner. Women did not see the situation in such a biased way. Equally, when men initiated the break-up they saw the relationship as completely over. When they were the ones who were broken-up with, they weren't so final about things; they described their partners' actions as manipulative, but didn't attribute the same descriptions to their own behaviour. The *researchers concluded this evidence tied into prior research that suggests men are more distressed by break-ups than women and that unwanted pursuit following a break-up is most commonly a male trait.*

The research conducted by Jordan et al. and the conclusions they drew seem to fly in the face of the assumptions that women invest more into committed relationships than men, at least on an emotional level. Most importantly for this book, what the research undoubtedly shows is that the perception of any given break-up will be coloured by gender tendencies. It seems men are more likely to develop self-serving assessments of the situation, while women are more likely to look at the circumstances in a more objective light. But putting psychological research, gender stereotypes or individual experiences aside, the truth of the matter is that, just like the song says – breaking up is hard to do.

From the first time you get shunned in the school playground to the endless hours of your adult life you spend worrying about how to stop thinking about your ex, everyone who has entered into a romantic relationship has probably found the ending of a relationship difficult. Relationships break down for all manner of reasons. Sometimes couples hurt each other to a point of disrepair. Sometimes people change and the relationship is not strong enough to adapt. Sometimes people suddenly confront underlying relationship or character flaws they perhaps always knew were there. And sometimes, frustratingly, the relationship just isn't right any more and both parties know they need to get out. Whatever the reason, the universal truth of the matter is that, at best, break-ups are awkward. And at worst, they can be painful, sad and downright heart breaking.

The thing is, when we enter into a relationship with someone we make certain investments, we make sacrifices and adapt our lives to accommodate our fantastic new partner. So if everything goes wrong, the transition from being that person's 'one' to being their ex can be tough to work through. The break-up of a relationship is never simple. And as the research we've looked at highlights, our gender will play a part in how we navigate through this transition. This goes some way to explain why following your traumatic break-up, you'll be listening to 1980s power ballads CDs and binging on chocolate in your pyjamas while he has a rowdy night in the pub with friends, lots of beer, seventy-five games on the fruit machine and a journey-home kebab. Or, if you agree with the researchers from the Francis Marion University, he'll be moaning about how conniving and scheming you were while you lament the gradual loss of a loving bond . . .

There are some phases and processes that are fairly universal, whether you are male or female, and which are similar to the phases we go through when we are grieving or mourning: heartbreak, resentment, anger, guilt and shame are common features of relationship breakdowns. The undeniable truth is that when we are going through these unavoidable break-up processes, we can never really view the whole story. Inevitably, the emotions that the deterioration of the relationship evokes get in the way of an impartial view of the situation. Our feelings are unlikely to be rational or unbiased, and that's before you even take into account those pesky gender-specific interpretations. This chapter is about separating your emotions from reality, and confronting, sharing and dealing with those emotions. It is about how you and your partner can develop a language you both understand to guide you through what has the potential to be a particularly nasty process. If neither of you can save your relationship by developing a common vocabulary, this chapter is about saving your own peace of mind by at least learning enough common ground to negotiate a way out.

Understanding Separation

People often talk about break-ups as coming as a shock or out of the blue. In fact, the signs of an imminent break-up are usually in evidence for a while before one or both partners decide to throw in the towel (Hayman, 2001). Most relationship breakdowns are gradual, if painful, processes – as opposed to events that suddenly occur. In order to understand this process, it is best to examine it in terms of its key features. Couples in distressed marriages or relationships experience a variety of feelings, thoughts and concerns that mainly reflect these underlying themes. Here we shall look in more detail at some of these underlying processes – infra-psychic/ psychological, dyadic and social processes – that usually occur when people contemplate and decide to separate.

Intra-psychic/Psychological Processes

Uncertainty

Anyone who's ever broken-up with someone else knows it doesn't happen overnight. You don't suddenly decide, 'This just isn't working, love, pack your bags, and close the door on your way out.' No, the 'let's not be boyfriend and girlfriend any more' moment usually follows a prolonged period of agonising and, crucially, a whole load of uncertainty. When people contemplate leaving relationships, they worry about the effect it will have on their lives, and also, the effect it will have on those around them. People worry about being lonely, about regretting their decision, about leaving a relationship that could potentially be perfect for them. This uncertainty means we often end up fighting for a relationship long after our instincts initially tell us it's over. And this can lead to the second key emotion of a relationship breakdown: resentment.

Resentment

When we are unhappy with the way a relationship is going, we often feel undervalued and unappreciated. Sometimes the relationship deteriorates because we feel these things, and sometimes we feel this way because the relationship is deteriorating. When we feel this way and these emotions are left unaddressed, they tend to fester and transform themselves into an ugly little specimen called resentment which spreads like cancer. At first, it is small and impossible to spot – perhaps it is a small concern you have about your relationship. But if is left unnoticed it will spread throughout the whole relationship. This often results in us withdrawing further from our partner, devoting less attention to the relationship and consequently applying our own interpretation of the situation to the problem – allowing the resentment to spread and grow.

Withdrawing from one's partner means that we are less likely to address issues that really need to be addressed. Instead, we dwell on them internally and consequently feed a range of emotions that actually make us feel worse. For example, Jodie's boyfriend Matt comes in later than promised for the sixth time that week. Outwardly she looks nonchalant and content, even though she is secretly fuming inside, but this is actually likely to provoke greater unhappiness in the long run. Let's take a look . . .

> Matt says: 'Hi there. You didn't need to wait up for me!'
> Jodie thinks: You could at least apologise for being so late, you selfish idiot.
> Jodie says: 'No, no, it's fine – I wanted to make sure you got home safely.'
> Matt says: 'Oh well, up to you. I'm off to bed now – night.'
> Jodie thinks: So you aren't even going to chat to me now you've finally arrived home – how can you treat me this way?
> Jodie says: 'Goodnight darling.'

If Jodie confronted the issue with her boyfriend, perhaps he would adapt his behaviour, or at least justify or explain it. Instead, Jodie feeds the feeling that she is being taken for granted with her inner monologue. Resentment manifests itself, Jodie feels worse about the situation, and blames the whole relationship, and her boyfriend, for her unhappiness.

Resentment is a common feature of a relationship breakdown. Individuals may resent their partner because they feel trapped, or because they blame them for causing such unhappiness. Perhaps you resent your partner because he has a new job causing him to work long hours and come home stressed. Perhaps you resent your partner because he is the reason you never took that holiday of a lifetime when you were younger. Whatever the reason, resentment is a big player on the break-up league tables.

Loneliness

The irony is that even when they are clutching their pillow sobbing their eyes out, or picking up the pieces of the millionth row about the same old thing, some people would still rather be in a destructive relationship than risk being alone. To some, a bad relationship is better than no relationship. It's certainly true that when we leave a relationship, the loneliness caused by the absence of our former partner in our lives is usually the first emotion we encounter.

As humans we are social beings who need to communicate with others. Biology, sociology and our upbringing tell us that the ideal situation for an adult is to be in a romantic relationship. It means the species can survive through reproduction, it helps with dinner-party seating plans and it makes the weekend food shopping slightly less of a chore. So the idea that we would leave this supposed ideal for the single life is a scary one. Loneliness is broadly defined as a complex affective response stemming from felt deficits in the number of one's interpersonal relationships (Buunk, 2001). For the reasons we've looked at, women are especially prone to worry about being lonely or meeting someone else in order to start a family (Crowe, 2005).

Blame and Anger

One of the most common characteristics of couple discord is blame directed at the partner for problems in the relationship, which often precedes declines in marital functioning (Bradbury and Fincham, 1990). Cognitive aspects of blame might include believing your partner to be completely blameworthy or even unworthy. For example, a symptom of this could be focusing on your partner's personality or character as opposed to his or her behaviour, so 'you are behaving in a selfish way' becomes 'you are a selfish pig'. This is a particularly common mistake made by the rejected partner.

Hopelessness

Going over the same ground repeatedly can cultivate the feeling that nothing will ever change, and things simply won't get better. When we come to expect arguments and resign ourselves to the fact that the situation can't be improved, we often hit a brick wall of hopelessness. This feeling is linked to cognitions that predict our vulnerability to depression regarding our relationships (Sayers et al., 2001). This suggests that hopelessness about the relationship is positively associated with the length of unhappiness in it. So, the longer an individual has been going through the motions, experiencing the same problems, the less hope they will have that the situation will improve.

Often this depressing hopelessness is down to the feeling of being trapped in a relationship with a spouse whom we blame, without the ability to problem solve or leave for a better situation.

Guilt

When discussing or analysing relationship break-ups, there is a tendency to focus on how to get through the separation, or how to cope when your partner leaves you. But of course, there is another side to the story. If the break-up is one-sided, the instigator doesn't get away scot-free. Oh no. Just because an individual no longer wants to be in a relationship, doesn't mean they no longer care about their partner's feelings or self-esteem. If someone is unhappier than his/her partner, he/she might feel guilty about wanting to separate. Knowing their partner may still love and need them can make them feel utterly miserable. The thought of how devastated the rejected partner will be can provoke feelings of immense guilt.

Shame

Sometimes people in distressed relationships or marriages experience shame. This could be because they feel ashamed that they have been unable to leave the relationship at a previous juncture (Wachtel, 1999). It could be because they feel useless and powerless in the face of the problems their relationship presents. Or the sense of shame could simply represent a sense of failure that things haven't turned out as expected.

Shame is one of the less obvious parts of the process, but a very important one. Shame can be emotionally debilitating if it is not dealt with in a challenging, honest manner.

Dyadic Processes

When we talk about dyadic processes, we're referring to the experiences you will go through as a couple. We've looked at the processes each partner is likely to go through individually, but, inevitably, when two people commit to a relationship, they commit to a union which means, good or bad, there are a number of processes they will go through together. Just as you share the happy moments – that first kiss, the first 'I love you' – you also share the not-so-great times.

So, once the resentment we've talked about comes to a head, what usually happens is a period of confrontation, where the problems with the relationship are aired and discussed. At this point the individuals do not necessarily know how it will end and may be motivated to resolve the issues and avoid breaking-up (Duck, 2005). Whatever the outcome, this is the moment of truth, the time when issues that may well have been bubbling for months surface, and this confrontation can make or break the relationship.

This can manifest itself in the form of an anxious period of to-ing and fro-ing, as each person attempts to reconcile their interpretation of events with their partner. And often there is a recognised pattern to events:

- Dealing with attempts at comprehension or self-justification – for example, 'I only shut you out because I feel you have given up on this relationship.'
- Reconstruction of the early days of the relationship – for example, 'Why don't we go down to the pub tonight and do the quiz, you know, like we used to?'
- Comparison of desirable behaviours – for example, 'I'd love it if you'd just come in and ask me how my day was for once!'
- Suggestion for increasing mutual satisfaction in the relationship – for example, 'Let's dedicate one night a week to going on a proper date.'

Of course, as anyone who's attempted to navigate what constitutes either a bad patch or the end of the road knows, this doesn't mean you and your partner will necessarily hit the mutual satisfaction part of the plan. If you can then that's great, but if you can't it may well be time to close the door on your time together.

Social Processes

After you've worked your way through the dyadic processes of the end of your relationship, there are a series of solo challenges to face. Once you've finally admitted to each other that it's over, deleted all his emails and taken to his place the collection of socks, pants and Bon Jovi CDs that seem to have accumulated in your flat, the next step is breaking the news to everybody else. Nothing else will drive home the fact that your relationship hasn't worked out more than the slow painful process of letting the world know you're not actually trying on bridal gowns any more, you don't come as part of a pair any more and, yes, you have started speed dating, blind dating, internet dating, or whatever the hottest new prefix for dating is these days.

Letting everyone else know can bring those feelings of shame and failure rushing back, particularly when you consider the pressures society places on us to be coupled up. It can cause us to grieve for the relationship all over again. After all, it's one thing for you and your partner to admit that the months of arguing have finally driven you both over the edge, but telling your granny she can put her favourite hat away, and igniting those less-than-subtle fears that you may in fact be a lesbian, is quite another. Suddenly, you aren't just experiencing a private rough patch with your partner, you are a single girl, back on the market.

Of course this varies with stages of life. Teen relationships and those we have in our early twenties are seen very much as practices for the real thing (Duck, 2005). Our younger years are seen as training grounds for developing the skills we will need for that one big serious commitment we will make later in life. But as we get older, each relationship is seen as potential for 'the one', and when that potential fails to realise itself it can be hugely disappointing. For various reasons, the consequences of separation in such cases are more severe and significant.

Because of the way we are socialised, this public acknowledgement of blame can feel very different for men and women. While a man might go out and pronounce, 'Yes! I'm a single man, the shackles are off – I'm playing the field again!' a woman is far more likely to shrug and reluctantly admit, 'It's back to the drawing board for me – we've broken up, so I guess I'm back on the shelf again.' This just serves as further evidence that women are socialised to see commitment as a goal, whereas men are socialised to see it as an evil trap.

Gender Differences

By this stage in the book, you should have picked up on the fact that men and women behave very differently in relationships. Women are usually more expressive and analytical, and tend to get emotionally attached more quickly. Even from that first date, a woman will be secretly, even sub-consciously, working out how her name rolls into his surname, or if his allergy to long-haired dogs is going to mean their children have to make do with hamsters. Women make scarily premature predictions for the future, and they search for emotional cues that will indicate their predictions are accurate. On the other hand, men tend to be logical, more independent and more solution-focused. When it comes to problems in a relationship, a man will usually prefer to withdraw and think, whereas a woman will usually want to talk about it. In the eyes of a man, once a problem has been aired, the onus is on finding a solution and getting on with it. Conversely, nothing appeals more to a stressed-out female than the chance to dissect, analyse and re-tell every moment of the disagreement or problem. If you don't believe it, just ask your hairdresser.

These differences immensely affect how each gender reacts in relationship crises. Studies have demonstrated that women are more likely than men to assume demanding roles in relationships (Christensen and Heavey, 1990). Findings from these investigations suggest a woman usually pushes for relationship issues to be addressed, and confirm that women have always assumed this role in society. However, this doesn't sit particularly well with a man's tendency to avoid confrontation on relationship issues. His reluctance to talk will often be interpreted as a lack of concern or effort. Equally, a man is likely to become increasingly irritated by the female push to discuss, discuss, discuss and will actually retreat further from the relationship. Consider Sarah and Jason. They've been going out for six years now and recently it feels as though there's a brick wall between them. They don't make each other laugh, they don't connect with one another and they don't share anything any more. Sarah tries to raise the issue with Jason after one particularly awkward night...

Sarah says: 'What's wrong with you?! We need to talk!'

Jason hears: 'You're making me unhappy! Explain yourself!'

Jason thinks: This is a two-way street and I'm not massively happy either, but what difference will talking make?

Jason says: 'Nothing – I'm fine.'

Sarah hears: 'I can't be bothered to discuss this.'

Sarah thinks: The only way to sort this out is to discuss it – so he obviously doesn't care enough to want to sort things out.

Sarah says: 'If you loved me you'd be honest with me.'

Jason thinks: Don't blackmail me.

Jason says: 'I'm going out.'

This situation serves as yet another example of how men and women address problems in entirely different ways. While a man's solution will usually be to get on with life regardless, a woman's will usually be to dissect, discuss and analyse. Neither is right or wrong, but everyone *is* adhering to their own gender stereotypes.

Thinking about Separation and Sharing it with Him/Her

There are few feelings worse than the daily drudgery of enduring a relationship that has lost its spark, is no longer based on love, or simply isn't right. While a serious committed romantic relationship is often seen as the pinnacle of our lives and a goal to be working towards, many people would argue they would rather be single than in a relationship that falls short of 100 per cent happiness. Many couples actually go as far as to describe themselves as chronically disappointed by their marriages or relationships. It is extremely hurtful and painful to be attached to someone whom we have ceased to love, or whom we feel can no longer give us what we want and need (Wachtel, 1999). But communicating these desperate feelings to a partner can seem impossible.

The first key thing here is to remember that your perception of the situation will undoubtedly be coloured by your own emotions and beliefs. As the research by the Francis Marion University suggested, the same break-up can be seen entirely differently through two pairs of eyes. It rarely occurs to us that our negative judgements could be wrong and that when we criticise our partner or the relationship, we are actually attacking a distorted image. CBT suggests that a person's interpersonal behaviour tends to 'invite' or 'pull' a predictable response, which is confirmatory of the original beliefs (Safran and Segal, 1990). For example, if we feel angry or hurt, these negative thoughts lead to emotional, behavioural and physiological reactions (Padesky and Greenberger, 1995). Consequently, our manner may provoke adverse reactions in our partner, and we interpret their behaviour as evidence to support our original theory. Couples should remember that their emotions are likely to affect their behaviour, and they should take this into consideration when jumping to conclusions about their partner's behaviour. It is useful to try to take a step back from the situation and establish an objective viewpoint. When you partner tries to communicate, try and listen to what they are actually saying, not what you assume they will say. You will never know what your partner is trying to say better than he does, so listen properly – not through a filter that blocks out words that disprove long-established assumptions.

Once negativity begins it can become all-encompassing and self-fulfilling. Several studies have shown that distressed couples respond to their negative emotions about their relationships by noticing the negative aspects of interpersonal situations (Epstein and Baucom, 2003). So, the more negative we feel about the situation, the more prone we are to noticing those little things. For example, if we are worn down, exhausted by and tired of the relationship we are far more likely to interpret an innocent sigh as a sign of contempt or boredom. If we are sick to the back of teeth with what we interpret as a constant stream of selfish behaviour from our partner, we are more likely to notice that once again, he left the toilet seat up. Vanzetti et al. (1992) found that individuals distressed by their relationship actually predicted their partners would behave more negatively during specific conversations. Moreover, they held more negative global assumptions about how people and relationships actually function and negative standards about how they should work (Epstein and Baucom, 2003).

Imagine the difference between these two situations. The first is Veronica and Mark, two months into their relationship:

Veronica: 'Are you hungry, darling? Would you like some lasagne?'
Mark: 'I'm good thanks – I had a massive lunch. I was thinking we could go over to Mum's tonight – what do you say?'
Veronica: 'Sure, I can always stick this in the freezer. I'll jump in the shower and be ready in ten?'

And now imagine the same scene after two years and a period of habitual conflict:

Veronica: 'Are you hungry? Would you like some lasagne?'
Mark: 'I'm good. I had a massive lunch. I'm heading over to Mum's tonight, if you want to come?'
Veronica: 'Oh I see – so you walk in, turn your nose up at my cooking and then assume I will slot into your plans and undoubtedly watch you tuck into a four-course meal at your mother's.'

The situation hasn't changed – but the general state of the relationship has. The personalities haven't changed, but the way actions and words are interpreted has.

So, negativity within our own relationship can actually alter the way we perceive the wider world. In its simplest sense, perhaps this can explain the difference between seeing a romantic film and weeping tears of gleeful emotion or making exaggerated vomiting sounds and shooting cynical looks at the screen. When we feel negatively about our love, we feel negatively about love in general. When we don't feel too great about our world, we don't feel too great about anything in the universe. When discussing the way forward with your partner, it's helpful if you can bear this in mind, and try to prevent general feelings of negativity from colouring your success in moving forward.

This is perhaps easier said than done. The problem is you never see it coming, you can never prepare for it. Back in the 'No you hang up. No *you* hang up' days, back when every moment together feels like a blessing, and you suddenly understand what Julio Iglesias was singing about all those years ago (and you lose all sense of irony when listening to his *Greatest 80s Ballads* albums), you can never anticipate these days when your relationship actually makes you feel worse about yourself and the world, not better. You're never prepared for the moment you realise that everything your partner does annoys you. And you never have an action plan for the disastrous realisation that the anticipation of seeing your other half has turned from a tummy-butterfly explosion to a sinking slump.

As things get worse, optimism is the first casualty. The arguments continue, the love and excitement slowly dwindles away, and it can feel as though you are on a one-way path to either a barren loveless marriage or the messiest break-up of all time. But these don't have to be your only options. Next, we'll look at some tips for navigating this huge decision with your partner. This isn't about ensuring you stay together, it's about developing the communication tools to empower you and your partner to look at the issues objectively and establish the right solution for both of you – whether that means working at your relationship or kissing it goodbye.

Tip 1 Be Willing to Compromise and See Things from Another Perspective

The first golden rule here is: no one can save a relationship by themselves. It requires effort and effective communication in abundance – from both partners. Thus, in order to put a relationship back on track both partners must seek to change their behaviour and work towards cooperation rather than competition or confrontation (Crowe, 2005).

Both partners need to think carefully about and concentrate on the strengths of his/her partner and reflect on their own contribution to the problems experienced in the relationship, in order to strive for a more balanced view. Research has shown that how one partner perceives and interprets what the other does can be far more important in determining satisfaction in one's relationships or marriage than the actions themselves (Epstein and Baucom, 2003). In other words, it isn't what your partner actually does that is the problem, it is the way you interpret it.

If you and your partner both want to save your relationship, you both have to be prepared to distance yourselves from your own interpretations of events, and accept that your view of things is not necessarily 100 per cent correct. If you can't start with that willingness to compromise and discuss without prejudice, it is unlikely your attempts at reconciliation will ever get off the ground.

Tip 2 Know what you Want and be Assertive

Many couples remain stuck in a rut because they shy away from articulating what it is they really want. This might be through fear of the response of their partner. Some individuals feel the limitations of self-sacrifice are preferable to the risk of causing pain or anger to the ones we love; they hold their own wants and needs inside, preferring to attend to those of their partner. However, in the long run, this will only contribute to those feelings of resentment and negativity we have already discussed. Problems also arise when people swing between passive and aggressive styles and find it hard to strike a balance (Flecknoe and Sanders, 2004).

For example, look at Vicky and John. Deep down, Vicky is scared that her dreams for the relationship are different from John's so rather than express what she actually wants, she devotes her efforts to meeting John's expectations. This is exhausting and unfulfilling, and after a few weeks or months, she tires of the continual attempt to please. Then she redresses the balance by making unreasonable demands of John, expecting him to emulate her submissive behaviour. The end result, particularly for John, is a big confusing mess.

Genuinely being able to assert oneself is not about irrationally reacting to a long-established situation like the one described above. It is about a general social and emotional ability to communicate clearly and confidently needs, wants and feelings while at the same time respecting others' needs, wants and feelings.

Being assertive encourages positive emotions and prevents painful emotions like anger, hurt, frustration and disappointment from developing in the first place. The more assertive a person becomes the more comfortable they will feel in any situation. Assertiveness in relationships is all about honest, open communication and compromise, where both parties feel understood and heard. Moreover, by being assertive, you express your feelings and your partner let your partner know how much you are affected by them. Even if your partner completely disagrees with your position he/she can at least appreciate your strong feelings on an issue.

Another important aspect of being assertive is the ability to say no to requests. For some people this is especially difficult because it means upsetting or disappointing others. However, saying no means that you set your limits on others' requests for your time and energy when such demands conflict with your own needs and desires (Bourne, 2005). It also means you can do what you want without feeling guilty or ashamed. For example, if your partner has invited some friends to spend the evening and you have just returned from the day from hell at work, you could be assertive and say to your partner, 'I understand you would like to spend the evening with your friends. It turns out that I have had a really long day and feel exhausted so I need to pass on tonight. Would there be another night when we could all get together?'

Tip 3 How to Criticise and How to Accept Criticism

A crucial element of every disagreement is the difference in the way partners perceive the same circumstances (Beck, 1988). Their perspective is filtered through their own special lens, or schemas, leading to opposing views. Partners quite often see each other's questions, requests or statements in a way that serves to blame, attack or deflate their partner. Using criticism may create more problems than it solves (Beck, 1988). For example, consider Judith and Brett, who have been married for five years now. They met through friends and initially couldn't believe their luck. They seemed so perfect for one another. He loved the left side of the bed, she had to sleep on the right. He loved dogs, she hated cats — you get the picture. However, things have staled lately and they are experiencing major communication problems. Here's a typical exchange after a heated row over, let's say, his friendship with an ex-girlfriend:

> Judith says: 'Let's talk about what happened.'
> Brett thinks: What's the point? We will just go round in circles. I know what I think.
> Brett says: 'Not now; it's not a good time.'
> Judith thinks: This is serious, why don't you want to work through it with me?
> Judith says: 'What's wrong with you?'
> Brett thinks: Why does everything have to be on her terms. I don't want to talk about this now.
> Brett says: 'Not now!'
> Judith thinks: How dare you patronise me! Don't talk to me like a child.
> Judith says: 'I have had enough of this!'

When someone feels they are being criticised by their partner, there are two common paths: the first is that they crumble and feel rejected; the second is that they defend themselves from criticism by becoming critical themselves. Criticism is perceived as a direct threat to one's self-esteem.

The real skill here is learning how to pass comment on negative elements of your relationships without resorting to blame and put-downs. Once you and your partner have mastered this, it means you have two new choices. Now, upon receiving criticism, you can stand your ground and assert your own opinion confidently, but without sniping or point-scoring; or, you can accept that the criticism might just be fair and look at how you can work on this aspect of your behaviour.

The best way to equip yourself with these options is by remembering to begin your sentences with 'I' rather than 'you'. I-statements acknowledge your responsibility for your own feelings, while you-statements generally judge, accuse or blame others, thus making them feel defensive (Bourne, 2005).

The difference between 'You make me feel insecure when you do that' and 'I feel insecure when this happens' is monumental. One statement is accusing and attributes the negative emotions to your partner. The other statement accepts your feelings are you own responsibility while asserting an issue you are unhappy with. If you and your partner get into the habit of using these prefixes, you will learn to offer and receive criticism more effectively.

Tip 4 Coping with Anger

It is normal to feel angry sometimes. However, anger is often problematic for many people. Sometimes the problems arise from an inability to control anger. For others, the problems lie in a tendency to shrug away and ignore anything unpleasant in fear of provoking anger or bad feeling. Anger is often most intense when experienced with someone with whom we are in close contact. Couples often present their dissatisfactions as merely expressions of how angry their partner made them. The links between intimate relations and anger can be understood by recognising that one is likely to hold specific personal expectations (Padesky and Greenberger, 1995). So we get most angry with those we are in close relationships with because we expect the most from them.

Anger can range from irritation to rage. How angry we become in a given situation is influenced by our interpretation of the meaning of that event. Therefore, there is great individual variation in the type of event that elicits anger (Padesky and Greenberger, 1995). The psychological explanation of anger recognises that one's mood is a key part of the anger but not the only part. In order to understand the causes of anger one needs to look at other factors in a systematic way. It is helpful to separate personal aspects of anger into mood, thoughts, bodily reactions and impulsive behaviour. The other part one also needs to consider is the outside world – for example, frustrating events or situations. Hence, one needs to be mindful about how changes in this affects him/her and how they may make changes in their behaviour that affect their environment.

According to CBT, all these parts of anger can affect each other, causing it to spiral out of control. Each person owns his/her feelings. It might seem ridiculous, and completely inaccurate when you consider how often we attribute negative emotions to other people's behaviour, but actually nobody else can single-handedly cause you to feel angry, resentful or frustrated. Other people may say or do all kinds of things but it is a person's *perception* – your interpretation – of their behaviour that causes one to feel whatever one feels (Bourne, 2005).

Assertive people may get angry with someone, but they never reject the person. They own their feelings and reactions rather than blaming them on the other person. They let the other person know that *what* they are doing at that particular time is very annoying but are willing to take ultimate responsibility for their feelings. They can express their anger without being demeaning or unloving. In contrast, aggressive behaviour threatens a person. Aggression impacts relationships, it often pushes people away and can make it difficult to connect.

You also need to remember that anger is best expressed when one feels it rising. When things are left unsaid, anger builds and continues to exist under the surface. When it eventually comes to the surface, it finally comes out as aggression, sarcasm or bitterness. Expressing anger does not predict divorce, but expressing criticism and contempt do (Epstein and Baucom, 2003). You can always let someone know how you feel by being brief and simple. Remember it is better to say less than more.

Tip 5 Considering a Trial Separation

A trial separation, for some people, is an easier way to begin a permanent separation. A study conducted with Relate findings showed that only a quarter of the couples in the study who were in a trial separation were still together six months after their counselling ended. There are several reasons for this (Hayman, 2001):

- Once separated it becomes far more difficult to come back together. Problems in the relationship have become public.
- It is usually better to work through problems in the relationship rather than out of it.
- Once couples have opted for a trial separation, they learn to fear a permanent separation less.

A trial separation can bridge the gap between being together and being apart. Often, this will give you time to reflect, to consider how your differences may be colouring your views, and work out what is really right for you. It might mean you and your partner call it a day, but equally it might show how you can restructure your relationship to ensure success in moving forward.

These tips suggest a few ways you and your partner can work through a rough patch to establish the best plan of action. You and your partner are the only ones who can establish what the right solution is for your relationship, but following some of these steps can help you establish communication that will get you there quicker and with the least heartache.

Conclusion

The research by the Francis Marion University highlighted the point that you can take one situation, one relationship and one break-up, filter it through two sets of eyes and the scene will appear completely differently.

What he sees as manipulation, you see as careful contemplation. What he sees as the end of the road, you see as a short break. Men and women will approach, negotiate and reflect on a break-up completely differently and this can make the process a million times more complicated.

Let's take Charley and Greg. After six months of hellish fighting they finally decide to call it a day. Decision made, bags packed and stuff returned, the two say their final goodbyes, which to Greg isn't really a big deal.

> Greg says: 'Right, catch you around. See you later, then.'
> Charley hears: 'I'm off! Yippee! Have a nice life!'
> Charley thinks: How dare he dismiss the dying embers of our love so
>   nonchalantly!

So what's happened here is, as expected – Charley is reading into the situation and ascribing to it a significance Greg just doesn't see. To him, the relationship is over, they've talked it to death and now is the time to get on with things. To Charley, this might be the last time they speak and she wants it to be amicable, memorable and provide closure on the relationship.

If the two meet in the middle, a crisis can easily be averted. Consider the difference between these two responses;

> Charley says: 'So that's it? "See you later." Is that how much this
>   means to you? This is how you ruined things in the first place.'
>
> Charley says: 'This is really hard for me. The reality of saying goodbye
>   is making it all hit home, and I feel really emotional about it. I wish
>   you all the best though – and hope one day we can be friends.'

By understanding Greg's reaction is largely down to him just being a man, and also understanding her emotions are largely down to her being a woman, Charley can put his response in perspective and be honest about her own. The second speech encourages openness and empathy, not bitterness and blame. This probably won't save the relationship – but it will make the separation easier to navigate.

Of course – before you get to Charley and Greg's point, there is the decision to make in the first place: should you and your partner be calling it a day or sticking with it? A good rule of thumb here is to plot your relationship on a metaphorical pie chart displaying happiness and unhappiness. If the amount of time you are unhappy because of your relationship greatly overshadows the amount of time you are happy because of it, then it's probably time to move on. After all, the point of a relationship is to enhance your life and if it has stopped doing this, then it's very hard to justify investing the necessary time and effort required to keep it going. But be ready to admit this isn't necessarily your partner's fault or the sign of a rubbish relationship doomed from the start. It may just be down to a basic flaw in communications, and your inability to tackle this as a couple is likely to be down to you as much as it is to your partner.

If you do want to stick with it, remember you can't do it by yourself. A relationship comprises two human beings and for it to flourish and survive, it must be nurtured, supported and strengthened by both. If a partner can't dedicate himself to the cause in the same way as you, then you're probably fighting an impossible battle anyway. Whatever your decision, the key to all of this is open, assertive communication that focuses on respect and negotiation rather than blame and resentment. Yes, be angry. Yes, be sad. But try to express these emotions in a way that won't provoke your partner or, indeed, prolong the inevitable. Don't let 'I can't believe it's over' turn into 'You've ruined the relationship'. Don't let 'I'm so angry we can't talk to one another like we used to' become 'You selfish, uptight, uncommunicative idiot'. If you and your partner can develop the communication tools to express your feelings in a non-aggressive, neutral manner then the process will be easier, less stressful, and likely to incorporate far fewer smashed hopes, smashed dreams and smashed photo frames.

Men Should Remember:

- You might not want to talk things through, but accept your partner might. That's not her being awkward, it's how she's psychologically built, so try to find a common ground that feels comfortable for both of you.
- Learn how to link what you think you need with what you are saying. Work out what will make you happy and find a way to articulate this so that it is clear for your partner. It will make things easier in the long run, whether or not they feature in your long-term plans.

Women Should Remember:

- Don't always see a relationship breakdown as a great loss. Sometimes it can open the door to a far more productive and healthy stage in your life.
- Don't play games – be honest. If you are sad, angry or jealous then be open. Holding back will only lead to resentment.

Chapter 10

Divorce

Many research projects have sought to ascertain the emotional implications of dramatic life events. Unsurprisingly, a large proportion of these studies have come to the conclusion that women are more prone to the emotional effects of a serious, life-changing event. Maciejewski et al. (2001) examined the incidences of depression over a twelve-month period and conducted structured interviews with 1,024 men and 1,800 women. They found women were approximately three times more likely than men to experience depression in response to a stressful life period or event.

However, these biases were closely tied to indirect, less personal life events. Women were at a far greater risk of suffering depression as a result of events within their 'network', for example, the death of a close friend or an external change such as moving house. This is most probably down to a higher level of investment into friendships and social networks. When it came down to the most distressing events anyone can personally go through, men and women drew level. Following a number of key events, men and women are at an equal risk of depression. In short, there are a number of life events that have huge emotional implications for both genders – for example, the loss of a loved one, a major relocation, the birth of a child, and divorce.

Research about divorce is becoming more and more commonplace in today's society as divorce spreads like wildfire. Getting married is one of the biggest decisions you will ever make. Essentially it constitutes a lifelong commitment to your partner – emotionally, financially and legally. It's a big deal. Increasingly, couples are deciding that, actually, it wasn't the best decision for them, and it isn't death doing them part, it's another big 'D' word – divorce. The figures are staggering. About 45 per cent of Australian, 55 per cent of American, 42 per cent of English and 37 per cent of German marriages end in divorce (Halford et al., 1997). That's right – in the UK you're almost as likely to end up at the divorce courts as you are to make it to the finishing post as man and wife. Likewise, in America, the 'best day of my life' is more likely to turn into the stuff of nightmares than happily ever after.

Sadly, divorce is becoming a fact of life, and one you can never really prepare yourself for. When you're beaming at the altar, all misty-eyed and brimming with sincere promises of for ever, divorce is a dirty word and the furthest thing from your mind. Likewise, five, six, seven years later when you're sitting at your dining-room table at four in the morning stoking the last dying embers of an argument about an issue that has become less of a problem and more of a theme in your relationship, confetti and wedding cake seem like a distant if not irretrievable memory. Of course, when you start throwing offspring into the mix, the situation becomes even more heart breaking and stressful for everyone involved.

The research mentioned recognises that divorce is indeed a stressful process for anyone to go through and men and women are equally prone to depression as a result of navigating that process. So it should stand to reason that two divorcing partners, even if they can't get on, would at least understand what the other is going through. Unfortunately, this is unlikely to be the case. Yes, men and women are equally as affected by that final split, but that doesn't mean they deal with it in the same way. After all, if a warring couple reacted to situations with matching harmonious responses, they probably wouldn't be divorcing in the first place.

It seems only right that divorce should be included in a guide that aims to help you through difficult and traumatic aspects of a romantic relationship. Whereas previous chapters have concentrated on how to avoid your relationship reaching this point, this chapter is about how you and your partner can work together, even if you just don't *work* together. We'll discuss how and why divorce occurs, how you can cope in general and how to start the process of change when it feels you and your partner talk different languages. We'll look at the difference between 'I need to move on' and 'I never loved you anyway' and the confusion between 'I need to take care of myself' and 'I want to hurt you'. In short, this chapter focuses on how to develop better means of negotiating this difficult transition, to ensure you both move away from the partnership with confidence, optimism and sense of perspective intact.

D.I.V.O.R.C.E – Bigger than Ever

It's sad but true, divorce is bigger than ever. It is no longer just a social taboo, an unromantic rarity or Liz Taylor's hobby. No, it is a fact of life, and the eventual conclusion of nearly half of all marriages. But why? Is the human race suffering a lack of enthusiasm for the till death do us part enthusiasm of yester year? Has a set of divorce papers become the latest fashion accessory? Or has the sanctity of marriage given up and gone home? A variety of explanations for the increasing frequency of divorce have been offered by researchers (Collard and Mansfield, 1994). These include:

- People (women in particular) have higher expectations and expect more personal fulfilment from marriage.
- There are easier divorce laws.
- More married women are economically active and therefore capable of supporting themselves.

These are just for starters. Consider the role of the church: we now live in a society far more concerned with science and self-help than religion and morality. Traditionally, marriage has been a religious ceremony, entered into with solemn vows to God that the marriage will last for ever. Pretty powerful stuff when you live in a society where religion is paramount. In modern society where, despite the broad spectrum of religious choices available, people are generally less likely to practise a religion devoutly, to many people marriage has become more of a legal and financial formality than a religious undertaking.

A factor possibly linked with the lessening religious presence in society is the fact that divorce has become far more acceptable. Whether divorce has become more popular because it has become more acceptable or vice versa is hard to say, but the fact is that in terms of social judgement it is far easier for you to get divorced than it was for your mother. And it was far easier for your mother to get divorced than it would have been for her mother. Being a divorcee no longer carries the social stigma it used to.

Collard and Mansfield's last point about increased female earning power is probably another key factor in the continuing rise of divorce. It wasn't such a viable option when women were entirely dependent on their husbands to earn the cash it takes to run a home and raise its inhabitants. But suddenly a wife is almost as likely to have a career as her husband, particularly before she has children or if she chooses not to have children. For many couples, financial dependency does not constitute a reason to keep a marriage together because they are both financially independent.

So divorce is easier, more accepted by society and a viable option for many couples who just can't seem to work things out. But what are those initial triggers that force a flagging relationship from the marital home to the law courts?

Throwing In the Towel – When and Why

Getting married doesn't freeze you into a permanent state of the happy, starry-eyed bride you were on your wedding day. Likewise your partner probably won't cry every time you walk into a room, or carry you to bed every other night after the big day: people change. A marriage is simply a sum of its parts, so it stands to reason that marriages change too. This change isn't necessarily a negative thing. The changes can test, strengthen and solidify your partnership, but sometimes they spell big trouble. Often it is not the change itself that triggers the deterioration, it is the resultant emotions and behaviour. Divorce happens not due to the fact of change but because the marital relationship is strained by conflict and negative emotions that cascade into a cycle of negativity (McCarthy and McCarthy, 2004). When people are asked what causes divorce they often cite major problems such as an adultery, alcoholism, or loss of job or status. While all these stimuli can damage the marital bond, it is really the daily issues and unresolved conflicts that spell the end. Your partner losing his job might not be a relationship-wrecker in itself, but if he becomes resentful, introverted and insecure as a result, the behaviour these emotions provoke may well kick off a downward spiral to divorce.

These changes, and the way we react to them, will be intrinsically linked to gender. In a study by Ponzetti et al. (1992), they found the most commonly and easily remembered reasons as reported by both ex-partners for divorce were ones such as physical separation, specific behaviour, health problems or violations of marital expectations, which all sounds fairly understandable and straightforward. But Ponzetti et al. also found that men were particularly guilty of focusing on particular instances within the marriage instead of looking at the wider picture. So a woman might look back and say, 'It didn't work out because we weren't really suited, we spent too much time apart and we didn't trust each other enough' while a man might say, 'It all fell apart that day she left my running shoes out in the rain and went for a drink with that creep she works with.'

Divorce – the Process

When we hear the word 'divorce' many of us think of the brief physical signing of divorce papers; the formalities of ending a marriage. Unless you've been divorced. If you have you know a divorce doesn't happen in a day. It is a long painful process. It isn't an event, it's a marathon, and none of the parties involved ever breeze through unscathed. Oh no. It represents a nodal phase in a family's history. In fact it can be said that divorce adds a whole stage to the family life cycle for those who must go through it (Beal, 1980) In other words, divorce isn't a fact of life that can be coped with as part of a family's day-to-day operation. It *becomes* the family's day-to-day operation, and a phase they must negotiate in order to function. Often, the longer the marriage has lasted, the more painful it can be to adopt this new way of life.

Unlike other major shifts in life, there are virtually no formal rites or rituals that can assist the individual or the family with the difficulties associated with a divorce. When we deal with a family death there are established rituals that represent normality and routine in a time of great emotional upheaval – for example, funerals and burials. There is no formal routine for coping with divorce, so every family must establish its own sense of normality. We invest a lot in the assumption that a marriage will work out – we live together, we forsake all others and we bring children into the world. When it all goes wrong, these very assumptions, these safe foundations are rocked to the core, and there is no social itinerary to guide you through the process.

Divorce clearly illustrates the concept of intense emotional and/or physical distance in the marital experience. This intensity is reflected in the fact that individuals believe their autonomy or ability to function cannot be achieved if they stay close to their spouse (Beal, 1980). When we decide to divorce, we turn a complete emotional 180 degrees. Part of getting married to someone is believing you will only be happy if you are committed to that person, in believing your personal growth and fulfilment is intricately linked to them. When we get divorced, we do so because we believe we can only be happy and achieve true contentment if we are independent of and separate from that person. When you look at the range of emotions we go through – experiencing a marriage, a marital breakdown and then a divorce – it's a wonder anyone makes it out the other end.

This massive emotional upheaval is just one of the reasons people shy away from divorce, even when it is probably the best solution, but there are a plethora of other reasons. One of the biggest is family: the family that brought you up and the family you may well be bringing up yourself. If you come from a long line of strong, long-term marriages, it can be really hard to break away from that example and leave a marriage. There are feelings of guilt, disappointment and failure. Likewise, having a family of your own, and wanting to keep that family together is one of the most common reasons for rejecting divorce as an option. Strong family values can make a decision to divorce very difficult, and especially when extended family networks are involved, there is the tendency to try to create stable families and strong kinship bonds. Where children are concerned, the pressure to stay in an unhappy marriage becomes more powerful for women. According to evolutionary psychology, women feel a strong obligation to provide a stable environment for their children due to their instinctive nurturing nature. Guilt is a common emotion for many women contemplating divorce. Moreover, since the burden of childcare most probably will remain their responsibility, this makes it more unlikely for them to terminate the marriage (Williams, 1987).

Another reason why people stay in unhappy, unhealthy marriages is the fear of being alone. When a relationship we have devoted time, energy and commitment to falls apart before our eyes, our sense of self-worth and our perception of our validity as a romantic partner can take a huge knock. Marriages break down for a million different reasons, but one of the most common effects of this deterioration is a lack of love and affection between two partners. Just as the comforting security of a loving partner's commitment builds our self-esteem and self-confidence, the lack of it can attack a healthy self-image. At the end of a relationship harsh words are exchanged, feelings are often neglected and in some cases infidelities and blatant violations of the relationship's boundaries occur. All these factors can leave both partners feeling they are unattractive, unlovable and unlikely to find another partner. So the fear of being alone makes the prospect of an unhappy marriage seem preferable to the prospect of facing life alone.

Pressures from our parents, children and wider family are often factors in the shunning of divorce as an option. Practical issues of finance, property and custody can also act as deterrents. The fear of ending up alone can cage people into an unhappy marriage. But that isn't what this chapter is about; it is about accepting that divorce, painful as it may be, is often the more sensible alternative to living through a marriage that is unfulfilling and unsatisfactory. It is about accepting divorce is the only way forward, and learning to negotiate the way forward with maximum diplomacy and minimum drama. We will explain how men and women experience divorce differently and discuss how to accept and work to those differences to ensure both partners can move on.

Moving On . . . Easier Said Than Done?

OK, so you've cut your losses and penned your name on the divorce papers. You've wept frustrated tears at the monotony of a relationship that has worn you down and left you bare. You've suffered the awkward silences of a dying bond, and you've cut a clear path through the barrage of advice ranging from 'You have a duty to your family' to 'If you're not happy, get out'. And now you have to grab onto a process called 'moving forward' and run with it.

Like it or not, property and childcare issues are usually part and parcel of a divorce and have to be dealt with. However, rather like asking a bull to sit down and talk through the issues of animal cruelty with a matador waving a red cape, often our instincts and emotions can cloud our rationality. It's rather idealistic to assume that an inked signature on a divorce paper will transform an emotionally charged feud into a calm, reasonable discussion. Just because you have come to an agreement that divorce is the way forward, it doesn't mean you will reach agreement on anything else.

Let's look at Dionne and Sean. They've been married for eight years, but following two years of constant rowing and relentless criticism, they've decided to separate. In an attempt to tie up the loose ends of their separation, they meet to discuss their next steps:

Dionne says: 'I think we need to sort out who gets to keep what.'
Dionne means: 'This is going to be a long painful process, let's start with the basics.'
Sean hears: 'I'm not losing out on anything, don't think you're keeping the TV.'
Sean says: (somewhat defensively) 'OK, what do you want?'

Dionne says: 'Well, I'd love to come by and pick up some old photo albums.'

Sean thinks: Thanks God for that – I thought you were going to fleece me for my hard-earned savings.

Sean says: 'Of course you can have those, what on earth would I want with them?'

Dionne hears: 'I don't care about those memories any more.'

Dionne says: 'Well, I didn't expect you to be quite so forthcoming, those photos mean a lot to me. It would be nice if they meant something to you too.'

Sean says: 'Oh, for God's sake, how did this turn into a character assassination? Why is everything always my fault?'

And before you know it, a simple discussion about romantic keepsakes has turned into the next episode in an ongoing series of disputes, simply because they view the end of the relationship in a different way. Ongoing acrimony and constant feuding like this make a painful process ten times worse. The legal rites of a divorce ensure that complete avoidance of confrontation and discussion is usually nigh on impossible, so you and your ex-partner should focus on ways to build a rapport that will enable you to work through the messy end of your relationship, and through these common misunderstandings. Couples who simply cannot reach this point often find their finances as depleted and wretched as their emotional stores, because the alternative is conducting every minute of your break-up through expensive lawyers. It seems futile to pay people to help you communicate so you can extract yourselves from a bond that was once based on one of the deepest forms of human connection – a romantic relationship.

Ultimately, having the dregs of your marriage played out by costly divorce lawyers won't help you gain the emotional closure you get when you put a distressing period to bed. Dealing with the issue head on might seem like an intimidating, undesirable option when there are people more than happy to deal with it for you, but true closure comes from knowing you have identified a problem, faced it, addressed it and resolved it, not from paying a lawyer enough for a lifetime's worth of Jimmy Choos and praying you never bump into your ex in the supermarket.

If there are children involved then you will always share a bond with your ex, and cooperation will be key to the emotional welfare of everyone involved. So it makes sense to start the process right at the beginning of the separation. If you can build an effective dialogue early on then you have the foundations for a relationship that will help you both move forward and sustain the security of a mother–father bond for your children. Cracking the crucial differences between male and female reactions to events like divorce will help you understand when your partner is being unreasonable and when their intended meaning is simply lost in translation.

How do we get to the light at the end of the divorce tunnel? How do we reach a point where we can look past our emotional distress and appreciate that the best way to protect ourselves is to compromise, understand and communicate? After all, the key elements in any divorce are a man and a woman, and those two ingredients don't always add up to cool, calm negotiations or harmonious understanding.

Inevitably men and women approach the conundrum of communicating their way through divorce in entirely different ways. When a man and a woman sit down to discuss, for example, who keeps their shared dog, two entirely different agendas are at play, purely because of our gender-specific emotions. A woman will approach this discussion thinking, 'I want to be listened to, I want him to appreciate my feelings, and understand that I feel lonely and vulnerable and giving up my pet dog feels as though I am surrendering my last vestige of comfort in the cold, dark world I am embarking upon as a newly single woman.' The man will think, 'I want to keep the dog. He keeps the kitchen floor clean and nobody else will play ball with me in the park.' Or let's look at Kevin and Allison – they're trying to decide what to do with their wedding rings:

Allison says: 'It's so hard to know what to do with the rings; I mean, I love mine so much – and it will always remind me of how happy we were on that day.'

Allison means: 'Let's take a minute to remember the good times. It's so sad this has all fallen apart, don't you think?'

Kevin hears: 'Kevin – what's the answer here? What shall we do with the rings?'

Kevin says: 'Well, that's great Ali, but it's not much use to anyone now is it? Let's put the engagement ring, and the two wedding bands on eBay, flog them as a job lot and then split the proceeds – then everyone's happy.'

Allison hears: 'Move on woman, it's over. Stop dwelling.'

Allison says: 'Happy?! Is that all these symbols of our marriage mean to you? Do you know how hard this is for me?! You're so heartless.'

Kevin thinks: Hang on a minute – how did this turn into a big emotional row about feelings? I thought it was about working out what to do with our now meaningless wedding bands?'

The basic premise is that a woman will usually look for understanding and discussion, a man will usually look for an action plan and a solution. Remember, these aren't usually one-off rows about whose turn it is to wash up, or why you insist on leaving the bathroom tap dripping every night. These are rows that follow on from weeks, months, maybe years of unhappiness, and are based on basic truths like: 'We don't love each other any more' or 'You hurt me so much that I have to leave this relationship'. It isn't as though you start off on a level playing field. But there are a few steps you can follow to ensure your discussions are as amicable, productive and painless as possible:

Moderate your Language

Think about the way your words will be interpreted. There is a huge difference between 'You are being so selfish' and 'This is hard for me to accept, because it seems a little unreasonable'. Effective communication is about developing the best way to express a sentiment through choosing your words carefully. Taking time before speaking will give you the breathing space to convey thoughts so they don't sound like accusations.

Facts, not Feelings

Try to stick to the hard undeniable facts of the situation. 'I'm screwing you over for every penny you've got because you showed me up and broke my heart when you sneaked off with that trollop from the office' doesn't sound half as powerful as 'Our marriage is no longer viable because one party chose to conduct a relationship that violated our vows, therefore a financial settlement must be reached.' Calm and factual will always win over aggressive and dramatic, so try to keep your emotions separate from the nitty gritty of your negotiations.

I, not You

To avoid aggression and causing offence, try to start sentences with 'I', so 'I feel let down' rather than 'You let me down'. The effect of this is that rather than sounding accusatory, you will sound explanatory. Your partner is more likely to listen to you explaining your feelings about a situation than if you accuse them of causing those feelings. The 'I' mode allows room for the suggestion that your partner is not solely responsible for your feelings, and consequently sounds less aggressive.

No Assumptions

Ban phrases like 'You know what I mean' or 'Before I tell you this, don't fly off the handle', because they are assumptive and pre-empt emotions that may not exist and situations that may not occur. Ask the obvious questions, don't assume you know your partner's position on everything – perhaps they are ready to compromise more than you think. Don't assume your partner knows your feelings on something either. Effective communication isn't about assuming your partner knows you well enough for you not to need to communicate.

Pick your Battles Wisely

Sometimes, it is more fruitful if partners give up an argument rather than go on until one wins or they abandon the argument through exhaustion (Crowe, 2005). Backing down in an argument you don't feel so strongly about can actually place you in a better position to negotiate an issue you do feel strongly about, because you can show your partner you are aware of their wishes, value their opinion, and won't labour over every single point of contention for the sake of arguing. Backing down at the appropriate time paves the way for future communication success.

Once you've established an effective platform for communication, the next step is using this communication to negotiate. In other words, once you are both speaking the same language, you can start to do business. Divorce negotiations often reach a frustrating stalemate where each issue becomes a symbolic battlefield, with both parties feeling that if they concede on any one point, they will lose the entire war. As we've pointed out, abandoning or conceding a point can be more powerful in establishing effective negotiations than fighting every argument to the last.

Some couples complain they never seem to reach a decision but instead become sidetracked by other issues. And at the same time, others feel their partner never listens to their preferences, needs or that he/she says something hurtful or sarcastic (Epstein and Baucom, 2002). The key here is to continue the dialogue without attacking each other. This is the only way to establish a dialogue that will leave both partners feeling their needs have been addressed and, where possible, met. Crowe (2005) has identified negotiation as an essential feature of an amicable divorce, and has identified the following steps to help couples overcome the difficulties this often presents:

Guidelines for Negotiation

State the Issue
Make sure both of you are clear on the issue to be resolved, whether it's who gets to keep the house, or who gets custody of the children. Be clear about what you are negotiating over, and the eventual desired

conclusion: 'We must decide how our finances should be divided. By the end of this discussion, we need to have come to a mutually agreeable conclusion.' Vague objectives such as: 'We need to sort out this mess' make it difficult to focus on the important issue, and leave the gate open for unrelated disagreements to be brought up.

Focus on the Future

This is important. It's hard to look to the future and resolve issues that will form your relationship in its new capacity if you are both bogged down with the behaviour, emotions and arguments that featured in your history. Change complaints into specific requests for the future, and ensure these requests are positive, repeatable and practicable. The more rational and specific a request is, the easier it is to understand and act on.

Give and Take

Requests and compromises should be reciprocal. It is unlikely that a satisfactory arrangement will be reached if one partner feels they are compromising far more than their ex. Ensure you are both displaying a degree of compromise and willingness to work to your partner's wishes. Expressing wishes should be a two-way process, as should fulfilling these wishes.

Make a Plan

The point of all of this discussion is that you should eventually reach a solution, or at least be in a position to implement a strategy that will cater to both sets of needs. So make a practical plan with clearly outlined responsibilities on both sides of the equation. This will make it obvious to each partner exactly what is expected of them. And make sure you are both agreed on your action plan, or the chances are that it won't be successful.

Monitor Your Progress

Once you have reached an amicable plan, look at your relationship honestly from time to time to ensure you are both adhering to it.

Regular checks shouldn't be used as excuses to start hurling accusations and blame around. They should act as meaningful bench-marks to evaluate the success of your negotiations and reminders that maintaining a healthy post-divorce relationship requires effort and commitment from everyone involved.

Realistically speaking, these techniques won't necessarily resolve all your communication problems. However, they do provide the kind of focus that can help you move away from the endless 'he says, she says' circles often created when two separated partners debate an emotional issue. Once you've mastered the basics of communication and negotiation, and established a routine where contentious issues are dealt with in a structured, calm way, you're ready to look at the biggest, and potentially most explosive issue that any separating couple will have to address. By definition, marriage means an amalgamation of two separate lives. It means you build things together, and create joint projects. Dividing these shared assets can be the hardest part of any divorce. And over the next few pages we'll look at possibly the most emotional example of this – childcare.

Childcare

The most significant joint project a couple can undertake is parenting. The emotional investment required to raise children is monumental and the idea of separation from a child is every parent's worst nightmare. Obviously, upon divorcing, a couple have made the decision that they can no longer live together as man and wife. But where does this leave the children? Resolving childcare issues often proves to be distressing, even heart breaking for parents, as it usually means that somebody ends up spending less time with their children than they would like. The key objective in this situation must always be to place the needs of the children before the needs of the adults involved.

For a child living through a divorce, the emotional effects can be varied, particularly depending on age. Research shows that very young children find it difficult to understand the motives behind divorce and often make the assumption that it is their fault that Mummy or Daddy do not live together or love each other any more (Crowe, 2005). Conversely, understanding the issue can be as damaging as not understanding the issue; older children, who are likely to have an awareness of the reasons behind the divorce, can sometimes be expected to make almost impossible decisions between parents. For example, some couples allow their children to decide who they want to live with. This places daunting pressure on children who feel they are forced to reject one parent. With age comes a desire to comfort parents when they are visibly distressed, but this can evoke feelings of disloyalty and guilt for the child, who again feels they are taking sides. Basically, divorce is painful for the children involved, and will inevitably have a huge impact on their lives. As a parent, your duty is to do all you can to minimise this impact and work with your ex-partner to ensure that, where possible, you cushion the blow. There are a few simple steps you can take to aid this process.

How to Explain

It's important both partners present a united front when explaining the key issues to their children. This avoids confusion and sends a clear signal: 'Despite the fact that we have decided we will both be happier if we separate, we are still united and very much a two-parent team when it comes to your upbringing.' If you can't agree on issues, then do your disagreeing – or with any luck, careful negotiating – away from your children, and only approach them with the issue once you have clarified and resolved it.

If this proves too hard, then at the very least, ensure your children don't get caught up in the blame and guilt that often flies around in these situations. They should be treated as innocent civilians in any conflict, not as ammunition or as allies. The divorcing couple are the adults in the situation and should behave as such. It is very easy to use children as excuses or to back you up as you argue with your spouse (Hayman, 2001). But this should be avoided at all costs.

When you tell your children your marriage is ending, you always need to use the simplest language and the message should be repeated many times to ensure they have correctly absorbed it (Crowe, 2005). Tell them with conviction, and constant reassurance that the split is not their fault and that they are still loved absolutely endlessly and unconditionally by both parents. Ensure the communication is a reciprocal process. Encourage questions, and do your best to answer them objectively. Children need to be able to discuss the situation with both of you and they need to be able to ask questions and have their own feelings appreciated and heard (Hayman, 2001). Their interpretation of the situation is key.

Lastly, don't make your children feel responsible for your feelings. Research shows it is extremely damaging to children to have to 'parent' his or her parent (Hayman, 2001). If a child is forced into a position where they feel responsible for the emotional welfare of their parent, it can have disastrous implications for their success in forming relationships in later life. Remember that the roles of parent and child have strict definitions and responsibilities; ensure that you and your partner remain united and in control, not sniping or needy.

Here are some useful tips on how to tell your children:

- Don't even mention divorce until you have made an absolute final decision.
- Explain the situation in simple language. Try not to confuse them.
- Address any worries or concerns.
- Present a united front when treating any arising issues – i.e. behaviour problems.

Shared Parenting

So we've established that even if you and your partner decide to go your separate ways you will always be linked if you have children together. You simply have to establish some kind of relationship and put some form of routine into practice to ensure the impact of your separation is minimal for your children. Divorced people often stop standing side by side on childcare issues. They may even find themselves taking opposing and/or contrasting views (Hayman, 2001).

In order to establish a strong parenting team, both partners must be able to step outside their relationship and concentrate on the real issues at stake. In implementing effective childcare, you must both realise the emotional hangovers from your relationship have nothing to do with the relationship both of you share with your offspring, and they should not be allowed to overshadow that bond. If you both maintain a united front, you can avoid forcing your children to feel they must take sides, and you can protect them from the emotional turmoil of watching the two people they love the most at war with one another.

Remember your children are just that – children. Don't make them responsible for decisions about their own childcare. If you allow your children to make vital choices over things like who they live with, you will put them under incredible pressure, and risk blurring the boundaries between child and parent which can inevitably lead to behavioural problems. If you let your eight-year-old choose where she lives, why shouldn't she choose who she goes out with, or where she hangs out, or whether she smokes? Remember that until your children are old enough to manage their own lives, the responsibility must remain with you.

Staying in Touch

Inevitably divorced parents must accept that one way or another they will probably end up seeing less of their children. That might mean missing out on doing the school run. It might mean missing out on weekends together. But there are ways you can minimise the impact this has on everyone involved.

Living within travelling distance makes a big difference. The further you live from your children, the harder it will be for you to contribute to their upbringing. Research has shown this applies especially to men; half of non-resident fathers have lost contact with their children after two years of separation regardless of where they live (Crowe, 2005). You can imagine what these statistics look like for fathers who choose to live in different countries or on different sides of the world to their children. This links back to the idea of minimising change for your children. Going from living in a house with two parents to living with one parent and only seeing the other at weekends, or dividing time in half with each parent is a massive change for a child. It would be a massive change for anybody. That change is all the more dramatic if one parent is an unattainable distance from home, and will encourage the potential for resentment, initially from the parent who feels they have been left behind to raise their children alone, and later from the children who will then go on to understand and experience rejection. If a distance is unavoidable, you really need to establish a system of regular contact, which might involve regular emails, phone calls or visits – anything that can work towards eradicating the emotion 'Mummy/Daddy wasn't there for me.'

Finally, in making arrangements to act as co-parents one needs to consider how to manage certain arrangements around childcare. The usual pattern is that women take on the day-to-day care of their children and men are responsible for their care at weekends and holidays. This may contribute further to the everyday stress of women, as they try to fulfil the multiple roles of worker, mother and care taker. Of course, the qualities of each of these roles are looked at differently through the eyes of women and men. Men may argue that they miss their everyday family interaction with their children and are stressed over financially supporting them.

Continuing to co-parent while managing and acknowledging that your marital relationship is over is a real challenge but one that can be achieved. Cooperation makes all the difference. Effective co-parenting relies entirely on being able to work with your ex-partner and to forge a new relationship that centres on your shared responsibility for your children. It is useful to involve your children as participants in this by actually considering their feelings when arrangements are set up. This doesn't mean they make the decisions, but it does mean their views count.

Conclusion – Life after Divorce

Life continues after divorce and it can be quite exciting to meet someone new. However, new relationships can bring their own conflict and confusion for ex-partners and your children. Divided loyalties often exist in this situation. There are also many other difficulties to be surmounted by an ex-spouse getting into a new relationship, especially when there has been an affair. Children may regard themselves as being disloyal to their biological parent. Closely related to the issue of loyalty is the problem of competition, which can take many forms (Beck, 1988). For example, rivalry between children and the new partner for the attention of the parent or rivalry between the new partner and the ex-partner over the attention of the children.

The many issues that might arise can be dealt with successfully by having some decision-making meetings. The skills of negotiation and communication can be useful in order to avoid any conflicts that could interfere with their work as co-parents (Beck, 1988). Compromises need to be made and new partners need to exercise a degree of patience and tolerance towards each other.

Although divorce might often be a relief, it can be like a bereavement (Crowe, 2005). How we move on and deal with the end of a relationship depends on a number of variables. Personality affects your ability to cope with grief and loss: people who are self-confident and optimistic manage to cope better. Acceptance is another important variable. It is healthier than feeling controlled by chronic anger or bitterness towards your ex-spouse. Divorcees can be reassured that although they need to assume some responsibility for their break-up, they need not believe there is something wrong with their personalities that makes future relationships prone to failure (Hulson and Russell, 1994).

Men Should Remember:

- Be open about your feelings. If the divorce is killing you, admit it – it may help you and your partner negotiate your way through.

- Try to banish bitterness – acceptance is a better emotion and will help you move on.
- Understand your partner will want to deal with this differently. When appropriate and possible, make time to listen to one another.

Women Should Remember:

- Try to deal in facts, not in emotions.
- Where possible, focus on the solution, not the problem
- Consider and learn to accept the possibility that your partner isn't deliberately trying to hurt you – he's just trying to make his own way through the separation.

Chapter 11

Living Happily Ever After

We all know how the fairy tale ends: after the trials and tribulations, the wicked witches and poisoned apples, the beanstalks and ivory towers, the boy gets his girl and rides off with her into the sunset. Then they settle down, he trades the white horse for a nice practical estate car, she cuts her long hair because while it's a godsend when you're stuck in a twenty-foot tower it's a nightmare to style once you're back on level ground, and they get out a substantial mortgage on a three-bedroomed detached place in the country. Where, of course, they live happily ever after. Children's fairy tales are one of the first examples we are given of romantic relationships, which is ironic, because it couldn't be further from an accurate representation of what love is really like.

The truth is that perfect couples don't exist, love is really hard work and romantic relationships require time, patience and regular maintenance. Oh, and Father Christmas isn't real either. Sorry. But these stark realities aren't necessarily negatives, they are just facts of life. By definition a romantic relationship features two personalities, which is what makes them so interesting but at the same time a trigger for conflict. Because one partner is male and one female, there will be disagreements. Because you were brought up in different homes, you are likely to see the world differently, and because you are both individuals with likes, dislikes, hopes, fears and expectations there will always be room for disagreement.

When a man and a woman decide to commit to each other, it's never going to be plain sailing. There is a temptation to assume that once you've got past all the awkward dating, the wrangling over cohabiting and even the big question, the hard work is done, and you can simply put your feet up and enjoy being blissfully in love. But the basic building blocks of who we are provide a constant breeding ground for conflict. This is healthy. After all, what would be the point of relationships if we all felt the same and could never learn anything from one another? Disagreeing with a partner is a great way of challenging their beliefs, your beliefs and affirming the strength of your relationship – as long as this dialogue is carried out in a constructive and open way.

Being a happy couple and developing a strong relationship is all about effective communication. Just because you feel that sometimes Mars and Venus are too far apart to reach a compromise, doesn't mean you can't bridge this gap with a calm, rational explanation of why your feelings are so different. What you need to recognise is that much of your frustration, disappointment, anger and uncertainty derive not from a basic incompatibility of the sexes but from unfortunate misunderstandings that are mainly the result of faulty communications and biased interpretations of each other's actions (Beck, 1988). Problems don't arise just because you are a woman and he is a man. They arise because you have not learnt to read each other correctly, and it is far easier to jump to false conclusions and make unjustified accusations. Clarity of communication is the first thing you should look at when evaluating the way you interact with each another.

The ability to communicate with each other successfully is a major criterion of a good relationship. Successful communication is necessary in nearly all stages of a relationship (Beck, 1988) as we've seen through our examination of dating, sex, divorce and everything in between. But, as we've also seen, all too often couples slip into a routine of bad communication, which is incredibly hard to escape. He sighs, you get angry, you tut, he leaves the room, you scream, he slams the door and so on and so on. We fall into a vicious circle that feels comfortable, even if it is making both partners unhappy. Your happy ever after should be about breaking that cycle and re-establishing good communication so it contributes to the strength of your relationship rather than destroying it. The good news is that really minor changes in your behaviour can dramatically improve your relationship, whether you are discussing marriage, babies or what takeaway to get that evening. When you feel you and your partner are talking entirely different languages you need to reassess not only what is being said but what is being heard, then you can begin to establish a more helpful communication structure and ensure you and your partner are one step closer to the happily ever after.

Language for Beginners – the Building Blocks of Common Vocabulary

A common mistake is assuming that problems begin with your first romantic relationship; in fact they usually begin about eighteen years prior to that. From the moment the midwife shouts 'It's a boy!' or 'It's a girl!' a large proportion of your destiny is already mapped out. We've talked throughout the book about the kinds of areas this pre-destiny and socialisation touches on, but more specifically there are a number of traits people expect you to display, merely by being male or female – some of these are mapped out below:

Characteristics of the Female Stereotype
- affectionate
- compassionate
- does not use harsh language
- eager to soothe hurt feelings
- gentle
- gullible
- loves children
- loyal
- sensitive to the needs of others
- soft-spoken

- sympathetic
- tender
- understanding
- warm
- yielding

Characteristics of the Male Stereotype

- acts as a leader
- aggressive
- assertive
- competitive
- defends own beliefs
- dominant
- forceful
- has leadership abilities
- independent
- individualistic
- makes decisions easily
- self-reliant
- willing to take a stand
- willing to take risks

Gender stereotypes

These beliefs can actually be extremely damaging to a channel of communication because they can lead couples to think they will never be able to change their partners' behaviour because it is rooted in deeply ingrained gender-assigned personality traits. So Jenny assumes 'My boyfriend is incredibly assertive and confident, so he can handle me telling it like it is – his jokes aren't funny and his feet smell.' Some of these stereotypes are completely incorrect and to assume your partner will be insensitive or thick-skinned, or, to give another example, to assume your partner will never understand your innermost feelings simply because he is a man, will construct a impenetrable barrier between you. It is actually far more useful to look at some more specific research into how men and women communicate differently, as we have done throughout the book. That way you can assess where the problems are occurring rather than assume your partner will never see your point of view. For example, identified a number of these key gender differences:

- Women seem to view questions as encouragement for discussion while men view them as requests for information.
- Women are more likely to share feelings and be more intimate. Men avoid discussing intimate issues and focus on topics such as work, politics, sport.
- Women seem to take aggression/arguments as a sign of relationship breakdown, whereas men seem to view conflict or disagreement simply as a form of conversation.
- Women tend to discuss, share experiences, concerns and offer reassurance and support. In contrast, when someone tells a man a problem, he tends to view that as an explicit request for a solution, rather than an excuse to talk about the problem for the sake of talking about it.

These variations in the meaning of communication between genders lead women and men to have very different and often quite opposite expectations. Take Susie and Jacob. Susie is having a tough time at work, and is finding it really hard to get on with one of her team members. The constant conflict is bringing her down, and when she comes home from work she wants to unburden herself of the day's stresses by talking to Jacob about them. So she sits him down and tells him the whole story, not because she thinks he can do anything about it but because it helps her to talk about it. Jacob, on the other hand, thinks the best way he can help here is to offer a solution: 'So, leave your job.' As far as he is concerned, he's listened, he's identified the problem and volunteered a solution that will most certainly knock it on the head. Job done, now he can go and watch *Match of the Day*. Well, he could if Susie would stop slamming doors and walking in front of the TV. Jacob has misinterpreted what Susie wanted from the exchange, and has consequently hurt her feelings.

Here you can see how our gender-specific communications can affect our expectations of our partner. Jacob expected Susie to react like a man, and say, 'Thanks for the advice, mate, nice one,' and go back to talking about boobs, beer and sport. Susie expected Jacob to react like a woman and analyse the situation for hours with her, even if they never reached a fail-safe strategy for confronting the problem. Partners should be able to discern these differences. They should keep in mind that the different expectations they hold can only impede their communication and their relationship overall.

To work through these kinds of problems, couples like Jacob and Susie need to look at their patterns of communication in a different way. Psychologists refer to this as reframing. Reframing consists of reconsidering these negative qualities in a different light (Beck, 1988). When Susie views Jacob's behaviour through her own female-biased standards, she automatically sees his reaction as negative, because it is different from hers. Consistently using this negative frame to view the relationship will eventually create misunderstandings and drive an emotional distance between the couple. By taking a step back from the situation and observing with the knowledge that your way isn't necessarily always the right way, you can frame your partner's actions in a more positive light. So if you stop viewing things as a woman, and start viewing them a little more neutrally, or even as a man would, you can understand why talking about the cricket is preferable to analysing the way that girl said 'Hello' at the Christmas party. It starts to become clear that him walking straight up the stairs and into the shower after work, without so much as an acknowledgement, doesn't necessarily mean 'I hate you and I can't be bothered to speak to you', it just means 'Let me have my shower. I smell. I'm tired – but I promise once I have de-stressed you will have my full attention.' Also, the more you try to look at the positives of your partner's behaviour, the more you will find. As this system of understanding and empathy develops it will result in even more positive behaviour. Just as you can get swept up in a cycle of negative communication, the opposite is also true.

In order to establish these good communication habits, couples must learn to see each other as team mates, rather than adversaries. Instead of puzzling through using their gender-specific languages and losing a great deal in fumbled translation, couples should learn to understand one another properly. Men do occasionally enjoy discussing problems, but they are still likely to go about it in a different way to women. Just because a long, blown-out analysis isn't their first port of call when things go wrong, doesn't mean they are incapable of being sensitive or attuned to their feelings. Men can develop more positive expectancies about expressing their feelings and needs (Epstein and Baucom, 2003). Equally, women can also learn to be more solution-focused. You and your partner have a great deal to teach one another, and the best environment for this process of learning is a channel of open, honest communication. More often than not, a great tool to equip you and your partner for the process can be CBT. We've talked about acceptance, perspective and the value of a balanced reaction throughout. CBT encompasses all these tools within a basic set of rules and tips.

CBT

As we've established, communication doesn't just occur when your lips are moving. Communication is constant. There is as much verbal communication as there is non-verbal communication (Crowe, 2005). All these non-verbal signs constitute communication: eye contact, avoidance of eye contact, a shrug, a frown, a grin, a sigh – the list is endless. Basically every move you make can be interpreted positively or negatively, rightly or wrongly. These interpretations form assumptions that people have about us. It is these assumptions that cause such conflict within romantic relationships: he assumes she is bored by his story because she stifles a yawn; she assumes he thinks she is boring because he fails to laugh at her favourite joke. These assumptions aren't based on fact, they're based on our interpretations.

This is important, because communication is so much more than just a transmission of a message from one person to another. Tied up in the process is the interpretative activity. Messages are adapted or misinterpreted by their recipient. Because of the strength of the feelings and the ambiguity that surrounds what is said or done, partners in romantic relationships are prone to misinterpret each other's actions. Failure to decipher the meaning of what is being communicated usually results in making erroneous conclusions, which in turn may result in conflict, arguments or hurt. Hence, the role of communication in relationships is critical and involves significant psychological processes.

Consider the following case: Fi and Morris have been out for a couple of dates. Fi is a successful interior designer and Morris is an architect. They get on really well and they both want to spend more time with each other. However, the fact that they are at such an early stage in their relationship prohibits them from expressing how they really feel. Their communication is based on assumptions or inferences about each other's genuine motives. So when she says, 'I had a really nice time with you tonight,' he thinks, 'What if she is just being polite?' So, he backs away and stays silent, for fear of making a fool of himself. Fi interprets this silence as a sign that she has been too full-on and worries she has misjudged the situation. So she backs off. Soon, both individuals have scared each other to a point of nervous anxiety, and the relationship is over before it has begun, simply because of a subtext that never even existed.

According to CBT, the coding system we use is guided by our beliefs. Thus, we try to decipher the meaning of our partner's communications using our beliefs as our lens of reality. These beliefs can be biased or coloured leading us to make unrealistic judgements, offer unjustified explanations and form illogical conclusions. Problematic feelings and behaviours arise from distorted, incorrect, maladaptive cognitions. A self-fulfilling cycle may establish itself, and individuals begin to act in a way they know will confirm or maintain their distorted beliefs. Moreover, problems occur because we tend to believe our inferences as much as we believe something we directly observe. Thus, we tend to treat our thoughts as observable facts: your boyfriend may have placed that mug on the table, and you may have seen it with your own eyes, but because you are convinced he is in a thunderous mood, you tell yourself he actually slammed it down with contempt. Particularly when we feel emotional about a situation, the vagueness of our perception can trip us up quite easily (Beck, 1988). Our interpretations are more likely to be based on our own internal states or insecurities rather than observable reality.

Cognitions (that is one's attributions, beliefs, expectancies or memories) are viewed as critical in determining feelings and behaviours. Thereby, cognitive therapy focuses on how we perceive (or rather misperceive) situations. It aims to remedy these distortions and deficits in thinking and consequently improve our communication (Beck, 1988). Couples can test their interpretations about each other and correct them accordingly rather than let them spoil their relationships. They can actually learn to speak the same language through examining their behaviour and the way it is perceived against the way they perceive their partner's behaviour, and the meaning behind it.

Ira and Mike have been engaged for a year, although lately they have started to argue regularly. On the way home from a party one night, Mike is uncharacteristically quiet as he drives. Ira begins to think, 'Mike's not talking to me – something's wrong, he must be mad at me.' She spends twenty minutes racking her memory to work out exactly what she could have done to inspire such rage. In her quest to explain Mike's silence, she attributes it to hostility towards her.

Essentially Ira is disregarding any other explanation for Mike's silence. She is mind-reading, assuming she knows what his silence means, when really there could be a million reasons he is so quiet. When your expectations are thwarted, you tend to jump to negative conclusions about your partner's state of mind. Relying on what is being called mind-reading is a common error: 'She is acting this way because she wants to get back at me' or 'He said that because he is hiding something and feels guilty.' As a result of such mind-reading, arguments, attack or misunderstanding can easily occur. Interpreting your partner's motives in this way is fraught with danger because people simply cannot read each other's minds (Beck, 1988). However much you think you might know your partner you can never tell what he or she really feels or thinks unless you ask them. Mind-reading can lead to isolation and withdrawal and eventually contribute to disconnection. So ask. And once you've asked, listen. No – really listen.

Speaking Sense – Finding a Common Language

No relationship guide would be worth its salt unless it actually offered you some really useful advice. The next few pages contain some practical advice you and your partner can employ to help you find a common dialect. What men say and what women hear may be two very different things, but with a little negotiation and a lot of communication you can bring them closer together.

How to Hear Differently – Challenging Your Ears

In almost any interaction between couples, each person will have automatic thoughts, or schemas, that influence what they say, how they say it and what they do. These thoughts may not be openly expressed, but inevitably affect tone of voice, facial expression and gestures (Beck, 1988). The good news is that although these automatic thought processes and their consequent behaviour are deeply ingrained, they are not completely resistant to change. Using a combination of technique and effort you can break the chain between your thoughts and their automatic reaction. Equally, using CBT you can actually transform the initial thoughts that are causing the problem in the first place. Some of these methods are outlined below.

Step 1: Making the Links between Emotional Reactions and Automatic Thoughts

When you and your partner hit a communication barrier, the first thing you can do is to examine your own behaviour. As you have an emotional reaction to something, try and catch the moment you switch from feeling hurt or angry to an inner dialogue or automatic thought. Try to match the event or the action to the thought process.

Step 2: Practice Identifying Automatic Thoughts

Learning to recognise your automatic thoughts is a skill that can be mastered through practice and persistence (Padesky and Greenberger, 1995). Recognition is an important tool because it helps you gain insight into your internal dialogue and to master your emotions and your reactions. By doing that you can actually start to gain some control over your relationship rather than be controlled by it (Beck, 1988).

Step 3: Question your Automatic Thoughts

Of course, simply recognising your automatic thoughts does not necessarily change them. In order to do that, you need to determine whether your thoughts are distorted or erroneous by putting them to the test. You need to understand that even though your thoughts appear to be valid and true, they may not stand up to scrutiny.

To check their validity, ask yourself this series of questions (Padesky and Greenberger, 1995):

1. What is the evidence in favour of my conclusion/interpretation?
2. What is the evidence against my conclusion/interpretation?
3. Is there any alternative explanation for his or her behaviour?
4. What are the advantages or disadvantages of holding a belief?
5. What is the worst possible outcome you think could occur?

Through the use of logic, argument, persuasion, ridicule or humour an effort can be made to challenge the irrational beliefs that cause the difficulties in the relationship. This requires you to be really honest with yourself, and it is hard work, but the emotional benefits of learning to put your thinking errors into perspective are invaluable.

Step 4: Use Rational Responses

Rational responses evaluate the rationality of your automatic thoughts. Finding the rational response helps to put your thoughts in some perspective; that means treating your thoughts as 'interpretations' and not as the 'absolute' truth (Beck, 1988). For example:

Automatic thought:	*'She is getting back at me.'*
Rational response:	*'She is angry. But that isn't necessarily affecting her behaviour towards me.'*
Automatic thought:	*'I am not important to him.'*
Rational response:	*'I don't know this for a fact because I cannot mind read. If I feel this way, I should ask him.'*

With rational responses, new information is created. These new meanings empower you to view your partner and your relationship in a different light, and pave the way for understanding.

Learning to Speak a New Language

When we talk about acquiring new behaviours, this doesn't mean you and your partner have to undergo personality transplants. You are who you are, and the little personality quirks you possess are probably the reason your partner fell in love with you in the first place. More commonly it is small, subtle changes that are required to turn your relationship around. As Beck (1988) states, small behavioural changes can lead to massive relationship changes and consequently reverse vicious circles. But changes, no matter how small, are often scary. The biggest fear is often that we will get it wrong. It can really help to accept that mistakes are commonplace for everybody, in every process of relationship therapy – and actually they can be hugely useful. So, if you are serious about changing the communication rut you and your partner have slipped into, perseverance is key. Some general hints to aid this process follow:

- **Keep trying:** no one said it would be easy. Major relationship changes do not occur overnight, so start with realistic expectations so you don't find yourself disappointed, disillusioned and despondent about the whole process. If you give up, your partner will feel their efforts are underappreciated and the process is likely to fail miserably.

- **Praise:** changing automatic thought processes and behaviours within your relationship is a two-way process, and it is important for both partners to recognise when the other is making a concerted effort to turn things round. Even when these gestures seem small and insignificant remember that dramatic relationship improvements start with small changes. Be positive about the progress – acknowledge that your partner is making an effort.
- **Challenge your negative thoughts:** as much as you should be positive about your partner's contribution, you should also be positive about your own. Stay in control of those negative thoughts that will make you feel the situation is hopeless, and pat yourself on the back when you know you have stopped the thought–action process and actively behaved in a way that is more productive for your relationship.

And if you Remember Nothing Else . . .

There are good elements in every relationship: the affection, the excitement, the tenderness. Then there are the more boring, stable elements: the security, the reassurance, the support. After a certain amount of time together, it is fairly common to discover that it is the latter set of elements that have the longest shelf-life. Sooner or later, the number of butterflies you feel in your tummy when he calls significantly reduces; eventually you can manage a whole shopping trip without holding hands down every aisle; every couple comes to realise that, actually, the bedroom has become about sleeping rather than wild passion. All of this is just the start, the wake-up call comes when you can't bear to be in the same room as each other, or the sight of him makes you grit your teeth.

Constant fighting, conflict and hurt are usually the signs of the end of the infatuation. When couples constantly misunderstand one another, this usually comes from an active process whereby they begin to see distorted, negative interpretations of each other and they come to expect the worse. It is a rare individual who is always aware of this misinterpretation. People simply are not in the habit of checking their interpretations or focusing on the clarity of their communications (Beck, 1988); instead, they misread their partner's behaviour, ascribe possibly imaginary motives to it and jump to illogical conclusions. It rarely occurs to us that the way we see things is wrong or that our behaviour could be based on a trigger that never existed. Cognitive therapy has shown that couples can learn to be more reasonable with each other and consequently strengthen their ties (Crowe, 2005). In a nutshell, what you need to remember is the following:

- Everyone uses his or her own 'coding' system, which may be biased and defective. Partners should take responsibility for subjectivity and possible distortions in their beliefs (Epstein and Baucom, 2003). This means examining your core beliefs, or schemas, and assessing how realistic they are.

- Avoid jumping to conclusions or assuming you have magically acquired the ability to read minds. Both of these errors produce highly inaccurate predictions and cause completely unnecessary stress for a relationship. Ask your partner what they think instead of telling them what you assume they think.

- Negotiate, negotiate, negotiate. If you are having problems communicating with your partner, then you must assess where you are going wrong and negotiate a solution that works for both of you. That means using I-sentences instead of you-sentences. For example, look at the difference between: 'You close me out of your life' and 'Sometimes I feel lonely.' It means using requests instead of complaints – and those requests should be positive, specific, future-orientated and practicable (Crowe, 2005). Aid the negotiation by suggesting ways you aim to contribute to the solution by changing your behaviour.

- Do not discuss problems abstractly and non-concretely. Couples usually discuss their problems in abstract, non-specific, non-behavioural language – for example, 'We have marital problems.' The use of this type of language does not lead to any understanding of the problem, particularly of the sort of behaviour involved (Weeks and Treat, 2005), and doesn't help you nail down a specific solution. If couples focus on the what, where and when, it is far easier to understand how change can be introduced.

- Any problem is an important problem. Partners are often reluctant to discuss complaints openly, honestly and with the intensity they feel about a problem (Weeks and Treat, 2005). This results in issues being understated or minimised. In order to be effectively happy with your partner, things should not be left unsaid. When problems are reported or identified, it is important you actually listen to what your partner wants or asks and that you encourage them to open up to you on any concerns they may have, big or small.

- The perfect solution, tempting as it might sound, is not for you and your partner to see things in exactly the same way. Your perceptions of situations will always be different because you are two separate individuals, and you should allow and encourage these differences. If you communicate your willingness to understand that your partner sees things differently, you are more likely to reach an amicable point where both partners feel secure in a relationship where opposing views are listened to and respected, even if they are not agreed with.

- Express your love and affection for your partner. As we've discussed, feelings of being supported or being secure usually take over from feelings of being desired or worshipped. But, when it comes to the crux of the matter, the most important feeling is being loved. Make sure you are still affectionate with one another. Make time to kiss, cuddle, pay compliments – anything that lets your partner know they are loved. Here, you can use powerful non-verbal communication to positive effect.

- Show sensitivity to your partner's concerns and vulnerable spots. While some people can be more sensitive than others, this is a quality that can be cultivated (Beck, 1988). When your mate is overreacting to certain things, avoid being critical or rejecting their concerns. Gently explore what their worries or fears are. Try to resist passing judgements or making global attributions. Instead, view these overreactions as signs of vulnerability, and accept your role as a team member in helping your partner work though them.

Once you get these things right, the results can be life changing. Halford et al. (1997), likened it to establishing a 'relationship account' like a bank account. Sharing positive thoughts and behaviours is like making deposits at the bank. Over time, a healthy, robust level of credit builds up and this safety net will see you and your partner through the tough times.

Turning 'Once Upon a Time' Into 'Happily Ever After'

'Happily ever after' is the most commonly used and least accurate story book cliché in existence. Not because everlasting happiness is unattainable, but because it gives the impression you and your partner will negotiate one initial tough battle (like a poisoned apple or a witchy stepmother), usually in the early stages of your relationship, and then everything else will be plain sailing. Oh yes, after you've mounted his white stallion, found the sunset and headed off into it, it's happy days for everyone.

In actual fact, men and women will never live in perfect story book harmony with one another because they just aren't built that way. For the same reason that you're good at discussing intricate emotional problems and he's good at reading a map, you and your man will also differ dramatically in the way you see each other, your relationship and the wider world. That will never change. He will never think, 'What should I do?' means 'I want to mull this over for hours, make a decision, cry because it's the wrong one and then talk about if for another six years.' Equally, you will never think, 'I'm tired' means 'I'm tired' – you'll probably think it means 'I've gone off you because you're ugly and boring.'

The good news is that these differences make relationships so much fun. And there's more: with a little acceptance and a game plan for dealing with the differences, you and your partner can overcome them – easily.

Using the advice in this book won't help you both become the same person and think the same way. That's called brainwashing. Or cult mentality. Or something like that. This book will help you realise you have your own opinions, and you have your own experiences, and that's OK. It will help you see that putting things in perspective is the way to deal with them, and it will help you to moderate your own communication in order to be compatible with your partner. And after that, you might just be one step closer to that big fat cliché – happily ever after.

References

Chapter 1 Dating

Baumeister, R. E., Catanese, K. R. and Vohs, K. D. (2001), 'Is There a Gender Difference in Strength of Sex Drive? Theoretical Views, Conceptions, and a Review of Relevant Evidence', *Personality and Social Psychology Review* 5, 242–73.

Beck, A. T. (1964), 'Thinking and Depression: II. Theory and Therapy', *Archives of General Psychiatry* 10, 561–71.

——(1967), *Depression: Clinical, Experimental, and Theoretical Aspects*, New York: Harper & Row.

Beck, A. T., Rush, J., Shaw, B. and Emery, G. (1979), *Cognitive Therapy of Depression*, New York: Guildford.

Bee, H. (1999), *The Growing Child: An Applied Approach*, New York: Longman.

Berscheid, E. (1985), 'Interpersonal Attraction', in G. Lindzey and E. Aronson (eds), *Handbook of Social Psychology* Vol. 2, (pp. 413–84), New York: Random House.

Bowlby, J. (1988), *A Secure Base*, New York: Basic Books.

Buunk, B. P. (2001), 'Affiliation, Attraction and Close Relationships', in M. Hewstone and W. Stroebe (eds), *Introduction to Social Psychology* (pp. 370–400), Oxford: Blackwell.

Caldwell, M. A. and Peplau, L. A. (1982), Sex Differences in Same Sex Friendship, *Sex Roles: A Journal of Research* 8 (7), 721–32.

Epstein, N. B. and Baucom, D. H. (2003), *Enhanced Cognitive-Behavioral Therapy for Couples: A Contextual Approach*, Washington, DC: APA.

Feeney, J. A. (2003), 'The Systemic Nature of Couple Relationships: An Attachment Perspective', in P. Erdman and T. Caffery (eds), *Attachment and Family Systems: Conceptual, Empirical and Therapeutic Relatedness* (pp. 139–63), New York: Brunner-Routledge.

Furman, W. and Flanagan, A. (1997), 'The Influence of Earlier Relationships on Marriage: An Attachment Perspective', in W. K. Halford and H. J. Markman (eds), *Clinical Handbook of Marriage and Couples Interventions*, New York: Wiley.

Hulson, B. and Russell, R. (1994), 'Psychological Foundations of Couple Relationships', in D. Hooper and W. Dryden (eds), *Couple Therapy: A Handbook* (pp. 37–56), Milton Keynes, UK: Open University.

Kobak, R., Ruckdeschel, K. and Hazan, C. (1994), 'From Symptom to Signal: An Attachment View of Emotion in Marital Therapy', in S. M. Johnson and L. S. Greenberg (eds), *The Heart of the Matter: Perspectives of Emotion in Marital Therapy* (pp. 46–71), New York: Brunner/Mazel.

McKay, M. and Fanning, P. (1991), *Prisoners of Belief: Exposing and Changing Beliefs That Control Your Life*, Oakland, CA: New Harbinger.

Morr, M. C. and Mongeau, P. A. (2004), 'First-Date Expectations: The Impact of Sex Initiator, Alcohol Consumption, and Relationship Type', *Communication Research*, 31 (1), 3–35.

Pervin, L. A. and John, O. P. (2001), *Personality: Theory and Research* (8th edn), New York: Wiley.

Rose, S. and Frieze, I. H. (1989), 'Young Singles' Scripts for a First Date', *Gender and Society* 3, 258–68.

——(1993), 'Young Singles' Contemporary Dating Scripts', *Sex Roles* 28, 499–509.

Shotland, R. L. and Craig, J. M. (1988), Can Men and Women Differentiate Between Friendly and Sexually Interested Behaviour? *Social Psychology Quarterly* Vol. 51, No. 1, 66–73.

Unger, R. K. (1979), *Female and Male: Psychological Perspectives*, New York: Harper & Row.

Workman, L. and Reader, W. (2004), *Evolutionary Psychology: An Introduction*, Cambridge: Cambridge University Press.

Chapter 2 First Sex

Alexander, M. G. and Fisher, T. D. (2003), 'Truth and Consequences: Using the Bogus Pipeline to Examine Sex Differences in Self-Reported Sexuality', *Journal of Sex Research*.

Beck, A. T. (1988), *Love Is Never Enough*, New York: Harper & Row.

Buss, D. M. and Schmidt, D. P. (1993), 'Sexual Strategies Theory: An Evolutionary Perspective on Human Mating', *Psychological Review* 100, 204–32.

Byers, E. S. (1996), 'How Well Does the Traditional Sexual Script Explain Sexual Coercion? Review of a Program Research', *Journal of Psychology and Human Sexuality* 8, 7–25.

Carlson, N. R. (1998), *Physiology of Behavior*, Boston: Allyn and Bacon.

Cohen, L. L. and Shotland, R. (1996), 'Timing of First Sexual Intercourse in a Relationship: Expectations, Experiences, and Perceptions of Others', *Journal of Sex Research* 33, 291–9.

Crowe, M. (2005), *Overcoming Relationship Problems: A Self-Help Guide Using Cognitive Behavioral Techniques*, London: Robinson.

Cupach, W. R. and Metts, S. (1991), 'Sexuality and Communication in Close Relationships', in L. McKinney and S. Sprecher (eds), *Sexuality in Close Relationships*, Hillsdale, NJ: Erlbaum.

DeLameter, J. (1987), 'Gender Differences in Sexual Scenarios', in K. Kelley (ed.), *Females, Males, and Sexuality: Theories and Research* (pp. 127–39), Albany, NY: State University of New York.

Edley, N. and Wetherell, M. (1995), *Men in Perspective: Practice, Power and Identity*, London: Prentice Hall.

Ferroni, P. and Taffee, J. (1997), 'Women's Emotional Well-Being: The Importance of Communicating Sexual Needs', *Sexual and Marital Therapy* 12, 127–38.

Ford, V. (2005), *Overcoming Sexual Problems: A Self-Help Guide Using Cognitive Behavioral Techniques*, London: Robinson.

Haavio-Mannila, E., Kontula, O. and Rotkirch, A. (2002), *Sexual Lifestyles in the Twentieth Century: A Research Study*, New York: Palgrave.

Herold, E. S. and Way, L. (1988), 'Sexual Self-Disclosure Among University Women', *Journal of Sex Research* 24, 1–14.

Joffe, H. and Franca-Koh, A. C. (2001), 'Parental Non-Verbal Sexual Communication: Its Relationship to Sexual Behaviour and Sexual guilt', *Journal of Health Psychology* 6 (1), 17–30.

Jong, E., Escoffier, J. and McDarrah, F. W. (2003), Sexual Revolution, New York: Thunder's Mouth Press.

Koblinsky, S. A. and Palmeter, J. (1984), 'Sex-Role Orientation, Mother's Expression of Affection Toward Spouse and College Women's Attitudes Toward Sexual Behaviours', *The Journal of Sex Research* 20, 32–43.

Leiblum, S. R. (2002), 'Reconsidering Gender Differences in Sexual Desire: An Update', *Sexual and Relationship Therapy* 17, 57–68.

Levant, R. F. (1997), 'Non-relational Sexuality in Men,' in R. F. Levant and G. R. Brooks (eds), *Men and Sex: New Psychological Perspectives* (pp. 9–27), New York: Wiley.

Marsiglio, W. (1988), 'Adolescent Male Sexuality and Heterosexual Masculinity: A Conceptual Model and Review', *Journal of Adolescent Research* 3, (3–4), 285–303.

Ofman, U. (2000), guest editor's note, *Journal of Sex Education and Therapy* 25, 3–5.

Pick, S. and Palos, P. A. (1995), 'Impact of the Family on the Sex Lives of Adolescents', *Adolescence* 30, 667–75.

Propper, S. and Brown, R. (1986), 'Moral Reasoning, Parental Sex Attitudes and Sex Guilt in Female College Students', *Archives of Sexual Behaviour* 15, 331–40.

Rose, S. and Frieze, I. H. (1993), 'Young Singles' Contemporary Dating Scripts', *Sex Roles* 28, 499–509.

Rubin, Z., Peplau, L. A. and Hill, C. T. (1981), 'Loving and Leaving: Sex Differences in Romantic Attachments', *Sex Roles* 7(8), 821–35.

Simm, W. and Gagnon, J. H. (1986), 'Sexual Scripts: Performance and Change, *Archives of Sexual Behaviour* Vol. 15, No. 2, 97–120.

Unger, R. K. (1979), *Female and Male: Psychological Perspectives*, New York: Harper & Row.

Williams, J. H. (1987), *Psychology of Women: Behavior in a Biosocial Context* (3rd edn), New York: Norton.

Chapter 3 Meeting Parents and Friends

Apter, Dr T. (1999), British Psychological Society's conference.

BBC News, 21 December 1999, 'The Real Trouble with In-Laws', http://news.bbc.co.uk/1/hi/uk/573446.stm.

Crowe, M. (2005), *Overcoming Relationship Problems: A Self-Help Guide Using Cognitive Behavioral Techniques*, London: Robinson.

Flecknoe, P. and Sanders, D. (2004), 'Interpersonal Difficulties', in J. Bennet-Levy, G. Butler, M. Fennell, A. Hackmann, M. Mueller and D. Westbrook (eds), *Oxford Guide to Behavioural Experiments in Cognitive Therapy* (pp. 393–409), Oxford: Oxford University Press.

McCarthy, B. and McCarthy, E. (2004), *Getting It Right the First Time: Creating a Healthy Marriage*, New York: Brunner-Routledge.

McGoldrick, M. (1980), 'The Joining of Families Through Marriage: The New Couple', in E. A. Carter and M. McGoldrick (eds), *The Family Life Cycle: A Framework for Family Therapy* (pp. 93–119), New York: Gardner.

Safran, J. D. and Segal, Z. V. (1990), *Interpersonal Process in Cognitive Therapy*, New York: Basic Books.

Scott, E. (2006), 'Stress Management. Top 10 Worst Ways to Handle Conflict', www.stressabout.com/b/2006/03/07.

Shucksmith, J., Hendry, L., Love, J. and Glendinning, T. (1993), 'The Importance of Friendship', *Research in Education* (52).

Chapter 4 Emotional Unavailability

Ainsworth, M. D. S., Blehar, M. C., Waters, E. and Wall, S. (1978), *Patterns of Attachment: A Psychological Study of the Strange Situation*. Hillsdale, NJ: Erlbaum.

Bowlby, J. (1980), *Loss: Sadness and Depression* in *Attachment and Loss Series* Vol. 3, New York: Basic.

——(1980), 'Attachment and Loss: Retrospect and Prospect', *American Journal of Orthopsychiatry* 52, 664–78.

Butler, G. and Surawy, C. (2004), 'Avoidance of Affect', in J. Bennett-Levy, G. Butler, M. Fennell, A. Hackmann, M. Mueller, D. Westbrook (eds), *Oxford Guide to Behavioural Experiments in Cognitive Therapy* (pp. 351–69), Oxford: Oxford University Press.

Buunk, B. P. (2001), 'Affiliation, Attraction and Close Relationships', in M. Hewstone and W. Stroebe (eds), *Introduction to Social Psychology* (pp. 370–400), Oxford: Blackwell.

Collins, N. L. and Read, S. J. (1990), 'Adult attachment, Working Models and Relationship Quality in Dating Couples', *Journal of Personality and Social Psychology* 58, 644–63.

Crowe, M. (2005), *Overcoming Relationship Problems: A Self-Help Guide Using Cognitive Behavioral Techniques*, London: Robinson.

Epstein, N. B., and Baucom, D. H. (2003), *Enhanced Cognitive-Behavioral Therapy for Couples: A Contextual Approach*, Washington, DC: American Psychological Association.

Mayer, J. D. and Salovey, P. (1993), 'The Intelligence of Emotional Intelligence', *Intelligence* 17, 433–42.

Padesky, C. A. (1994), 'Schema Change Processes in Cognitive Therapy', *Clinical Psychology and Psychotherapy* 1 (5), 267–78.

Reis, H. T. and Patrick, B. C. (1996), 'Attachment and Intimacy: Component Processes', in E. T. Higgins and A. W. Kruglanski (eds), *Social Psychology: Handbook of Basic Principles* (pp. 523–63), New York: Guilford.

Shaver, P. and Hazan, C. (1988), 'A Biased Overview of the Study of Love', *Journal of Social and Personal Relationships* 5, 473–501.

Shaver, P., Hazan, C. and Bradshaw, D. (1988), 'Love as Attachment: The Integration of Three Behavioral Systems', in R. F. Sternberg and M. L. Barnes (eds), *The Psychology of Love*, New Haven: CT: Yale University.

Simpson, J. A. and Gangstead, S. W. (1991), 'Individual Differences in Sociosexuality: Evidence for Convergent and Discriminate Validity', *Journal of Personality and Social Psychology* 60, 870–83.

Simpson, J. A., Rholes, W. S. and Nelligan, J. S. (1992), 'Support Seeking and Support Giving Within Couples in an Anxiety-Provoking Situation: The Role of Attachment Styles', *Journal of Personality and Social Psychology* 62, 434–46.

Street, E. (1994), 'Couple Therapy in the Family Context', in D. Hooper and W. Dryden (eds), *Couple Therapy: A Handbook* (pp. 12–36), Milton Keynes, UK: Open University.

Williams, S., Connolly, J. and Segal, Z. V. (2001), 'Intimacy in Relationships and Cognitive Vulnerability to Depression in Adolescent Girls', *Cognitive Therapy and Research* 25 (4), 477–96.

Young, J. E., Klosko, J. S. and Weishaar, M. (2003), *Schema Therapy: A Practitioner's Guide*, New York: Guilford.

Chapter 5 Infidelity

Atwater, L. (1982), *The Extramarital Connection*, New York: Irvington.

Bailey, J. M., Gaulin, S., Agyei, Y. and Gladue, B. A. (1994), 'Effects of Gender and Sexual Orientation on Evolutionary Relevant Aspects of Human Mating', *Journal of Personality and Social Psychology* 66, 1081–93.

Baucom, D. H. and Epstein, N. (1990), *Cognitive-Behavioral Marital Therapy*, New York: Brunner/Mazel.

Baumeister, R. E, Catanese, K. R. and Vohs, K. D. (2001), 'Is There a Gender Difference in Strength of Sex Drive? Theoretical Views, Conceptual Distinctions, and a Review of Relevant Evidence', *Personality and Social Psychology Review* 5, 242–73.

Beck, A. T. (1988), *Love Is Never Enough*, New York: Harper & Row.

Betzig, L. (1989), 'Causes of Conjugal Dissolution: A Cross-Study', *Current Anthropology* 30, 654–76.

Brown, E. M. (2001), *Patterns of Infidelity and Their Treatment*, Philadelphia, PA: Brunner-Routledge.

Buunk, B. P. and Dijkstra, P. (2004), 'Gender Differences in Rival Characteristics that Evoke Jealousy in Response to Emotional Versus Sexual Infidelity', *Personal Relationships* 11, 395–408.

Buunk, B. P. and van Driel, B. (1989), *Variant Lifestyles and Relationships*, London: Sage.

Buus, D. M. and Shackelford, T. K. (1997), 'Susceptibility to Infidelity in the First Year of Marriage', *Journal of Research in Personality* 31, 193–221.

Buus, D. M., Larsen, R. J., Westen, D. and Semmelroth, J. (1992), 'Sex Differences in Jealousy: Evolution, Physiology and Psychology', *Psychological Science* 3, 251–5.

Buus, D. M., Shackelford, T. K., Choe, J., Dijkstra, P. and Buunk, B. P. (2000), 'Distress about Mating Rivals', *Personal Relationships* 7, 235–43.

Carnes, P. (1983), *Out of the Shadows*, Minneapolis, MN: CompCare.

Crowe, M. (2005), *Overcoming Relationship Problems: A Self-Help Guide Using Cognitive Behavioral Techniques*, London: Robinson.

DeSteno, D. A. and Salovey, P. (1996), 'Jealousy and the Characteristics of One's Rival: A Self-Evaluation Maintenance Perspective', *Personality and Social Psychology Bulletin* 22, 920–32.

Epstein, N. B. and Baucom, D. H. (2003), *Enhance Cognitive-Behavioral Therapy for Couples: A Contextual Approach*, Washington, DC: American Psychological Association.

Glass, S. P. and Wright, T. L. (1985), 'Sex Differences in Type of Extramarital Involvement and Marital Dissatisfaction', *Sex Roles* 12, 1102–20.

——(1992), 'Justifications for Extramarital Relationships: The Association Between Attitudes, Behaviours and Gender', *Journal of Sex Research* 29, 361–87.

Hayman, S. (2001), *Moving On: Breaking up Without Breaking Down*, London: Vermilion.

Lawson, A. (1988), *Adultery: An Analysis of Love and Betrayal*, New York: Basic.

Leahy, R. L. (2003), *Cognitive Therapy Techniques: A Practitioner's Guide*, New York: Guilford.

Lefrancois, G. (1990), *The Lifespan* (3rd edn), Belmont, CA: Wadsworth.

Murphy, A., Vallacher, R., Shackelford, T., Bjorklund, D. and Yunger, J. (2005), *Relationship Experience as a Predictor of Romantic Jealousy*, Florida Atlantic University, Department of Psychology.

Okami, P. and Shackelford, T. K. (2001), 'Human Sex Differences in Sexual Psychology and Behavior', *Annual Review of Sex Research* 12, 186–241.

Parrott, W. G. and Smith, R. H. (1993), 'Distinguishing the Experiences of Envy and Jealousy', *Journal of Personality and Social Psychology* 64, 906–20.

Scarf, M. (1987), *Intimate Partners*, New York: Random House.

Spanier, G. B. and Margolis, R. L. (1983), 'Marital Separation and Extramarital Sexual Behaviour', *Journal of Sex Research* 19, 23–48.

Chapter 6 Moving in Together

Willitts, M., Benzeval, M. and Stansfeld, S. (2004), 'Partnership History and Mental Health Over Time', *Journal of Epidemiology and Community Health* 58, 53–8.

Baucom, D. H., Epstein, N., Sayers, S. L. and Sher, T. G. (1989), 'The Role of Cognitions in Marital Relationships: Definitional, Methodological, and Conceptual Issues', *Journal of Consulting and Clinical Psychology* 57, 31–8.

Beck, A. T. (1988), *Love Is Never Enough*, New York: Harper Perennial.

Collard, J. and Mansfield, P. (1994), 'The Couple: A Sociological Perspective', in D. Hooper and W. Dryden (eds), *Couple Therapy: A Handbook* (pp. 12–36), Milton Keynes, UK: Open University.

Crowe, M. (2005), *Overcoming Relationship Problems: A Self-Help Guide Using Cognitive Behavioral Techniques*, London: Robinson.

Leahy, R. L. (2003), *Cognitive Therapy Techniques: A Practitioner's Guide*, New York: Guilford.

— (2005), *The Worry Cure: Stop Worrying and Start Living*, New York: Piatkus.

Lefrancois, G. (1990), *The Lifespan* (3rd edn), Belmont, CA: Wadsworth.

Lewis, J. (2001), *The End of Marriage? Individualism and Intimate Relations*, Cheltenham, UK: Edward Elgar.

McGoldrick, M. (1980), 'The Joining of Families Through Marriage: The New Couple', in E. A. Carter and M. McGoldrick (eds), *The Family Life Cycle: A Framework for Family Therapy* (pp. 93–119), New York: Gardner.

Prinz, C. (1995), *Cohabiting, Married, or Single*, Hants, UK: Avebury.

Rindfuss, R. R. and VandenHeuvel, A. (1990), 'Cohabitation: A Precursor to Marriage or an Alternative to Being Single?' *Population and Development Review* 16 (4), 703–26.

Thomson, E. and Colella, U. (1992), 'Cohabitation and Marital Stability: Quality or Commitment?', *Journal of Marriage and the Family* 54, 259–67.

Chapter 7 Marriage

Beck, A. T. (1988), *Love is Never Enough*, New York: Harper Perennial.

Berger, P. and Kellner, H. (1964), 'Marriage and the Construction of Reality', *Diogenes*, 49–72.

Collard, J. and Mansfield, P. (1994), 'The Couple: A Sociological Perspective', in D. Hooper and W. Dryden (eds), *Couple Therapy: A Handbook* (pp. 12–36), Milton Keynes, UK: Open University.

Dafoe Whitehead, B. and Popenoe, D. (2006), 'State of Our Unions', annual assessment for the National Marriage Project at Rutgers, the State University of New Jersey.

Erber, R. and Gilmour, R. (1994), 'Courtship Antecedents of Marital Satisfaction and Love', in R. Erber and R. Gilmour (eds), *Theoretical Perspectives on Personal Relationships* (pp. 43–65), Hillsdale, NJ: Erlbaum.

Haley, J. (1963), 'Marriage therapy', *Archives of General Psychiatry* 8, 213–34.

Halford, W. K., Kelly, A. and Markman, H. J. (1997), 'The Concept of Healthy Marriage', in W. K. Halford and H. J. Markman (eds), *Clinical Handbook of Marriage and Couple Interventions* (pp. 3–12), West Sussex, UK: Wiley.

Heaton, T. B. and Blake, A. M. (1999), 'Gender Differences in Determinants of Marital Disruption', *Journal of Family Issues* 20 (1), 25–45.

Horwitz A. V., White H. R. and Howell-White, S. (1996), 'Becoming Married and Mental Health: A Longitudinal Study of a Cohort of Young Adults', *Journal of Marriage and the Family* 58 (4), 895–907.

Mansfield, P. and Collard, J. (1988), *The Beginning of the Rest of Your Life?* London: Palgrave Macmillan.

McCarthy, B. and McCarthy, E. (2004), *Getting it Right the First Time: Creating a Healthy Marriage*, New York: Brunner-Routledge.

McGoldrick, M. (1980), 'The Joining of Families Through Marriage: The New Couple', in E. A. Carter and M. McGoldrick (eds), *The Family Life Cycle: A Framework for Family Therapy* (pp. 93–119), New York: Gardner.

Unger, R. K. (1979), *Female and Male: Psychological Perspectives*, New York: Harper & Row.

Chapter 8 First-Time Parenting

Belsky, J., Lang, M. E. and Rovine, M. (1985), 'Stability and Change in Marriage Across the Transition to Parenthood: A Second Study', *Journal of Marriage and the Family* 47, 855–65.

Burgess, A. and Ruxton, S. (1996), *Men and Their Children: Proposals for Public Policy*, London: Institute for Public Policy Research.

Carter, E. A. and McGoldrick, M. (1989), *The Changing Family Life Cycle: a Framework for Family Therapy* (2nd edn), Boston: Allyn & Bacon.

Collins, N., Dunkel-Schetter, C., Lobel, M. and Scrimshaw, S. (1993), 'Social Support in Pregnancy: Psychological Correlates of Birth Outcomes and Postpartum Depression', *Journal of Personality and Social Psychology* 65, 1243–58.

Crawford, D. (1993), 'The Impact of the Transition to Parenthood on Marital Leisure', *Personality and Social Psychology Bulletin* 18, 39–46.

Crowe, M. (2005), *Overcoming relationship problems: A Self-Help Guide Using Cognitive Behavioral Techniques*, London: Robinson.

Epstein, N. B. and Baucom, D. H. (2003), *Enhanced Cognitive-Behavioral Therapy for Couples: A Contextual Approach*, Washington, DC: American Psychological Association.

Feeney, J., Alexander, R., Noller, P. and Hohaus, L. (2003), 'Attachment Insecurity, Depression and Transition to Parenthood', *Personal Relationships* 10, 457–93.

Felder, L. (1990), *When a Loved One is Ill: How to Take Better Care of Your Loved One, Your Family and Yourself*, New York: New American Library.

Gbrich, C. (1987), 'Primary Caregiver Fathers: A Role Study, Some Preliminary Findings', *Australian Journal of Sex, Marriage and Family* 8, 2.

Green, J. (1998), 'Postnatal Depression or Perinatal Dysphoria? Findings From a Longitudinal Community-Based Study Using Edinburgh Postnatal Depression Scale', *Journal of Reproductive and Infant Psychology* 16, 143–6.

Haddock, S. A., Zimmerman, T. S., Ziemba, S. and Current, L. R. (2001), 'Ten Adaptive Strategies for Families and Work Balance: Advice From Successful Families', *Journal of Marital and Family Therapy* 27, 445–58.

Hulson, B. and Russell, R. (1994), 'Psychological Foundations of Couple Relationships', in D. Hooper and W. Dryden (eds), *Couple Therapy: A Handbook* (pp. 37–56), Milton Keynes, UK: Open University.

Kalicki, B., Fthenakis, W., Peitz, G. G., Engfer. A., 'Gender-Roles at the Transition to Parenthood', poster presented at the XVth Biennial International Society for the Study of Behavioural Development ISSBD Meetings, Berne, 1998.

Lewis, C. (1996), 'Fathers and Preschoolers', in M. E. Lamb (ed.), *The Role of the Father in Child Development* (3rd edn), Chichester, UK: Wiley.

McCarthy, B. and McCarthy, E. (2004), *Getting it Right the First Time: Creating a Healthy Marriage*, New York: Brunner-Routledge.

McHale, S. (1985), 'The Effect of the Transition to Parenthood on the Marital Relationship: A Longitudinal Study', *Journal of Family Issues* 5, 409–33.

Murray, L. and Cooper, P. J. (1997), 'The Role of Infant and Maternal Factors in Postpartum Depression, Mother-Infant Interactions and Infant Outcome', in L. Murray and P. J. Cooper (eds), *Postpartum Depression and Child Development* (pp. 111–35), New York: Guilford.

Ruble, D. N., Fleming, A. S., Hackel, L. S. and Stangor, C. (1988), 'Changes in the Marital Relationship During the Transition to First-Time Motherhood: Effects of Violated Expectations Concerning Division of Household Labour', *Journal of Personality and Social Psychology* 55, 78–87.

Unger, R. K. (1979), *Female and Male: Psychological Perspectives*, New York: Harper & Row.

Walker, A. (2002), 'Pregnancy, Pregnancy Loss and Induced Abortion', in D. Miller and J. Green (eds), *The Psychology of Sexual Health* (pp. 304–19), Oxford: Blackwell.

Chapter 9 Separation

Beck, A. T. (1988), *Love is Never Enough*, New York: Harper & Row.

Bourne, E. J. (2005), *The Anxiety and Phobia Workbook* (4th edn), New York: New Harbinger.

Bradbury, T. N. and Fincham, F. D. (1990), 'Attributions in Marriage: Review and Critique', *Psychological Bulletin* 107, 3–33.

Buunk, B. P. (2001), 'Affiliation, Attraction and Close Relationships', in M. Hewstone and W. Stroebe (eds), *Introduction to Social Psychology* (pp. 370–400), Oxford: Blackwell.

Christensen, A. and Heavey, C. L. (1990), 'Gender and Social Structure in the Demand/Withdraw Pattern of Marital Conflict', *Journal of Personality and Social Psychology* 59, 73–81.

Crowe, M. (2005), *Overcoming Relationship Problems: A Self-Help Guide Using Cognitive Behavioral Techniques*, London: Robinson.

Duck, S. (2005), 'How Do You Tell Someone You're Letting Go?', *The Psychologist* 18 (4), 210–13.

Epstein, N. B. and Baucom, D. H. (2003), *Enhanced Cognitive-Behavioral Therapy for Couples: A Contextual Approach*, Washington, DC: American Psychological Association.

Flecknoe, P. and Sanders, D. (2004), 'Interpersonal difficulties', in J. Bennett-Levy, G. Butler, M. Fennell, A. Hackmann, M. Mueller and D. Westbrook (eds) *Oxford Guide to Behavioural Experiments in Cognitive Therapy*, (pp. 392–409), Oxford: Oxford University Press.

Hayman, S. (2001), *Moving On: Breaking Up Without Breaking Down*, London: Vermillion.

Jordan, M., Proot, C., Flemg, C. and Jernigan, M., Methods to End Relationships: Typical Behaviours and Statements Used to End a Romantic Relationship, presented at the annual convention of the American Psychological Society, New Orleans, 2002.

Jordan, M., Shriner, M., Proot, C., Bledsoe, K. and Mahoney. A., 'Six Dimensions of the Breakup of Romantic Relationships', presented at the annual convention of the American Psychological Society, New Orleans, 2002.

Leahy, R. L. (2003), *Cognitive Therapy Techniques: A Practitioner's Guide*, New York: Guilford.

Padesky, C. and Greenberger, D. (1995), *Mind Over Mood*, Palo Alto, CA: Guilford.

Safran, J. D. and Segal, Z. V. (1990), *Interpersonal Process in Cognitive Therapy*, New York: Basic.

Sayers, S. L., Kohn, C. S., Fresco, D. M., Bellack, A. S. and Sarwer, D. B. (2001), 'Marital Cognitions and Depression in the Context of Marital Discord', *Cognitive Therapy and Research* 25 (6), 713–32.

Vanzetti, N. A., Notarious, C. I. and NeeSmith, D. (1992), 'Specific and Generalised Expectancies in Marital Interaction', *Journal of Family Psychology* 6, 171–83.

Wachtel, E. (1999), *We Love Each Other but . . . : Simple Secrets to Strengthen Your Relationship and Make Love Last*, New York: St Martin's Griffin.

Chapter 10 Divorce

Beal, E. (1980), 'Separation, Divorce and Single-Parent Families', in E. A. Carter and M. McGoldrick (eds), *The Family Life Cycle: A Framework for Family Therapy* (pp. 241–64), New York: Gardner.

Beck, A. T. (1988), *Love is Never Enough*, New York: Harper & Row.

Collard, J. and Mansfield, P. (1994), 'The Couple: A Sociological Perspective', in D. Hooper and W. Dryden (eds), *Couple Therapy: A Handbook* (pp. 12–36), Milton Keynes, UK: Open University.

Crowe, M. (2005), *Overcoming Relationship Problems: A Self-Help Guide Using Cognitive Behavioral Techniques*, London: Robinson.

Eidelson, R. J. and Epstein, N. (1982), 'Cognition and Relationship Maladjustment: Development of a Measure of Dysfunctional Relationship Beliefs', *Journal of Consulting and Clinical Psychology* 50, 715–20.

Epstein, N. B. and Baucom, D. H. (2002), *Enhanced Cognitive-Behavioural Therapy for Couples: A Contextual Approach*, Washington, DC: American Psychological Association.

Fincham, F. D., Beach, S. and Nelson, G. (1987), 'Attribution Processes in Distressed and Nondistressed Couples: Causal and Responsibility Attributions for Spouse Behaviour', *Cognitive Therapy and Research* 11, 71–86.

Halford, W. K., Kelly, A. and Markman, H. J. (1997), 'The Concept of Healthy Marriage', in W. K. Halford and H. J. Markman (eds), *Clinical Handbook of Marriage and Couple Interventions* (pp. 3–12), West Sussex, UK: Wiley.

Hayman, S. (2001), *Moving On: Breaking Up Without breakding Down*, London: Vermilion.

Hulson, B. and Russell, R. (1994), 'Psychological Foundations of Couple Relationships', in D. Hooper and W. Dryden (eds), *Couple Therapy: A Handbook* (pp. 37–56), Milton Keynes, UK: Open University.

Maciejewski, P. K., Prigerson, H. G., Mazure, C. M. (2001), 'Sex Differences in Event-Related Risk for Major Depression', *Psychological Medicine*, Cambridge: Cambridge University Press.

McCarthy, B. and McCarthy, E. (2004), *Getting it Right the First Time: Creating a Healthy Marriage*, New York: Brunner-Routledge.

Niehuis, S. and Smith, S. (2001), 'Courtship and the Newlywed Years: What They Tell Us About the Future of a Marriage', *Social Psychology and Personality Review* 16, 55–178.

Ponzetti, J. J., Zvonkovic, A. M. and Cate, R. M. (1992), 'Reasons for Divorce: A Comparison Between Former Partners', *Journal of Divorce and Remarriage* 17, 183–201.

Wachtel, E. (1999), *We Love Each Other But . . . : Simple Secrets to Strengthen Your Relationship and Make Love Last*, New York: St Martin's Griffin.

Williams, J. H. (1987), *Psychology of Women: Behavior in a Biosocial Context* (3rd edn), New York: Norton.

Chapter 11 Living Happily Ever After

Beck, A. T. (1967), *Depression: Clinical, Experimental, and Theoretical Aspects*, New York: Harper & Row.

——(1988), *Love is Never Enough*, New York: Harper Perennial.

Crowe, M. (2005), *Overcoming Relationship Problems: A Self-Help Guide Using Cognitive Behavioral Techniques*, London: Robinson.

Dindia, K., Fitzpatrick, M. A. and Kenny, D. A. (1989), *Self-Disclosure in Spouse and Stranger Dyads: A Social Relations Analysis*, San Francisco: International Communication Associations.

Epstein, N. B. and Baucom, D. H (2003), *Enhanced Cognitive-Behavioral Therapy for Couples: A Contextual Approach*. Washington, DC: American Psychological Association.

Halford, W. K., Kelly, A. and Markman, H. J. (1997), 'The Concept of a Healthy Marriage', in K. W. Halford and H. J. Markman (eds), *Clinical Handbook of Marriage and Couples Interventions* (pp. 3–12), West Sussex, UK: Wiley.

Leahy, R. L. (2003), *Cognitive Therapy Techniques: A Practitioner's Guide*, New York: Guilford.

Padesky, C. and Greenberger, D. (1995), *Mind Over Mood*, Palo Alto, CA: Guilford.

Weeks, G. R. and Treat, S. R. (2005), *Couples in Treatment: Techniques and Approaches for Practice*, Philadelphia, PA: Brunner-Routledge.